Language
Development
in a
Bilingual Setting

NATIONAL MULTILINGUAL MULTICULTURAL
MATERIALS DEVELOPMENT CENTER
California State Polytechnic University, Pomona
Pomona, California

NATIONAL DISSEMINATION AND ASSESSMENT CENTER
California State University, Los Angeles
Los Angeles, California 90032

ISBN: 0-89755-009-9

Library of Congress Catalog Card Number: 78-061051

The project reported herein was performed pursuant to a Grant from the U.S. Office of Education, Department of Health, Education, and Welfare. However, the opinions expressed herein do not necessarily reflect the positions or policy of the U.S. Office of Education, and no official endorsement by the U.S. Office of Education should be inferred.

This publication was developed and printed with funds provided by the Bilingual Education Act, Title VII of the Elementary and Secondary Education Act of 1965, as amended by Public Law 93.380.

Developed by
NATIONAL MULTILINGUAL MULTICULTURAL MATERIALS
DEVELOPMENT CENTER
California State Polytechnic University, Pomona
Pomona, California

Published and Disseminated by
NATIONAL DISSEMINATION AND ASSESSMENT CENTER
California State University, Los Angeles
Los Angeles, California 90032

Office of Bilingual Education, H.E.W.

Printed in USA 1979

Language
Development
in a
Bilingual Setting

The NMMMDC acknowledges the editorial efforts of Dr. EUGÈNE J. BRIÈRE, University of Southern California, and the editorial assistance of John L. Figueroa, Ramon S. Holguín, and Roberto L. Ortiz.

ACKNOWLEDGMENTS

The National Multilingual Multicultural Materials Development Center is a cooperative effort involving many people in many roles. The following people have made significant contributions to the development of our materials: ADMINISTRATION:*Roberto L. Ortiz,* Director; *Vera Martínez,* Coordinator; RESEARCH and CURRICULUM: *Ramon S. Holguín,* Coordinator; *William J. Rivera, *David S. Siegrist, *Harriet Archibald-Woodward, *Gloria Gómez;* EVALUATION: *Frank S. Romero,* Coordinator; *Leo López, *Eugène J. Brière;* PRODUCTION: *John L. Figueroa,* Coordinator; *Oscar R. Castillo, Carol Newsom;* COMMUNITY DEVELOPMENT: *Alfred A. Swaim;* SUPPORT STAFF: *Barbara Miller,* Secretary; *Edith Cuevas, Lucy Fernández, Rebecca Kavanaugh, Priscilla Lifton, Vivien Martínez, Adela Williams, *Maggie Pérez, *Miroslava Reimers, *Alvina Sías.*

AUTHOR-CONSULTANTS AND SYMPOSIUM PARTICIPANTS:
JOAQUIN GUADALUPE AVILA, Mexican-American Legal Defense Education Fund; RAMONA GODOY, United States Commission on Civil Rights; JOSHUA A. FISHMAN, Yeshiva University; EDUARDO HERNÁNDEZ-CHÁVEZ, Stanford University; PEG GRIFFIN, University of Southern California and Center for Applied Linguistics; DELL HYMES, University of Pennsylvania; MURIEL SAVILLE-TROIKE, Georgetown University; STEPHEN D. KRASHEN, University of Southern California; MERRILL SWAIN, Ontario Institute for Studies in Education; GUSTAVO GONZÁLEZ, University of California, Santa Barbara; COURTNEY B. CAZDEN, Harvard University; BERNARD SPOLSKY, University of New Mexico; ARNULFO G. RAMÍREZ, Center for Educational Research, Stanford University, RICARDO J. CORNEJO, Center for the Study of Evaluation, University of California, Los Angeles; ERNEST M. BERNAL, JR., University of Texas at San Antonio; LUCILLE GONZALEZ, Chino Unified School District; LEY YEAGER, Cucamonga School District; LARRY YTUARTE, LaVerne College; JUANITA CIRILO, Hacienda-La Puente Unified School District; SANDRA BRICK, California State Polytechnic University, Pomona.
In addition to the major effort by the NMMMDC permanent staff, the following have also contributed in a variety of ways to this book: MARCIA ALBIOL, Chino Unified School District; DOLORES RAEL, Los Nietos School District; JULIAN VILLASEÑOR, Pomona Unified School District; DOLORES VILLASEÑOR, Pomona Unified School District; RUTH YOON, Los Angeles Unified School District.
*Former staff members

PREFACE

The purpose of bilingual/bicultural education is to serve the academic needs of students from different linguistic and cultural backgrounds. This goal, however, need not be attained at the expense of monolingual English-speaking students; the bilingual classroom should benefit the monolingual English speaker as well.

In the bilingual classroom the student will encounter the opportunity not only to learn another language but also to learn about another culture. In a pluralistic society, bilingual education offers the possibility of going beyond a mere gesture in the striving to encourage understanding among varied cultures by establishing a viable line of communication. Educators who foster this concept of education and participate in it will have accepted an exciting and difficult challenge. The implementation of bilingual/bicultural education requires that we search for the answers to many of the questions that have plagued educators. We must examine and scrutinize our former educational theories, hypotheses, and principles.

We hope the reader will find answers to his/her questions, become informed about current developments in bilingual education, and become aware of the concerns of those who study bilingual education. Finally, we hope the reader comes to feel informed on those aspects of bilingual education about which we are now certain and those about which we still have much to learn.

The 1976-1977 fiscal year was a significant year for bilingual education. Under the direction of Dr. John Molina, the Office of Bilingual Education implemented a national network for bilingual education. The National Network of Centers for Bilingual Education is composed of three types of centers, whose prime functions are to disseminate thoroughly evaluated bilingual and multicultural products nationwide for all levels of education. Curriculum products are being designed and developed in French, Portuguese, Greek, Spanish, Native American languages, Asian languages, and languages spoken in Alaska. Some centers, such as the Dissemination and Assessment Center for Bilingual Education (Austin), Spanish Curricula Development Center (Miami), and the Santa Cruz Project (Tucson), were in operation before the Network was conceptualized. The National Bilingual Network presently has grown to a total of 42 national centers.

The National Multilingual Multicultural Materials Development Center at California State Polytechnic University, Pomona, California, was funded in July, 1976. The Center's primary responsibility is to develop Spanish/English bilingual products for grades seven through twelve: in science for grades seven through nine and in social studies for grades ten through twelve. The target population consists primarily of Mexican-American, Puerto Rican, and Cuban students.

In preparing for the design and development tasks, more questions had to be explored than there were answers. Many were related to general bilingual education issues, and others were of more immediate concern and very program-specific, centering on the needs of the target population. The curriculum areas and the language proficiency of students and teachers at the intermediate and secondary levels also needed to be established.

As a result, a symposium on the general topic of "Language Development in a Bilingual Setting" was held in March, 1976 in Los Angeles in an effort to seek answers and to provide the Center's staff with direction in developing bilingual products. Fourteen papers by prominent scholars from the United States and Canada were presented on specific topics relating to language development in a bilingual setting. The formal delivery of these papers was followed by discussions that provided the authors with a basis for final revisions of their papers.

Roberto L. Ortiz

INTRODUCTION

Shortly after the discovery of America by Columbus, Spain, France, Holland, and England established colonies in what is now the United States. Not only did the four major Indo-European languages spoken in those countries come into contact with the many Native American languages, but Baltic, German, and Polish artisans also emigrated to the English settlements as early as the beginning 1600's, bringing their native languages with them (Morison, 1965). As time passed, then, a growing number of languages came into contact in this country. The need for scholastic instruction in different languages, therefore, began very early in our history.

Classes in German were taught in the Carolinas, Maryland, Pennsylvania, Virginia, and Wisconsin as early as the 1700's. Spanish, in conjunction with English, was the language of instruction in California and New Mexico in the 1800's. During that same period, the Cherokees were operating a bilingual education program in Oklahoma (Gonzalez, 1975). Even the first Bible published in the United States, the Eliot Bible, was in Massachusetts, "a relatively minor (Native American) language" (Gleason, 1961). However, during the late 1880's and early 1900's, the movement toward "a nationalistic, isolationist policy in the United States led to a nationwide imposition of English-only instructional policies" (Gonzalez, 1975). Although these policies have been challenged in the courts since the 1920's with varying degrees of success, it was not until the 1974 landmark *Lau* v. *Nichols* Supreme Court decision that bilingual education became the right of non- or limited-English-speaking children throughout the United States.

Despite the lack of bilingual programs in this country over such a long period of time, some scholars did conduct applied and basic research studies of bilingual programs in other countries or of bilingual groups in this country.* Nevertheless, there is still a great need for research in all phases of bilingual education. It is not too surprising, then, that a majority of the authors in this volume express concern over the current lack of applied and basic research in so many areas of bilingual education and either implicitly or explicitly suggest that this need be met quickly.

---

*For examples of the former, see Balkan, 1970; Fishman and Lueders-Salmon, 1972; Lambert and Tucker, 1972; Lewis, 1972; Macnamara, 1966; and Weinreich, 1953. For examples of the latter, see Andersson and Boyer, 1970; Cohen, 1975; Fishman *et al.* 1971; Gaarder, 1970; Haugen, 1953, 1956; Kjolseth, 1972; and Sanchez, 1934.

Another area of general concern is that of community involvement. Concurrent with the increasing awareness of the need for bilingual education programs in this country, an increasing awareness has grown of the need for community involvement in planning and conducting these programs.

Therefore, although the authors address themselves to specific problems of bilingual education in their particular areas of expertise, it is interesting to note that the two most common concerns of the authors are *research* and *community involvement* — regardless of the particular subjects they discuss.

A third area of common concern of the authors is a fear that bilingual education programs might cease to exist. Although the Supreme Court has made bilingual education a legal right of non- or limited-English-speaking children, Avila and Godoy point out that it is a civil rather than a constitutional right and, furthermore, that the right is collective rather than individual. The legal basis for bilingual education in the United States is therefore not as all-encompassing as might be believed. (For a corroboration of Avila and Godoy's interpretation, see Justice Blackmun's assenting opinion to the *Lau* v. *Nichols* decision in which he specifically refers to numbers and not individuals.)

Avila and Godoy further suggest that the courts have historically depended on the testimony of school boards in making decisions concerning education. Since school boards frequently feel that special programs such as bilingual education are an unneeded economic burden to the taxpayer, it is up to the members of the academic community to furnish empirically based, expert testimony concerning the positive values of bilingual education to the majority and minority groups.

Fishman also feels that the "marked" (minority) groups have a need to convince the "unmarked" (majority) group of the benefit of enrichment aspects of bilingual education to the unmarked group if bilingual education is to survive. Hernández-Chávez seems convinced that bilingual education in our society today is doomed to failure since the majority, who control the schools, are only interested in maintaining the status quo, which does not involve the betterment of culturally and linguistically different groups unless total assimilation into the dominant group takes place. Hymes asserts that schools are a tool of society to maintain social stratification through language and that any major gains through bilingual education will involve a re-education of the controlling group in each society. Spolsky sees the political considerations of bilingual education as even more important, perhaps, than the educational considerations since it is clear that bilingual education programs lead to remedial reallocation of economic and political power.

Ignoring the legal and political threats to bilingual education, if any bilingual program is to survive, it must accomplish the goal of teaching subject matter in two languages. Previously successful educational programs have been those that met the needs of a particular situation and that were based on viable philosophies and adequate theories that had been honed and sharpened on the basis of the results of rigorous multidisciplinary research.

This volume brings together the latest thinking in five areas important to the success of bilingual programs: legal aspects of bilingual education, philosophies of bilingual education, social factors in bilingual education, language and content in bilingual education, and assessment in bilingual education. A final paper discusses the latest innovation for actually providing a multitude of services and materials for bilingual education — The National Network for Bilingual Education.

Addressing themselves to the legal aspects of bilingual education, Avila and Godoy discuss the limitations and capabilities of the judicial process, the interpretations of the major court decisions, and the implications of these decisions for bilingual education in terms of community members, educators, and the school boards involved.

Fishman and Hernández-Chávez discuss philosophies of bilingual education. Fishman suggests that the needs of marked and unmarked populations differ, thereby resulting in philosophical diversity. The political, cultural, and educational goals of the marked and unmarked populations in a bilingual situation are discussed, and Marxian, Weberian, and Herderian theoretical positions are reviewed to clarify some of the philosophical disagreements. In a discussion following a fairy tale used to describe the role of bilingual education in our society, Hernández-Chávez reaches the conclusion that since our schools are designed to maintain the status quo, bilingual education will contribute to the assimilation process rather than to cultural and linguistic pluralism.

Griffin, Hymes, and Saville-Troike discuss the area of social factors in bilingual education. Griffin feels that educators involved in bilingual/bicultural education programs should be aware of the sociology of language, ethnography of speaking, and pragmatics of natural languages to thoroughly understand language factors in relation to social factors. Having this knowledge prior to writing curriculum materials would enable educators to make intelligent decisions about such problems as which variety of a language to use in a school and which materials are culturally appropriate.

In a careful and thorough discussion of the contributions of ethnography to the planning, conduct, evaluation, and justification of bilingual programs, Hymes presents those ethnographic considerations that are needed to analyze such variables as linguistic norms of the community, language varieties used in the community, people's reactions to these language varieties in various social contexts, and the cultural appropriateness of specific varieties of the target language.

Saville-Troike discusses the affective component of bilingual education in relation to biculturalism and contrasts various English programs on the basis of the different cultural emphases in each. Her paper concludes with a plea for research in the areas of student proficiency in both languages, cultural appropriateness of curriculum materials, and the attitudes of students and parents toward themselves and their group. This last area is particularly frustrating because a fair number of attitudinal studies have been performed. In the case of Mexican-Americans, for example, such studies as Carter (1968), Church (1971), Cooper (1971), Murillo (1976), Padilla (1976), and Politizer and Ramírez (1973) all deal with attitudes of Mexican-American children in the United States. However, this apparent wealth of information is misleading. Carter (1970) states:

> A year-long effort by . . . graduate students . . . failed to uncover much written material to enlighten a researcher on the interaction of cause and effect among the three important variables — the school, the community social system and the Mexican-American subcultural group. (p. 3)

Brière, Cromshow, Flynn, and Lehman (1976) reviewed all the literature available on attitudes of Mexican-Americans and discovered a glaring lack of sophisticated, rigorous research, particularly in the area of Mexican-American adolescents. Nathaniel Murillo, a psychologist, stated: "The Mexican-American adolescent represents one of the least studied groups in psychology." In short, those who have spent a great deal of time reviewing the existing literature view the enormous lack of empirical information as one of the most important, immediate research needs.

Krashen, Swain, González, and Cazden discuss various aspects of language and content in a bilingual classroom. In discussing various aspects of language acquisition before and after the critical age period, Krashen hypothesizes that adults use a consciously learned system and a subconsciously acquired system. The learned grammar is utilized as a monitor to inspect and alter utterances before they are actually spoken. Krashen feels that the adolescent learning a second language should be provided with both acquisition and learning situations and makes specific recommendations for classroom activities that will promote the desired environments.

Swain found that secondary grade students in a French bilingual program did learn subject matter in the second language (though certain subject areas are learned better than others) and that students in the bilingual program learned French better than those who did not take the program. In observing the types of corrections that teachers make in the classrooms, Swain found that the correction of content areas took precedence over the correction of linguistic errors.

González suggests that no language corrections be made during the presentation of content areas and that the only skill required of the student be the communication of accurate information in the content area. He also suggests that parallel content areas are needed in the first and second languages and that the same content areas be presented in different levels of grammatical complexity.

Cazden addresses the question of teachers' patterns of language usage from the standpoint of code switching in the bilingual classroom, emphasizing the subliminal messages concerning language prestige that the students might derive from the teacher's pattern shifts. Cazden also contrasts language usage in the subject areas of science and mathematics and explores the effects of subject matter on first and second language usage.

Assessment in bilingual education is discussed by Spolsky, Ramírez, and Cornejo. Spolsky, addressing the broad, overall assessment of bilingual programs, suggests that bilingual education also involves psychological, sociological, economic, political, religio/cultural, and linguistic factors. To properly evaluate a bilingual program, all the factors pertinent to a specific program should be considered. Since all the factors are of unequal importance in a particular program, it is necessary to establish different kinds of measurements requiring interdisciplinary and community input.

Ramírez reviews previous attempts to assess the language abilities of children in English and Spanish and some of the problems involved in those assessments, and discusses the Ramírez-Politizer language dominance measure in terms of Zirkel's model of bilingualism. He also presents pedagogical applications of dominance information.

Cornejo discusses a specific area of assessment — the evaluation of reading materials. After a general discussion of the background of such evaluations, he presents a detailed example of the kinds of considerations that should go into the evaluation of programs and into the development of instructional materials.

In the final section of this volume, the materials development centers, resource centers, and dissemination and assessment centers of the National Network for Bilingual Education are discussed by Bernal in terms of their functions and their interrelationships to each other, to the local education agencies, and to institutes of higher learning. Since the network spans such a vast geographical area, Bernal expresses the hope that the network will provide an integrated view of the needs and priorities of all local bilingual situations.

Although it is our sincere hope that bilingual education will continue in the United States and that cultural pluralism will replace narrow ethnocentrism, it is not certain that these goals will actually be achieved. Great assistance would be given to the attainment of these goals if both the majority and the minority groups in this country viewed bilingual programs as desirable. Successful promotion of this viewpoint will require sophisticated and rigorous research; careful, informed planning; intelligent operation of programs; active community involvement; enthusiastic participation of teachers and students; cooperative endeavors among local education agencies, institutions of higher learning, and the centers in the national network; proper training of teachers and teachers' aides; and a favorable attitude among citizens to ensure that the necessary federal and local funding will be forthcoming.

The papers in this volume furnish a carefully considered set of guidelines to accomplish most of these objectives. However, perhaps the biggest step in achieving the last objective came from a very popular writer rather than from a scholar involved in bilingual education. The explosive impact of Alex Haley's *Roots* (1976) on the entire nation has led not only to an enormous interest by a tremendous number of Blacks in their genealogical histories but also to a similar "White roots" phenomenon. Haley's work, and its resulting effects on a vast number of people in the United States, prompted a recent essay by Kanfer in *Time* in which he makes the statement: "After Haley . . . not only Blacks but all ethnic groups saw themselves as whole. . . ." *(Time,* March 28, 1977, p. 54.) He also states that the immigrants to this country were primarily concerned with their total assimilation in the prevalent culture and language. Much later, this "melting pot" concept of total assimilation came to be seen by various immigrant groups as an enormous loss of unique cultural backgrounds and language heritages. Kanfer's statement: "They lost an unrecoverable currency: their language." *(Time, ibid.)* is precisely one of the major concerns of proponents of bilingual education today. We need to return that "currency" and replenish it.

The papers in this book not only provide guidelines for a good starting point but also outline the theoretical and practical aspects that must be considered to make bilingual education a success.

Eugène J. Brière

REFERENCES

Andersson, Theodore, and Mildred Boyer. *Bilingual Schooling in the United States*. 2 Volumes. U.S., Educational Resources Information Center, ERIC Document ED 039 527, January, 1970.

Balkan, Lewis. *Les Effets du Bilinguisme Français-Anglais sur les Aptitudes Intellectuelles*. Bruxelles: AIMAV, 1970.

Brière, Eugène J., J. Cromshaw, T. Flynn, and C. Lehman. *Student Profiles in Bilingual Education: A Necessary First Step*. Pomona: National Multilingual/Multicultural Materials Development Center, 1976.

Carter, Thomas P. *Mexican Americans in School: A History of Educational Neglect*. New York: College Entrance Examination Board, 1970.

_____. "The Negative Self-Concept of Mexican American Students," *School and Society*, XCVI (March, 1968), 217-219.

Church, Virginia K. *A Comparative Study of the Attitudes and Aspirations of Bilingual Mexican American Students with Monolingual Mexican American Students*. U.S., Educational Resources Information Center, ERIC Document ED 085 136, July, 1971.

Cohen, Andrew D. *A Sociolinguistic Approach to Bilingual Education: Experiments in the American Southwest*. Rowley: Newbury House, 1975.

Cooper, James G. *Perception of Self and Others as a Function of Ethnic Group Membership*. U.S., Educational Resources Information Center, ERIC Document ED 057 965, September, 1971.

Fishman, Joshua A., Robert L. Cooper, Roxana Ma, et al. *Bilingualism in the Barrio*. Bloomington: Indiana University, 1971.

_____, and Erika Lueders-Salmon. "What Has the Sociology of Language to Say to the Teacher? On Teaching the Standard Variety to Speakers of Dialectal or Sociolectal Varieties," *Functions of Language in the Classroom*, eds. Courtney B. Cazden, Vera P. John, and Dell Hymes. New York: Teachers College Press, 1972, pp. 67-83.

Gaarder, A. Bruce. "The First Seventy-Six Bilingual Education Projects," *Monograph Series on Language and Linguistics*, ed. J. E. Alatis. No. 23, 21st Annual Roundtable. Washington: Georgetown University Press, 1970, pp. 163-178.

Gleason, Henry A., Jr. *An Introduction to Descriptive Linguistics*. Rev. ed. New York: Holt, Rinehart and Winston, 1961.

Gonzalez, J. "Coming of Age in Bilingual/Bicultural Education: A Historical Perspective." *Inequality in Education*, XIX (February, 1975), 5-14.

Haley, Alex. *Roots*. Garden City: Doubleday and Co., Inc., 1976.

Haugen, Einar I. *Bilingualism in the Americas: A Bibliography and Research Guide*. Gainsville: American Dialect Society, 1956.

_____. *The Norwegian Language in America: A Study in Bilingual Behavior*. 2 Volumes. Philadelphia: University of Pennsylvania Press, 1953.

Kjolseth, Rolf. "Bilingual Education Programs in the United States: For Assimilation or Pluralism," *The Language Education of Minority Children: Selected Readings*, ed. Bernard Spolsky. Rowley: Newbury House, 1972, pp. 94-121.

Kanfer, Stefan. "Climbing All Over the Family Trees," *Time*. [New York]. March 28, 1977, p. 54.

Lambert, Wallace E., and G. Richard Tucker. *Bilingual Education of Children: The St. Lambert Experiment*. Rowley: Newbury House, 1972.

Lau v. Nichols, 414 U.S., 563 (1974).

Lewis, E. Glyn. *Multilingualism in the Soviet Union. Aspects of Language Policy and its Implementation*. The Hague: Mouton, 1972.

Macnamara, John. *Bilingualism and Primary Education: A Study of Irish Experience.* Edinburgh: Edinburgh University Press, 1966.

Morison, Samuel Eliot. *The Oxford History of the American People.* New York: Oxford University Press, 1965.

Murillo, Nathan. "The Mexican American Family," *Chicanos: Social and Psychological Perspectives.* 2d ed. eds. Carrol A. Hernández, Marsha J. Haug, and Nathaniel N. Wagner. St. Louis: C. V. Mosby Co., 1976, pp. 15-25.

Padilla, A. M. "Psychological Research and the Mexican American," *Chicanos: Social and Psychological Perspectives.* 2d ed. eds. Carrol A. Hernández, Marsha J. Haug, and Nathaniel N. Wagner. St. Louis: C. V. Mosby Co., 1976, pp. 152-159.

Politzer, Robert L., and Arnulfo Ramírez. *Judging Personality from Speech: A Pilot Study of the Effect of Bilingual Education on Attitudes Toward Ethnic Groups. Research and Development Memorandum No. 106.* U.S., Educational Resources Information Center, ERIC Document ED 076 278, February, 1973.

Sánchez, George I. "Bilingualism and Mental Measures — A Word of Caution," *Journal of Applied Psychology,* XVIII (1934), 765-772.

Weinreich, Uriel. *Languages in Contact, Findings and Problems.* 6th Printing. New York: Linguistic Circle of New York. The Hague: Mouton & Co., 1968.

CONTENTS

PART ONE
Legal Aspects of Bilingual Education

PART TWO
Philosophies of Bilingual Education

PART THREE
Social Factors in Bilingual Education

Contents

PART FIVE
Assessment in Bilingual Education

PART SIX
The National Network for Bilingual Education

PART ONE

Legal Aspects of Bilingual Education

Bilingual/ Bicultural Education and the Law*

Joaquin Guadalupe Avila and Ramona Godoy

Although bilingual education existed in the 1700's in the United States, increasing nationalism and isolationism led to a nation-wide imposition of English-only instruction by the early 1900's. Since the educational institutions ceased to provide equal opportunities to large numbers of linguistic minorities, many of them have sought assistance from the legal system to secure a more meaningful access to the educational process. This discussion centers on the limitations and capabilities of the judicial process, the interpretations of the major court decisions, and their implications for community members, educators, school boards, and educational policies in general. It is suggested that because of the limitations of some of our major court decisions, the only way to assure that the needs of *all* linguistic-minority children are met is through student-parent-teacher involvement in the schools' daily affairs.

EDUCATION HAS become an essential prerequisite for individual advancement and survival in today's complex society. Equal educational opportunities, however, have eluded large numbers of minorities in this country. Since the educational institutions have not provided these opportunities, many minorities have sought assistance from the legal system to secure a more meaningful access to the educational process. This paper will discuss these efforts as well as present the limitations and capabilities of the judicial process in adequately responding to the needs of linguistically and culturally excluded minorities.

---

*The views expressed in this paper are those of the authors and do not necessarily reflect the position or policy of the United States Commission on Civil Rights nor that of the Mexican American Legal Defense Education Fund.

Before discussing the legal developments, a brief description of the judicial process is necessary to assess properly the court's role in requiring school districts to provide a meaningful educational opportunity. Courts in our society have functioned as conflict resolution mechanisms whereby individuals seek an objective determination of an existing conflict. In this capacity courts have developed a variety of legal doctrines to adjudicate controversies.

In the application of the legal principles, courts are presumed to decide in an impartial manner. In reality, however, such an objective decision-making process simply may not exist. Technically, courts cannot depart from well-established principles of law. An "unjust"[1] decision usually does not result from a disregard of the legal principle; the deviation may result from the application of the law. A court's application of the law is based on its perception of the factual controversy, its perception of the court's role in resolving societal disputes,[2] and most importantly, a judge's background and experiences.

On many occasions trial courts are swayed by all the aforementioned factors. When a reviewing appellate court determines that a trial court has employed reasons other than those based on sound judicial discretion, the lower court decision will be reversed. The same reviewing procedure is utilized until the case reaches the United States Supreme Court — the court of final resort.

This overly simplified description of the legal process explains, but does not justify, the court's negative views concerning bilingual/bicultural education. The decisions in *Keyes*,[3] *Morales*,[4] and *Otero*[5] (to be discussed subsequently) demonstrate court reluctance to second-guess school board actions by failing to order implementation of extensive educational plans that would remove the incompatibilities between a school system and the Chicano student. This reluctance is based primarily on the court system's perception of its role in resolving matters viewed as lying within the scope of educators. If educators cannot agree on the proper course or methodology of instruction, the courts, so the reasoning goes, are even less capable

---

[1]Justice, as we all know, is a relative term. What may appear to be justice to one group is an injustice to another. Prevailing notions of justice are a mixture of existing majority societal perceptions of right and wrong coupled with fundamental notions of natural law and fairness.
[2]The term *societal dispute* as used in this paper is any conflict involving major social movements in which the court determines it is not the proper forum for adjudication of the dispute. If the court is the forum of last resort and the court denies an audience, then for all practical purposes, a complaining minority group has no alternative other than seek protection of its rights from the very group that denies those rights.
[3]*Keyes* v. *School District No. 1*, 521 F. 2d 465 (1975).
[4]*Morales* v. *Shannon*, 516 F. 2d 411 (5th Cir. 1975).
[5]*Otero* v. *Mesa County Valley School District No. 51*, 408 F. Supp. 162 (D. Colo. 1975).

of deciding which is the program best suited for linguistically excluded students. However, before proceeding to discuss court decisions in the aforementioned cases, a short discussion of the historical development of bilingual education is necessary to demonstrate to society[6] and the courts that the United States has its roots in a multilingual society and culture. The recognition of this historical foundation can serve as a basis for creating judicial receptivity to classroom instruction in languages other than English.

In a short but comprehensive article, Gonzales (1975) describes the extensive use of scholastic instruction in a language other than English. For example, German was the primary language in Pennsylvania, Maryland, Virginia, and the Carolinas during the 1700's. Similar German classes were taught in Wisconsin. Spanish, in conjunction with English, was the language of instruction in California during the 1800's and in New Mexico as late as 1884. Moreover, the Cherokees in the 1800's had developed a bilingual education program that produced Oklahoma Cherokees with a higher English literary level than Anglos in Texas or Arkansas.

However, during the late 1800's and early 1900's there was a movement "towards a nationalistic, isolationist policy in the U.S. [which] led quickly to a nationwide imposition of English-only instructional policies" (Gonzales, 1975, p. 6). These policies resulted in English literacy tests as a prerequisite for voting, as well.[7] These policies did not go unchallenged. One of the early challenges to this English-speaking policy occurred in *Meyer* v. *Nebraska*.[8] In *Meyer*, the Supreme Court declared unconstitutional a state statute that prohibited the teaching of foreign languages to children below the eighth grade. Essentially the *Meyer* v. *Nebraska* decision established the "right of the individual to contract, to engage in any of the common occupations of life, to *acquire useful knowledge*"[9] (emphasis added). Unfortunately, the decision cannot be construed as requiring the state to provide an opportunity for the right to acquire knowledge to be meaningful. As a result of the *Nebraska* case, a state could not prevent by statute the teaching of a foreign language if the teacher decided to teach a class in Spanish; however, the state could not be required to provide such

---

[6]Societal perceptions influence court decisions involving significant social issues.
[7]The use of English-literacy tests has served to disenfranchise non-English-speaking citizens and other minorities:
    English literacy tests, having their origins in anti-immigrant feelings, are today used to discriminate against minorities that are readily identifiable by color: Chicanos, Blacks, Indians and Boricuas.
Project Report, *Chicano School Desegregation*, 7 HARV, CIV. RTS-CIV. LIB.L. REV. 307, 353 (1972).
[8]262 U.S. 390 (1923).
[9]*Id.* at 399-400.

instruction. There were a series of other cases that affected the prohibition of English-only instruction.[10]

The early decisions affecting educational policy did not seriously infringe upon the authority of local school boards to implement their educational programs. The intrusion of the courts into the school systems' decision-making policies was not instituted on a national basis until 1954 with *Brown v. Board of Education of Topeka*[11] and its progeny.[12] *Brown* established that school systems, pursuant to state law, could not racially segregate its students. This decision had a monumental impact, and the repercussions of *Brown* are presently felt in places such as Boston, Massachusetts.

In *Brown* the Court recognized the necessity to intervene in what were at one time considered matters lying within the exclusive domain of the school board. This intervention in school affairs provided the judicial framework for future school litigation involving more complex issues than the mere reshuffling of persons. As a result of this intervention, the Court recognized that state mandated segregation could not continue to exist in view of the equal protection clause of the Fourteenth Amendment.[13]

The Supreme Court decision in *Brown* was not well received by school districts in the South. Furthermore, federal district courts had not significantly altered the patterns of racial segregation in Southern schools.[14] Thus, in the early 1960's, Congress passed Title VI of the Civil Rights Act of 1964[15] to administratively combat racial segregation. Title VI provided:

> . . . [no] person in the United States shall, on the ground of race, color, or national origin, be excluded from participation in, be denied the benefits of, or be subjected to discrimination under any program or activity receiving Federal financial assistance.

Primary responsibility for enforcing Title VI rested with the Office for Civil Rights of the Department of Health, Education, and Welfare (H.E.W.).

Regarding Chicano segregation, H.E.W. did not commit any substantial resources; moreover, its enforcement efforts were not rigid:

---

[10]Compare *Pierce* v. *Society of Sisters*, 268 U.S. 529 (1925); *Farrington* v. *Tokushige*, 273 U.S. 284 (1926); *Yu Cong Eng* v. *Trinidad*, 271 U.S. 500 (1926). There were also a series of voting cases that established a right to bilingual elections and assistance. These cases were primarily aimed at the Puerto Rican communities in New York City, Chicago, and Philadelphia. See *United States Commission on Civil Rights, Ten Years After* (1975).

[11]347 U.S. 483 (1954).

[12]The second *Brown* decision, 349 U.S. 294 (1955), dealt primarily with the remedy stage of a desegregation case.

[13]This clause provides that no state shall "deny to any person within its jurisdiction the equal protection of the laws." This clause was interpreted to allow separate but equal treatment in the provision of public transportation. *Plessy* v. *Ferguson*, 163 U.S. 537 (1896).

[14]*United States* v. *Jefferson County Board of Education*, 372 F. 2d 836 (5th Cir. 1966), *cert denied*, 389 U.S. 840 (1967).

[15]42 U.S.C. §2000d to 2000d-4.

The Office for Civil Rights has been severely criticized for neglect of Chicano integration problems. Prior to the 1967-68 school year, H.E.W. required racial school statistics only for Blacks and whites. Only then was the category "other" added to its statistical forms and defined to include all "significant minority groups in the community" and specifically Mexican-Americans. Not until 1968-69 were separate statistics collected for "Spanish Surnamed Americans."

HEW's on-site review practices were as negligent and ineffective as its statistical oversight. Even where the Department had initiated its cumbersome administrative process, all too often real enforcement was left to others.[16]

After 1970, H.E.W. began to secure compliance plans for Title VI. These plans were based on the now famous May 25, 1970 memorandum in which H.E.W. dealt with the issue of bilingual education in its enforcement efforts:

Where inability to speak and understand the English language excludes national origin minority group children from effective participation in the educational program offered by a school district, the district must take affirmative steps to rectify the language deficiency in order to open its instructional program to these students.

In lawsuits filed to desegregate schools based on Title VI, lower trial courts were, as a result of the May 25th Memorandum, considering the implementation of bilingual education as part of the remedy. In *United States* v. *State of Texas*,[17] a federal court ordered the implementation of a comprehensive bilingual/bicultural education plan.

Unfortunately, this educational plan is stated in very broad language. Since the educational process is often difficult to categorize into neat compartments, general terms such as "bilingual/bicultural" are utilized. The problem with general terms in any court decree arises with monitoring the degree of compliance. These general terms permit a wide latitude of interpretation that may have a significant educational impact but which a court may fail to perceive. This latitude of interpretation has special significance in appreciating the role of the court system in resolving educational policy disputes. Essentially a court decree sets up a general framework in which to operate. The fleshing out of the decree ultimately falls upon the parties and the local community. This aspect of a bilingual case will be discussed extensively in a later section.

---

[16]Project Report, *Chicano School Desegregation*, 7 HARV. CIV. RTS-CIV. LIB. L. REV. 365-366 (1972).
[17]342 F. Supp. 24 (1971).

The *United States* v. *Texas*[18] bilingual/bicultural plan was part of a desegregation order. The case was not a so-called straight Title VI case, which would occur only when Chicano students institute an action against a school district for failing to provide programs to meet the language deficiencies of non-English-speaking students.[19] The only significant Title VI bilingual case to reach the Supreme Court is *Lau* v. *Nichols*.[20]

Lau was filed in the United States District Court for the Northern District of California by seven non-English-speaking Chinese students (representative of 1,800 other non-English-speaking Chinese students in the San Francisco Unified School District) against the Superintendent, members of the Board of Education of the school district, and members of the Board of Supervisors of the City and County of San Francisco. The aggrieved parties alleged that they were unable to speak, understand, read, or write English. They contended that, in essence, they were completely excluded from receiving the benefits of public school education. They further alleged that:

> . . . [A] school district, when it precludes non-English speaking children of Chinese ancestry from any opportunity to obtain an education by refusing to provide any instruction that would permit them to comprehend and benefit from classes taught in the English language, violates the First Amendment and the Due Process and Equal Protection clauses of the Fourteenth Amendment . . . [and] Section 601 of the Civil Rights Act of 1964, 42 U.S.C. §2000d.[21]

On May 26, 1970, the District Court issued an order denying petitioners' motions for relief. From this order, petitioners appealed to the United States Court of Appeals for the Ninth Circuit. On January 8, 1973, the Court of Appeals issued its opinion affirming the judgment of the District Court. The United States Supreme Court agreed to hear the case, and on January 21, 1974, Justice Douglas delivered the opinion of the court.

The opinion was not based on the argument that non-English-speaking students were being deprived of their equal protection rights under the Fourteenth Amendment to the United States Constitution. Rather, the Court relied solely on Title VI and its accompanying guidelines and regulations, which included the May 25th, 1970 Memorandum. According to the Court, the San Francisco School District, upon receipt of federal funds, contractually agreed to comply with Title VI of the Civil Rights Act of 1964

---

[18]*Ibid.*
[19]The degree of non-English-speaking ability needed to trigger the application of Title VI is uncertain at this time.
[20]414 U.S. 563 (1974).
[21]Brief for Petitioner at 2, 16, *Lau* v. *Nichols*, 414 U.S. 563 (1974).

and all the requirements imposed by the Department of Health, Education, and Welfare guidelines issued pursuant to that title. On this basis the Court reversed the Court of Appeals decision.

No indication was given by the Court as to the nature of an acceptable program for non-English-speaking students. Justice Douglas explained the Court's omission in establishing remedial criteria:

> This class suit . . . seeks relief against the unequal educational opportunities which are alleged to violate . . . the Fourteenth Amendment. No specific remedy is urged upon us. Teaching English to the students of Chinese ancestry who do not speak the language is one choice. Giving instructions to this group in Chinese is another. There may be others. Petitioners asks only that the Board of Education be directed to apply its expertise to the problem and rectify the situation. [22]

In response to this decision, the Secretary of the Department of Health, Education, and Welfare established a task force in 1975 to outline the kinds of "affirmative steps" that would be appropriate under the 1970 guidelines (United States Department of Health, Education, and Welfare, Office of the Secretary, Undated Memorandum). At the moment, it is unclear whether the Task Force Remedies can serve to establish a violation of Title VI or whether they are guidelines for formulating an appropriate remedy once a Title VI violation has been independently established. Since these recommendations were formulated by a highly respectable team of educational experts, the Task Force guidelines should be given great weight by courts in evaluating whether a school's treatment of linguistically excluded students may amount to a violation of Title VI.

The Task Force concluded in their recommendations that school districts should implement a bilingual program tailored to a child's linguistic and educational capabilities and that:

> A program designed for students of limited-English-speaking ability must not be operated in a manner so as to solely satisfy a set of objectives divorced or isolated from those educational objectives established for students in the regular school program. (United States Department of Health, Education, and Welfare, Office of the Secretary, 1975, p. 194)

While acknowledging various instructional methods, the Task Force explicitly stated that an ESL program for non- and limited-English-

---

[22]*Id.* at 564-565.

speaking children at the elementary school level was insufficient to meet minimal educational requirements. Something more had to be provided for the education of these students (United States Department of Health, Education, and Welfare, Office of the Secretary, 1975). The Task Force Remedies outline at least four steps for compliance with its recommendations. (A copy of these remedies is provided in the Appendix.) These steps include student identification, student language assessment, analyses of achievement data, and program offerings. Additional items involve student placement, parent communications, and other requirements.

In addition, after the *Lau*[23] decision, Congress passed the Equal Educational Opportunities Act in 1974.[24] This act declared:

> No State shall deny equal educational opportunity to an individual on account of his or her race, color, sex, or national origin, by . . . the failure by an educational agency to take appropriate action to overcome language barriers that impede equal participation by its students in its instructional programs.[25]

This Federal statute is applicable to all school districts and state educational agencies regardless of their funding sources.

As previously mentioned, the Supreme Court has yet to identify the proper remedy for addressing the needs of students who have been linguistically excluded from the educational process. The strongest appellate opinion that defined the *Lau* remedy came down in *Serna v. Portales Municipal Schools*.[26] In *Serna*, the appellate panel approved a Title VI court-ordered bilingual/bicultural education plan.

To briefly summarize this discussion concerning the development of a right to bilingual/bicultural education, the following are four approaches whereby students deficient in English can seek to require school districts to implement adequate educational plans:

1. *constitutional approach:* This approach seeks to require that denial of bilingual/bicultural programs amounts to a separate constitutional violation. Parties utilizing this strategy seek to establish the violation irrespective of whether there is a segregated school system.

2. *hybrid constitutional approach:* Under this strategy, parties institute an action to desegrate the schools. If the school systems contain a significant number of English-deficient students, then bilingual programs are implemented as part of a desegregation order.

3. *Title VI approach:* Under this approach, the complaining parties seek

---

[23]*Lau v. Nichols*, 414 U.S. 563 (1974).
[24]20 U.S.C. §1701 *et. seq.* (Supp. IV, 1974).
[25]20 U.S.C. §1703 (Supp. IV 1974).
[26]499 F. 2d. 1147 (10th Cir. 1974).

to secure by a statutory basis the right to a bilingual/bicultural education.

4. *Equal Educational Opportunities Act approach:* Although similar to number 3, the receipt of federal funds is not a prerequisite to the lawsuit.

Under all four approaches, an attorney must secure the same type of evidence and make similar evaluations. The first evaluation concerns the methodology used to identify students who are deficient in English. According to the Task Force recommendation, there are three criteria for determining which students are potentially in need of special programs: (1) identification of language first *acquired* by the student, (2) identification of the language most often spoken in the student's home, (3) identification of the language most often spoken by the student. As attorneys, we must rely on educators for advice in establishing standards to be utilized for identification. The next inquiry concerns assessing the level of linguistic ability of the students. These linguistic abilities are categorized as follows:

A. Monolingual speaker of the language other than English (speaks the language other than English exclusively).

B. Predominantly speaks the language other than English (speaks mostly the language other than English, but speaks some English).

C. Bilingual (speaks both the language other than English and English with equal ease).

D. Predominantly speaks English (speaks mostly English, but some of the language other than English).

E. Monolingual speaker of English (speaks English exclusively). (United States Department of Health, Education, and Welfare, Office of the Secretary, 1975, p. 193)

Health, Education, and Welfare Task Force Findings — Lau Remedies

As with the identification of students, the law must rely on educational experts to establish criteria for assessing English proficiency. The biggest problem in this area is the lack of consensus among experts concerning standardized tests.

The next evaluation involves an examination of the number of students involved. *Lau* involved 1,800 students. One of the Justices stressed the importance of numbers as a key factor in determining whether the school district was under an obligation to provide a remedial education:

> I merely wish to make plain that when, in another case, we are concerned with a very few youngsters, or with just a single child who speaks only German or Polish or Spanish or any language other than English, I would not regard today's decision, or the separate concurrence, as conclusive upon the issue whether the statute and the

guideline require the funded school district to provide special instruction. For me, numbers are at the heart of this case and my
concurrence is to be understood accordingly.[27]

The question of determining the appropriate numbers is difficult to
answer. The *Lau* remedies recommend that Health, Education, and Welfare should require a *Lau* plan when the district has 20 or more students of
the same language group identified as having a primary or home language
other than English. However, courts will probably focus more on the
numbers of English-deficient students. Moreover, a court will also
examine the number of linguistically-excluded students in comparison to
the overall student body percentage. Consequently, a school system that
contains well over 100,000 students may not be required by a court to
implement a bilingual plan if 150 students are deemed to be deficient in
English. Conversely, a school system consisting of 300 students may be
required by a court to institute a bilingual program if 20 students are
determined to be deficient in English.

The problem with a numbers approach as presented in the *Lau* concurring opinion is that it treats the right to a meaningful education as a
collective right rather than an individual right. This treatment is reflective
of the prevailing dogma upon which our educational system is based:

> This dogma projects a classroom situation in which thirty children are
> marched in lockstep through identical instructional activities. Obvi-
> ously, all children, regardless of ethnicity or language, have different
> learning abilities ranging perhaps from retarded to genius, varying
> past achievement rates ranging from retained-in-grade to child pro-
> digy, differing interests, aspirations, motivations, pressures, and
> learning styles. Yet, in spite of their differences, children are sub-
> jected to common instructional activities directed at the mythical
> average or typical child. It is this methodology, based on an out-
> moded dogma, that cannot fail to produce the mediocrity for which
> our schools are becoming famous. (Cardenas, 1975, p. 20)

Arguments for an individual right to a bilingual/bicultural education are
very compelling.[28] Since a child is forced to attend school, the state should
be obligated to provide the student with a meaningful educational experi-

---

[27]*Lau* v. *Nichols*, 414 U.S. at 572 (1974).
[28]See Grubb, *Breaking the Language Barrier: The Right to Bilingual Education*, 9 HARV.
CIV. RTS-CIV. LIB.L. REV. 52 (1974); Project Report, *De Jure Segregation of Chicanos in
Texas Schools*, 7 HARV. CIV. RTS.-CIV. LIB. L. REV. 307 (1972); Comment, *The Con-
stitutional Right of Bilingual Children to an Equal Educational Opportunity*, 47 SO. CAL.
L. REV. 943 (1974).

ence. A logical extension of the argument would lead a student to sue the school system for damages if the district failed to insure that the student could pass certain standardized tests. As the following discussion will show, it appears that courts are not ready to affirm bilingual/bicultural education as an individual right.

As previously mentioned, courts have very fixed views concerning their roles in resolving societal disputes. Establishing an individual cause of action against a school system for failing to provide a relevant education runs counter to a court's belief that it should not enter a field where judicial resolution is not suitable. Even if a cause of action were permitted, the problems of establishing a direct causal connection between the schools' actions and the failure of the graduating senior to read at the eighth grade level are monumental. A complaining party would have to show that only the schools' actions were directly responsible for the student's failure. Such a case of individual deprivation would be more manageable if the cause of action were based on a linguistic exclusion theory.

English-only instruction to a child who is deficient in the English language constitutes a total exclusion. This exclusion is analogous to the situation presented in *McLaurin v. Oklahoma S. Regents*.[29] In *McLaurin* the court focused on the importance of communication in acquiring an education. The school allowed a Black graduate access to the same physical facilities but nevertheless excluded him from interacting with his peers by requiring him:

> . . . to sit apart at a designated desk in an anteroom adjoining the classroom . . . to sit at a designated desk on the mezzanine floor of the library, but not to use the desks in the regular reading room . . . and to sit at a designated table and to eat at a different time from the other students in the school cafeteria.[30]

The Court held these efforts by the university to block student interaction as unconstitutional. Similarly, an English-deficient student is in the same situation as *McLaurin*. As the Court noted in *Lau*:

> Basic English skills are at the very core of what these public schools teach. Imposition of a requirement that, before a child can effectively participate in the educational program, he must already have acquired those basic skills is to make a mockery of public education. We know that those who do not understand English are certain to find their classroom experiences wholly incomprehensible and in no way meaningful.[31]

---

[29]339 U.S. 637 (1950).
[30]*McLaurin v. Oklahoma S. Regents*, 339 U.S. at 640 (1950).
[31]*Lau v. Nichols*, 414 U.S. at 566 (1974).

Despite this strong language, establishing an individual right to a bilingual education is still repugnant because of the cost to the school system to provide an extensive educational program to serve the needs of one child.

This repugnance was vividly illustrated in the case of *Otero* v. *Mesa County Valley School District No. 51.*[32] In *Otero*, 8.2 percent of the student body was Mexican-American. Of this percentage, relatively few students were deficient in English. In reviewing the facts, the trial court determined that the school system was making a conscientious effort to recognize and solve these linguistic problems. The Court also focused on the numbers: "Our case involves a very few, if any, students who have real language deficiency."[33] The Court further added:

> Plaintiffs want to restructure the curriculum of Mesa Valley School District No. 51, and they want to tailor it to accommodate plaintiffs' concept of the alleged needs of an astonishingly small number of students. What plaintiffs really want is to substitute their judgment for the thoughtful, independent judgment of the elected school board which, for the most part, has acted only after obtaining recommendations of qualified, duly appointed school officials and recommendations of qualified independent experts hired by the school board.[34]

This extreme deference to school board action is indicative of the Court's limited view of its role in resolving significant educational policy issues. A similar view was expressed in *Morales* v. *Shannon.*[35] *Morales*, unlike *Otero* and *Lau*, involved a desegregation issue with a bilingual/bicultural education component. The Court in remanding the case for more factual inquiries also expressed a reluctance to substitute the judgment of the court for that of educators:

> It is admitted that most Mexican American students enter school with English language deficiencies and this brings us to the next contention of appellants, that a bilingual-bicultural education program is necessary to permit the Mexican-American students to continue and develop intellectual capacity in Spanish while gradually becoming proficient in English. They point out that the school district has never applied for federally-funded programs although available, and that the refusal of the district to meet the special needs of its Mexican-American students is a form of continuing discrimination. *This again may involve a teaching technique.* (Emphasis added)

---

[32]408 F. Supp. 162 (D. Colo. 1975).
[33]*Id.* at 171 (1975).
[34]*Id.* at 164 (1975).
[35]516 F. 2d 411 (5th Cir. 1975).

It strikes us that this entire question goes to a matter reserved to educators.[36]

Although *Otero* and *Morales* give restricted views of the court's role in the educational process, other trial courts have not been so restrictive. For example, the previously discussed *United States* v. *Texas*[37] case demonstrates to what extent a court can determine the formulation of educational policy. The *Aspira* v. *Board of Education of the City of New York*[38] consent decree detailed in a comprehensive manner the type of bilingual/bicultural programs which school districts have a responsibility to provide to their minority constituencies. The city of New York has agreed to the following: identify children in need of bilingual/bicultural education; recognize its responsibility to cultural education; recognize its responsibility to provide bilingual/bicultural education by developing the child's knowledge of English, by providing instruction in any substantive subject in the child's native language, and by developing the child's knowledge of English; promulgate minimum educational standards that include bilingual education; distribute materials, tests, measuring devices, and other instructional materials concerning bilingual education; recruit and hire bilingual/bicultural educators; retain personnel in bilingual/bicultural education; establish pilot schools for bilingual/bicultural education; provide full implementation by September, 1975; generate funds from city, state, and federal sources for bilingual/bicultural education; and provide detailed monthly compliance reports.

Finally, the Tenth Circuit Court of Appeals, in *Keyes* v. *School District No. 1*,[39] reversed the trial court's adoption of a comprehensive educational plan designed to minimize the incompatibilities existing between Chicano students and the school system; part of the plan consisted of the implementation of a bilingual/bicultural plan. With respect to the issue of bilingual/bicultural education, the Court remanded the case for further factual findings. All of these decisions indicate that the remedy aspect of a desegregation suit with a bilingual component or a straight bilingual Title VI lawsuit is still in the process of development. Future cases that do establish a violation will have to demonstrate that the school's proposed plan of compliance with the law is not enough. The court's acceptance of the plaintiffs' criticisms of the school's program will depend upon the degree to which the court perceives that its ruling may constitute an unwarranted intrusion into the decision-making process of a school board.

---

[36]*Id.* at 414-415 (1975).
[37]342 F. Supp. 24 (1971).
[38]No. 72 Cir. 4002 (filed August 29, 1974) (Frankel, J.).
[39]521 F. 2d 465 (1975).

Even if a good remedy is secured, the process of monitoring and assuring compliance both with the spirit and letter of the law will be a demanding task. A decree without adequate monitoring and community participation is merely a paper victory. Judicial decrees at best establish a framework and define parameters delineating the basic responsibility of a school board to provide a meaningful educational opportunity. Coupling a highly involved community with an experienced attorney, the Chicano community could exert political pressure and require the school board to initiate programs which the school would not ordinarily be legally obligated to adopt. Under these circumstances, it is absolutely critical that educators, students, and parents participate in the process of monitoring a court decree.

State and Federal Legislation

In 1959 California State law declared that, "All schools shall be taught in the English language." It was not until 1967 that the law was amended to allow for instruction in a language other than English.[40]

More recently, the California legislature began to recognize the need for programs to assist limited non-English-speaking students. In 1971, the Bilingual Pilot Program (AB 116) was passed.[41] The following year, the legislature enacted the Bilingual Education Act of 1972, (AB 2284), a more expansive bilingual program.[42] Next came the Bilingual-Cross Cultural Teacher Preparation and Training Act of 1973 (SB 1335)[43] and the Bilingual Teacher Corps Program enacted in 1974 (AB 2817).[44] Other programs enacted during this time such as the Early Childhood Education Act of 1972,[45] the Educationally Disadvantaged Youth Program of 1972,[46] and the Miller-Unruh Basic Reading Act of 1965,[47] though not primarily for bilingual/bicultural education, can be utilized to assist limited and non-English-speaking children. Participation by school districts, however, in any of these programs is on a voluntary basis.

With the exception of the Bilingual-Cross Cultural Act, which is administered primarily by the Commission for Teacher Preparation and Licensing, the legislature directed the State Board of Education and the State Department of Education to administer these programs. Generally,

[40]Cal. Educ. Code §71 (West's 1975), *amending* Cal. Educ. Code §71 (West's 1957).
[41]Ch. 1521, Statutes of 1971, California Legislature, Regular Session.
[42]Cal. Educ. Code §5761 *et. seq.* (West's 1975).
[43]Cal. Educ. Code §5768 et. seq. (West's 1975).
[44]Cal. Educ. Code §5766 *et. seq.* (West's 1975).
[45]Cal. Educ. Code §6445 *et. seq.* (West's 1975).
[46]Cal. Educ. Code §6499 *et. seq.* (West's 1975).
[47]Cal. Educ. Code §5770 *et. seq.* (West's 1975).

the State Board of Education functions as the policy-making entity approving rules and regulations for these programs.[48] The legislature charged the department, on the other hand, with monitoring local program activities to ensure compliance with state laws and board regulations. Thus, responsibility for compiling surveys, reviews, and evaluations of programs mandated by the legislature is generally conferred upon the State Department of Education by statute.[49]

The Federal government also established educational programs to assist non- or limited-English-speaking children. In 1965, Congress passed the Elementary and Secondary Education Act (ESEA).[50] Title I of the ESEA is directed at educationally deprived children. This title, as amended in 1974, provides funds that may be used for the hiring of bilingual aides. Title VII of the ESEA funds bilingual education programs throughout the country.

Populations and Programs

More than 30 percent of California's 4.4 million students in grades K-12 were members of racial and ethnic minorities during the 1973-1974 school year, according to survey results published in the fall of 1974 by the California State Department of Education's Bureau of Intergroup Relations. The Spanish-surname population was 765,419 or 17.2 percent of the total student population. Black students were 432,418 or 9.7 percent of the total student population, Asian-Americans were 133,430 or 3 percent, and Native Americans were 22,316 or .5 percent (California State Department of Education, 1974).

In accordance with state law enacted in 1972, local school districts conducted surveys during the 1973-1974 school year on the numbers of non- or limited-English-speaking students in grades K-12.[51] A sample survey instrument, prepared by the State Department of Education Bilingual Bicultural Task Force, was mailed to each school district as a recommended method for identifying language-minority students. Each district conducted and compiled its own survey. That survey identified approximately 225,000 students as non- or limited-English speaking.[52]

During the fall of the 1974-1975 school year, the Office of the Legislative Analyst undertook a review of the department's administration of bilingual

[48]Cal. Educ. Code §151, 152 (West's 1975).
[49]41 Ops. Cal. Atty. Gen. 105.
[50]20 U.S.C. §241 et. seq. (1970).
[51]Cal. Educ. Code §5761.3 (West's 1975).
[52]The actual number tabulated by the State Department of Education was 202,000. According to Mary Burdette, legislative coordinator, Office of Governmental Affairs, State Department of Education, the department increased this number to 225,000 to allow for undercounts.(Staff interview with Mary Burdette, June 24, 1975.)

programs. This was the first time in the state's history of bilingual education
that such a thorough review of bilingual programs had been conducted.
The analyst's report stated that the department had identified 11 State and
Federal programs with approximately $36,320,046 in funds for possible use
in assisting language-minority students (State of California, Office of the
Legislative Analyst, 1975). The department used the term *program* to refer
to each funding source.

For several of the major programs (Educationally Disadvantaged Youth,
Early Childhood Education, Miller-Unruh Basic Reading Act, and
Emergency School Aid Act), the department had no data on a student
enrollment of 124,229; of these, 77,906 students were non- or limited-
English speaking. Forty-three percent or 33,713 of the non- or limited-
English-speaking students were enrolled in English-as-a-Second-
Language programs. The department could not identify the kinds of in-
structional programs made available to these language-minority students
from each of the above resources, nor whether these programs were full or
part time.

It should be noted that these department figures compiled in late 1974
may have been inflated, since students may participate in more than one of
the 11 programs simultaneously and could have been counted for each
program. Also, the figures do not indicate the extent to which a limited- or
non-English-speaking child actually participated in a program. Some programs entailed only a few hours of bilingual instruction each week, but
there was no indication which programs were full time or which were part
time. Even assuming that the figures were not inflated or that all the
programs were full time, the 77,906 non- or limited-English students
enrolled in these programs represented fewer than half of the 225,000
students the department had identified as needing such assistance.

According to the Analyst's report, few of the 11 programs funded bilingual projects.[53] The report identified only three programs as specifically
bilingual: State Bilingual Pilot Programs, State Bilingual Education Act,
and Federal Title VII of the Elementary and Secondary Education Act. If,
as cited in the Analyst's report, bilingual projects are primarily funded by
these three programs, only 21,693 students or fewer than 10 percent of the
225,000 non- or limited-English-speaking students participated in bilingual education in the school year 1974-75.[54] The cost in that year for these
three programs was $17,933,968 — $13,800,000 of which came from
Federal funds.

[53]Nowhere in the Analyst's report are bilingual programs defined. The department clearly
stated the distinction between a bilingual program and a bilingual/bicultural program.
[54]The Bilingual Pilot Program with $133,968 for fiscal year 1974-1975 was due to terminate at
the end of that fiscal year.

Because of the apparent inadequacies of the 1974 data, the legislature requested that the department conduct a second survey during the same school year, 1974-1975, to obtain an unduplicated count of non- and limited-English-speaking students to identify how many of these students were receiving a bilingual education. The department conducted this survey in the spring of 1975. The results, published in November, 1975, were prefaced by a statement explaining that the survey of state and federal programs was a one-time special study initiated at the request of the legislature to identify the numbers of non- and limited-English-speaking students participating in the various bilingual services programs (State of California, State Department of Education, 1975). The survey identified 233,520 non- and limited-English-speaking students in grades K-12, 62,851 of which were "served in bilingual programs."

Although 62,851 is an increase of 18,658 students from the previous figure of 44,193 obtained during the same school year, several comments on the second survey should be noted. The figures contained in the Analyst's report included 33,713 students in ESL programs funded by Federal Title I and Educationally Disadvantaged Youth (SB 90). In the April, 1975, survey, 42,922 students were recorded as receiving "English as a Second Language, Title I, SB 90, ECE, etc." Yet in another table of the same survey, a nearly identical number, 41,868 students, was reportedly served by "bilingual components of any individual or combined categorical programs — local, Title I, SB 90, ECE, etc." The survey report's preface conceded that local officials "had considerable difficulty in making the distinctions about language proficiencies and the allocation of program funds based on such distinctions . . . " (State of California, State Department of Education, 1975). The survey data raise the possibility that students were counted more than once.

It should also be noted that data for student participation in the Emergency School District Aid Act (ESAA) were not available in the 1974 report. Thus, the figure of 21,693 students receiving a bilingual education did not contain ESAA student figures. However, the second report in 1975 identified 3,291 non- and limited-English-speaking students as receiving a bilingual education from ESAA out of a total of 20,983 students served by bilingual programs. Even with the inclusion of the ESAA student figures compiled in the 1975 survey (20,983), bilingual programs served 700 fewer students than were reported in the fall of 1974 (21,693).

This total is less than nine percent of the 233,520 non- and limited-English-speaking students, a smaller percentage than was identified as receiving such assistance in the first survey.

Finally, and of significance, the second survey taken in 1975 indicates that the average expenditure per pupil for providing English-as-a-Second-Language instruction was $352, while the average per pupil cost of providing bilingual education instruction was $331.

1975-1976 Legislative Efforts

In 1975, the California State Assembly established the Special Subcommittee on Bilingual Bicultural Education to review state funded and/or state administered bilingual education programs. The subcommittee conducted six public hearings throughout the state to receive documents and testimony on this issue. On March 15, 1976, the subcommittee noted the following needs relative to the improvement of bilingual services in the state:

1. coordination of state and federal regulations governing the provision of bilingual services;
2. use of state-local program funds generated through a student's average daily attendance as primary funding for local bilingual education programs;
3. involvement of parents and teachers in the administration of bilingual programs, including implementation, evaluation, and funding decisions.

Other preliminary findings of the subcommittee stated the following:

1, California has no bilingual program services mandated on either the pre-kindergarten, elementary, or secondary levels;
2. the only state-funded bilingual program is AB 2284, the Bilingual Educational Act of 1972.[55] However, the extent of bilingual program services provided by this Act remains questionable.

After the collection of this initial data, the chairperson of the subcommittee, Assemblyman Peter Chacon, introduced legislation AB 1329, regulating bilingual education in California's public schools. Under the provisions of AB 1329, each district is required to offer bilingual/bicultural learning opportunities to each limited-English-speaking pupil enrolled in the public schools where ten or more such students are enrolled in the same grade level or in the same age group. All teachers for these classrooms are required to hold a bilingual cross-cultural certificate of proficiency or a bilingual cross-cultural specialist credential. Any teacher for these classes must be fluent in the primary language and familiar with the cultural heritage of the limited-English-speaking pupils in the bilingual classes he or she conducts. The pupil enrollment, however, remains on a voluntary basis. The bill also requires that each district provide adequate supplemental financial support to achieve such purposes. Assemblyman Peter Chacon states that the bill requires all local school districts to use the state and local

---

[55]Cal. Educ. Code §5761 et. seq. (West's 1975).

monies received from the enrollment of non- and limited-English-speaking children toward payment of the costs of an education that will meet their specific needs.

In addition, the legislation directs the districts to provide for programs to qualify existing and future personnel with the necessary bilingual/bicultural skills for teaching California's limited- and non-English-speaking students. Finally, the bill requires that public institutions of higher education establish programs to enable teachers to qualify for the bilingual/bicultural certificate, a prerequisite for teaching in a state bilingual program funded under the provisions of this bill.

Conclusion

This paper has shown the development of case law in bilingual/bicultural education. It has also demonstrated the state's failure to respond adequately to the needs of Spanish-speaking students. Unfortunately, there are no easy solutions toward solving the problems of institutional insensitivity. Lawsuits have limited applications; in the long run the determining forces will be student-parent involvement in the daily affairs of schools to assure that linguistic minority children receive an equal educational opportunity.

REFERENCES

California State Department of Education. "Racial and Ethnic Distribution of Pupils and Staff in California Public Schools." Fall, 1973. (Mimeographed November 29, 1974.)

Cardenas. Jose A. "Bilingual Education. Segregation, and A Third Alternative," *Inequality in Education,* Center for Law and Education. Harvard University. No. 19 (February. 1975), 19–22.

Gonzalez, J. "Coming of Age in Bilingual/Bicultural Education: A Historical Perspective," *Inequality in Education,* No. 19 (1975).

State of California, Office of the Legislative Analyst. *Report of the Legislative Analyst to the Joint Legislative Budget Committee, Analysis of the Budget Bill of the State of California for the Fiscal Year, July 1, 1975 to June 30, 1976.* Sacramento, California, 1975, p. 635. (Hereinafter cited as *Analysis of the Budget.*)

State of California, State Department of Education. "Limited English Speaking and Non-English Speaking Students in California." Sacramento, California, 1975. (Mimeographed.)

United States Department of Health, Education, and Welfare, Office of the Secretary. "Evaluation of Voluntary Compliance Plans Designed to Eliminate Educational Practices Which Deny Non-English Language Dominant Students Equal Educational Opportunity." (Undated Memorandum.)

United States Department of Health, Education, and Welfare, Office of the Secretary. "Task Force Findings Specifying Remedies Available for Eliminating Past Educational Practices Ruled Unlawful Under *Lau* v. *Nichols.*" Summer, 1975 (Mimeographed.)

PART TWO

Philosophies of
Bilingual Education

Philosophies of Bilingual Education in Societal Perspective

Joshua A. Fishman

A review of the literature on bilingual education reveals degrees of concern with three major goals: the political, the cultural, and the educational. Since the needs of marked and unmarked populations differ, these goals are pursued in various degrees of separation and combination that result in a philosophical diversity. Even when transitional/compensatory bilingual education is viewed as a device for reaching remedial economic and political goals, philosophical complexities and ambiguities exist. A review of Marxian, Weberian, and Herderian theoretical positions serves to clarify some of the philosophical disagreements. Since unmarked populations are already politically and economically dominant, their support is needed and can be attained by justifying bilingual education as an alternative to monolingual education for the unmarked child rather than simply as a factor in the social mobility or cultural protection of the marked child.

THE VOLUMINOUS literature on bilingual education reveals degrees of concern with three major goals: the political, the cultural, and the educational. These goals are not only pursued in various degrees of separation and combination, but they are variously evaluated by spokesmen of the different speech communities involved. The diversity of philosophical views on bilingual education is thus a result of each community's social diversity. Most complex societies normally reveal a variety of educational goals, even when monolingual education is the focus of attention. Bilingual education often presents an even more diversified philosophical scene, not only because it is commonly of more recent vintage (and, presumably, has had less time to achieve consensus) but also because it is much more commonly an intergroup enterprise. The groups involved in bilingual education often differ markedly in their resources, in their outlooks, and, therefore, in their goals. As a result, they favor or oppose bilingual education for different reasons. They want or fear different things. Where bilingual education has been in effect for many years (e.g., in Wales or in Dade County, Florida) there has been an opportunity for "the dust to settle" and for the major dimensions and difficulties to be clarified, understood, and in large measure to be overcome. Thus, American "viewers" must realize that the bilingual education around them is also philosophically far more "unsettled" than it is in most other parts of the world.

Marked and Unmarked

Because of the greater recency of bilingual education, particularly in the public sector, as well as because of its more common intergroup character, it is recurringly obvious that one of the two languages involved would *not* be a medium of instruction were it not for bilingual education. That language which is utilized as a medium of instruction only because of the introduction of bilingual education will be referred to here as the *marked* language. The designation "marked" implies special, unusual, different. However, it also implies problematic, most likely to be discontinued, most conflicted, less well established, and, therefore, at least temporarily weaker than the *unmarked* language. The distinction between marked and unmarked also applies to the populations involved in bilingual education. That population whose vernacular would *not* be recongnized were it not for bilingual education will be referred to here as the *marked* population. This population is often a disadvantaged minority (e.g., Chicanos in the United States or Ultra-Orthodox Yiddish-speaking Jews in Israel), but it may be a disadvantaged majority (e.g., "Bantus" in the Republic of South Africa) or even an advantaged minority (e.g., "European" resident foreigners in Latin America). Marking is contextually determined in terms of power, precedence, and prevalance. However, marking is reversible. If hitherto marked groups become dominant (in governmental, economic, educational, or other spheres), they become unmarked; and unmarked languages that were hitherto the main or only media of education may become marked (e.g., English, today, in bilingual education in the Philippines) or even discontinued entirely.

The distinctions between marked and unmarked (languages, populations) permeate the philosophies of bilingual education as well as the frequent differences in views with which bilingual education is regarded by marked and unmarked spokesmen (Fishman, 1976).

The Remedial Goals of Bilingual Education

The most tangible (and perhaps the most common) goals of bilingual education entail a remedial reallocation of political and economic power.

Disadvantaged populations often view bilingual education as a means of gaining entrée to better positions in the work force, to professional or technological expertise, and to greater participation in the political processes whereby societal priorities are set and resources are allocated. Unmarked spokesmen too often rationalize a long established lack of social mobility on the part of marked populations as being caused by a lack of unmarked language mastery on the part of those populations. Seemingly, both marked and unmarked spokesmen agree that bilingual education can provide a surer and a more humane route to unmarked language mastery than does unrelieved monolingual education in the unmarked language alone. As a result, the bulk of transitional/compensatory bilingual education in the United States is justified and rationalized on these manifest grounds. Nevertheless, as in most other areas of human endeavor, the manifest and the latent are not necessarily in agreement. Even in connection with the remedial goals of bilingual education, the views of unmarked and marked populations and their spokesmen are often in disagreement.

Unmarked spokesmen often suspect that bilingual education ostensibly undertaken for the purposes of fostering greater economic and political participation on the part of peripheral populations will really bring about not national integration but its opposite: the political and economic solidification of cultural discontinuities. Unmarked spokesmen often oppose bilingual education, even when its goals are avowedly transitional and compensatory, as having undesired side-effects in terms of cultural separatism and its politicization. In order to avoid such side effects, unmarked spokesmen usually advocate monolingual education in the unmarked language for disadvantaged minorities as a less threatening and more direct route to the amelioration of social problems encountered by marked populations.

If unmarked spokesmen fear marked cultural *resurgences* as unanticipated side effects of transitional/compensatory bilingual education, marked spokesmen commonly fear unanticipated cultural *dislocations* as a result of such education. Marked spokesmen accuse transitional/compensatory bilingual education of being no more than a palliative or placebo in the political-economic realm at the same time as it is viewed by them as disruptive and destructive in the cultural realm. While bilingual education is viewed as being too little and too late in bringing about any real reallocations of societal power (marked spokesmen point out that populations acquire new languages if and when they are admitted to new social roles requiring these languages rather than vice-versa), it is considered a hidden subverter of the domains of intimacy (home, family, friendship, community), which are the last and only ones usually available to the marked language. Thus, marked spokesmen often view transitional/compensatory bilingual education as leading to a particularly crippling brand of double marginality: raising expectations that cannot be satisfied in the political and economic realm at the same time as undermining the ethno-cultural defenses of the marked community *vis-à-vis* its own "internal life" (Gaarder, 1970; Kjolseth, 1973).

Transitional/compensatory bilingual education is thus not without its philosophical complexities and ambivalences. These, however, derive not only from the manifest or avowed goals of such bilingual education but from its putative latent goals or side effects in the cultural sphere interpreted in diametrically opposite ways by marked and unmarked spokesmen.

Marx vs. Weber: A Classic Disagreement

The philosophical suspicions pertaining to the cultural entanglements of transitional/compensatory bilingual education underscore the impossibility of treating bilingual education merely as a device for reaching remedial economic and political goals. Cultural questions are inescapable, not only because two different ethno-cultural constellations so commonly need to be recognized in bilingual education, but also because the causal priority of ethnic and economic resources is a well-established dilemma in Western social theory. Bilingual education planners and practitioners rarely realize that Karl Marx and Max Weber have very substantially anticipated their own concerns in this connection (Fishman, 1977a). Thus, a review of the now-classical Marxian and Weberian theoretical positions may serve to clarify some of the philosophical disagreements that practitioners and planners so often encounter in connection with compensatory/transitional bilingual education.

The classical Marxian view claims that material resources are causally prior and primary in societal behavior (even above values and ideologies). The allocation or distribution of these resources elicits a cultural superstructure for their protection both between ethnic categories as well as within them. Thus, ethno-cultural grouping and the behaviors that distinguish them are considered to be merely epiphenomenal devices and defenses, secondary by-products created by the material facts of life. In bilingual education terms, this may translate either into a defense of transitional/compensatory programs (if they *do* assure access to new resources) or into an opposition to such programs (if they do *not* assure such access). In either case, it is that access to resources which is the basic desideratum from which the cultural consequences will flow. A genuine reallocation and equalization of resources will lead to a necessary equalization of cultural identities. There are no inherent cultural advantages, as there *are* inherent material advantages. As soon as material advantages are equalized then there is no need for emphasizing cultural differences since the latter are merely resultants of the former rather than a reality in their own right. In both instances, those who favor the amalgamation of marked and unmarked populations should favor transitional/compensatory bilingual education; and those who do not, should not. But in both instances, *it is actual reallocation of resources that is the crucial variable* rather than bilingual education *per se;* and for both the marked and unmarked groups, a class purpose and a class bias must be recognized. Thus, the Marxian view is basically that bilingual education in itself is useless for social mediation since such mediation requires direct action in the social (particularly in the economic/political) arena. Marxism and capitalism thus share a characteristic emphasis on material considerations.

The Weberian view as to the interaction between material and cultural dynamics is quite different from the foregoing. It does not so much attend to the chicken-and-egg problem of "which comes first — material or cultural differences" as to the belief that cultural dynamics, once set into motion, cannot be considered epiphenomenal or derived. Indeed, Weber points out that ethno-cultural factors are fully capable of fashioning and altering the means of production and the directions of resource allocation. The classical Hindu, Chinese, and Judaic cultures produced very different and very characteristic treatments of resources, as did the Protestant ethic. All cultures generate their own resource allocation systems, as all resource developing systems generate their own cultural legitimations. From this point of view, transitional/compensatory bilingual education might very well have major remedial consequences, by design or by accident, precisely because of its ethno-cultural impact. Bilingual education should be supported or opposed not on the basis of any purported one-way model of necessary priorities in the relationship between material and cultural resources, but rather in the awareness that interactions and influences in both directions are constant and inescapable. These interactions and influences in both directions are responsive to planning. Those who oppose or favor cultural homogenization should oppose or favor transitional/compensatory bilingual education not because of any mistaken notion as to the putative primacy of material factors in societal life but on the basis of the impact of such bilingual education as *cultural planning.* The Weberian view thus holds out more hope than does the Marxian view that remedial bilingual education can be the beginning of social remediation. However, it also stresses that culture and politics are inescapably linked.

Herder and the Ethno-Cultural Goals of Bilingual Education

If Marxism possibly leads to overstressing the material bases of social reality as a philosophical point of departure for bilingual education, then

Herderism may overstress the ethno-cultural bases of social reality as an alternative philosophical point of departure. For Herder, ethno-cultural diversity is a supreme good that requires cultivation, protection, and devotion. Ethno-cultural uniqueness, originality, and authenticity are viewed as the very bases of societal functioning at a truly human level. These bases constantly require strengthening, particularly in view of the dehumanizing and leveling influences flowing from modern technology. Technologically disadvantaged languages and cultures are in constant danger of displacement and replacement by technologically stronger and more useful ones. Thus, while there is no gainsaying the *practical* utility of regional or international languages of wider communication such as English, French, Russian, Spanish, Arabic, or Chinese, these must never be permitted to displace languages of narrower communication, no matter how restricted an ethno-cultural validity they possess. Bilingual education, therefore, can become the means whereby these more powerful languages are acquired at the same time that marked languages are protected from oblivion, particularly for use in the spheres of ethnic intimacy and originality. Bilingual education for the purpose of language-and-culture maintenance thus becomes not only a major opportunity within the confines of alternative philosophies of bilingual education, but also a potential contributor to the betterment of modern life and to the very preservation of that which is most precious in human existence: ethno-cultural fidelity, creativity, and diversity (Fishman, 1972).

Not unexpectedly, the Herderian vision is not without its opponents. Even marked spokesmen are far from being unanimous adherents of language-and-culture maintenance. There are certainly many who consider bilingual education as being primarily justified by what it can "deliver" in terms of superior unmarked language mastery rather than in terms of marked language maintenance. Indeed, there are marked language spokesmen who consider marked language maintenance as inherently unattainable as a school-based endeavor. They would much rather struggle against the obvious dangers of schooling entirely in the unmarked language than confront a school that claims interest in maintaining the marked language but which, under that guise, is successful only in advancing mastery of the unmarked language while fostering *varieties* of the marked language and *functions* for the marked language in conflict with or inconsistent with those of the marked home and community. Marked spokesmen have long pointed out that schooling is a two-edged sword with respect to the ethno-cultural continuity of marked speech communities (Fishman, 1966). Even when schooling is fully under the marked community's own control, in terms of personnel, curriculum, and methodology (which is seldom the case in connection with remedial/bilingual education), it normally leads to greater exposure to unmarked functions and interactions. This becomes more evident when schooling is not under the marked community's control. Under these circumstances, its marked language emphasis easily becomes minimized and trivialized. The marked language becomes no more than "words" — the marked culture becomes no more than "things." Thus, the delicate web of authentic beliefs, values, observances, and pursuits is lost and (even worse) caricatured by heavy-handed reliance on stock phrases and stereotyped foods. Thus, there are not only marked language spokesmen who are not greatly interested in pursuing bilingual education along Herderian philosophical lines but there are also some who oppose any such pursuit precisely on the grounds that bilingual education tends to subvert such principles even when it seeks to advance them. That being the case, it should certainly come as no surprise to find that there are unmarked spokesmen who oppose bilingual education oriented toward maintaining marked languages and cultures at public expense. The usual stance adopted by such opponents is that such an orientation is politically dangerous, culturally romantic, and fiscally frivolous. Basically, it is the Herderian glorification of diversity that is rejected and a counter-image that is enthroned: a world that is efficiently prosperous and pacified on the basis of a minimal number of major languages (preferably including — if not restricted to — the mother tongues of the unmarked opponents of Herderian thought). More surprising, perhaps, is the recurring appearance of unmarked spokesmen who *do* adopt the Herderian stance — in broader or narrower terms — and *do* champion the cause(s) of the marked language(s). Frequently, these unmarked spokesmen are themselves of marked background and their championship of the marked cause is part of a personal odyssey of returning to their own roots as well as part of their attempt to organize others to do so. However, there is also no dearth of genuinely unmarked spokesmen who have altruistically dedicated themselves to the advancement of marked languages and cultures and who have advocated and utilized maintenance-oriented bilingual education. Indeed, if there is today bilingual education for language-and-culture maintenance purposes involving Romansch in Switzerland, Navajo in New Mexico and Arizona, or Spanish in a few points in the Southwest, it is largely because of the efforts and the dedication of genuinely unmarked spokesmen of the Herderian ideal. On the other hand, language-maintenance oriented bilingual education programs in Ireland, Wales, among several American immigrant-derived populations, among Frisians in Holland, among Catalans in Spain, etc., are based, in large part, upon the efforts and devotion of re-ethnicized leaders who had previously experienced considerable "unmarking."

Although Herderians stand at the opposite extreme from Marxists, they recognize the potential contribution of politics and economic resources to their ethno-cultural goals. Whereas Marxists are still likely to deride Herderian arguments as objectively specious and logically inverted — thereby completely missing the Herderian point that life is more than materially based objectivity and logic — Herderians are by no means reluctant to admit the need for political and economic protection if language-and-culture maintenance is to succeed and if bilingual education for that purpose is to be effective (Gaarder, 1977). Herderian thought (historically influential among marked populations in Central, Eastern, and Southern Europe and spreading from there to marked populations throughout the world) is now coming into a new vogue among academic anthropologists, ethnographers, and ethnicity specialists in the United States and in Western Europe. Herderian concepts and Herderian ideals will obviously remain part of the permanent intellectual and emotional reservoirs of social philosophy and of bilingual education.

Educational Enrichment Goals

The Marxian-Weberian-Herderian debate attracts by far the lion's share of philosophically relevant attention within the bilingual education fold. As a result, an exploration of the strictly educational (as distinct from economic or cultural) goals of bilingual education may well become the sleeping beauty of this entire realm of discourse. A philosophical approach to bilingual education that views it from the point of view of education *per se* may well be crucial if unmarked populations are to be interested in bilingual education for themselves and their children. Since unmarked populations are already politically and economically dominant, the Marxian-Weberian debate is not really relevant to their concerns or interests. Furthermore, since unmarked populations are either ethno-culturally neutralized or ethno-culturally dominant, the Herderian pathos may be equally lost upon them. Thus, a distinctly unmarked approach to bilingual education is needed if it is to have anything to say to the unmarked population of the United States and of the world at large. Even those whose concern for bilingual education originated in a concern for marked populations should appreciate the tactical importance of co-opting unmarked support for bilingual education. However, such support is most assuredly attainable only if unmarked populations *themselves* have something to gain from bilingual education. If this view is to be developed, then bilingual education must justify itself philosophically as *education*, i.e., that it must justify itself as an alternative to monolingual education for the unmarked child, rather than as a factor in the social mobility or in the cultural protection of the marked child (Fishman, 1977b).

Overlooked though it may have been, the educational (as distinct from the political or cultural) philosophy of bilingual education is, nevertheless, not entirely an unplowed field. The approach commonly taken is akin to that frequently employed in foreign language instruction: an additional avenue for expansion of intellect, emotional capacity, aesthetic sensitivity, and communicative-intuitive development (Fishman, 1976). As a philosophical position, it is necessary to distinguish between the claim that any or all of the above desirable enrichment goals are more fully attainable via two (or more) media of introduction on the one hand, and Whorfianism on the other hand. This philosophical position distinguishes between grammar and culture. Whorfianism claims that the structural differences between languages lead to different cognitive styles or linguistic Weltanschauungen (Fishman, 1976). An enrichment philosophy of bilingual education claims that it is language, as the prime carrier of culture, that leads to distinctive sensitivities, values, appreciations, and understandings. Whorfianism claims that the ultimate determinants of human cognition — perception, thought, memory, and problem solving — are morpho-syntactic. Enrichment bilingual education claims that these ultimate determinants are found in the web of ethno-cultural creativity and usage to which languages are particularly attuned by virtue of being imbedded conveyors, expressors, and co-participants.

Enrichment bilingual education is certainly the traditional form of elitist education from time immemorial (Lewis, 1976) and is the type of bilingual education most widespread throughout the world today (Fishman, 1976). It is realized through special language schools in the Soviet Union and China, via immersion in French for Anglophone children in Quebec and Ontario, via expatriate schools throughout the third world for children of the indigenous middle class as well as for children of resident foreigners, via private schools stressing French (more rarely, Spanish, German, or Italian) for middle- and upper-class children throughout the West, etc. Just as with Russian princelings in an earlier era, and with Roman elites in an even earlier one, and with Sumerian elites in a still earlier one, bilingual education involving both a major local and a major extra-local ("world") language is viewed as providing an additional asset in life. Thus far, enrichment education has been available primarily to those who would *safeguard* the advantages of their favorable social status. It has rarely been made available to the masses during the past century in which public education has become predominant throughout the world. Nevertheless, there are already beginnings of bilingual education at public expense for unmarked children, and it is in this very context that the adherents of enrichment bilingual education see the major contribution that their philosophy can make. The movement toward "one world" requires bilingual education so that all children can benefit from the "additional window on the world" that bilingual education espouses. Indeed, enrichment bilingual education seeks to harmoniously interrelate the two most powerful educational trends of the post war era: the trend toward vernacularization and the trend toward internationalization. The first trend continues the 19th century European tendency to provide at least mother tongue education for all unmarked children. The second trend, in its most recent reincarnation, is intimately associated with the world-wide spread of English (just as it was formerly associated with the spread of French and other languages of wide communication) and reflects the growing realization of many new and struggling third world educational systems that vernacularization alone cannot solve the educational lag with which they are faced. However, the strongest barricades against enrichment bilingual education are encountered in the Western world where both vernacularization of education for unmarked populations and local technological control are both well established and well advanced. Under these circumstances (both characteristic of the United States), enrichment bilingual education receives its most dubious reception whereas it is precisely here that it requires acceptance.

The opposition to enrichment bilingual education in the United States (or in Britain, France, Italy, etc.) reveals the extent to which additional languages and cultural perspectives remain unreal for the unmarked mainstreams. The gains attributed to enrichment bilingual education are often viewed as marginal and minimal by the dubious. The expenses involved are considered disproportionately great for the benefits derived. The entire philosophical premise of enrichment bilingual education is simply disbelieved and reacted to as dealing with esoterica and exotica. This is not to say that enrichment bilingual education does not exist in these advantaged mainstream settings but that it has remained elitist in scope and orientation and that it appears destined to remain so until other languages and cultures become more widely recognized, experienced, and valued in the life of the advantaged unmarked citizenry. This *did* occur in antiquity and could occur again in modern times.

Ideal Types and Real Cases

Philosophical distinctions have a tendency to gravitate toward ideal types. Such distinctions often engage in a kind of "distortion for the purpose of clarity" and the philosophical positions become increasingly purified and separated from each other. In the real world, however, syncretism is more common than orthodoxy. Types of bilingual education come into being that combine philosophical positions that are separate and different in theory, just as others come into being that make differentiations that seem to be philosophically unmotivated or unjustified. One and the same bilingual education program may serve transitional compensatory ends for some children and language maintenance ends for others. Similarly, one and the same program can very easily serve language maintenance purposes for certain students and enrichment purposes for others. Indeed, the three major philosophical positions discussed above often correspond to sequentially connected stages of bilingual education in practice. Thus, in recent years, bilingual education has frequently gotten underway as a remedial compensatory enterprise that unmarked authorities have instituted for the benefit of marked populations. Subsequently, as marked populations have come to enjoy upward political and economic mobility, they have exerted increased leverage upon the unmarked power structure to permit an alternative form of bilingual education to be made available, namely, one that had language-and-culture maintenance emphasis. A still subsequent stage in the developmental cycle occurs, normally after still further growth in the political and economic power of the marked population, when members of the unmarked population seek enrichment bilingual education (involving the marked language as a co-medium) as an option for themselves at the same time that maintenance bilingual education is continued as an option for the marked population. The latter development is an about-face for the unmarked population, since the distance between offering bilingual education to marked populations as a way of overcoming their handicaps on the one hand, and desiring bilingual education for one's self and one's own children on the other hand, is a very considerable one in intellectual, emotional, social, political, and economic terms. The past decade of bilingual education in Canada and in Wales provides many examples of the sequence sketched above. If the socio-educational progression is viewed as a linear continuum with feedback, branching, and reversal possibilities, then it should come as no surprise that in actuality a large number of models exist in which several of the philosophies sketched above in their pristine purity are represented in varying practical proportions (Fishman, 1976). The transmutation of theory into practice is not only wondrous to behold but full of surprises as well.

REFERENCES

Fishman, Joshua A. *Bilingual Education: An International Sociological Perspective.*
    Rowley: Newbury House, 1976.
_____. "Ethnicity and Language," *Language, Ethnicity and Intergroup
    Relations,* ed. H. Giles. New York: Academic Press, 1977a.
_____. *Language and Nationalism.* Rowley: Newbury House, 1972.
_____, *et al. Language Loyalty in the United States; the Maintenance and
    Perpetuation of Non-English Mother Tongues by American Ethnic and Religious
    Groups.* The Hague: Morton, 1966.
_____. *Social Science Perspective on Bilingual Education.* Arlington: Center
    for Applied Linguistics, 1977b.
Gaarder, Bruce. "Political Perspective on Bilingualism and Bilingual Education," *Bilingual
    Schooling and the Survival of Spanish in the United States.* Rowley: Newbury House,
    1977, pp. 95-128.
_____. "The First Seventy-Six Bilingual Education Projects," *Georgetown
    University Monograph Series on Languages and Linguistics.* Vol. XXIII, 1970, pp.
    163-178.
Kjolseth, R. "Bilingual Education Programs in the United States: For Assimilation or
    Pluralism?" *Bilingualism in the Southwest,* ed. Paul R. Turner. Tucson: University of
    Arizona Press, 1973, pp. 3-27.
Lewis, E. Glyn. "Bilingualism and Bilingual Education: The Ancient World to the Renais-
    sance," *Bilingual Education: An International Sociological Perspective,* ed. Joshua A.
    Fishman. Rowley: Newbury House, 1976, pp. 150-200.

Meaningful Bilingual/ Bicultural Education: A Fairy Tale

Eduardo Hernández-Chávez

A pessimistic fairy tale advances the idea that schools as they exist today are basically designed to maintain the status-quo. Many educators feel that bilingual education contributes to the assimilation process needed by this society to maintain the power structure. Rather than concern ourselves with such issues as alternate days versus alternate periods, or transitional versus maintenance bilingual programs, attention should be focused on the more fundamental questions that deal with the role of education and the place of cultural and linguistic diversity in society.

ONCE UPON a time, in that great land of Dreams and Plenty, there lived a powerful King, Queen, and Royal Family, along with their subjects. The subjects toiled in the vineyards and the workshops of the Kingdom to provide sumptuous meals and fine furnishings for the Royal Family. The King, whose name was Government, had a voracious appetite; and the Queen, named the American People, who had wrested this land from the barbarians, was accustomed to her fine clothes and gems.

The Royal couple were stern and strict with their subjects for they thought them envious of their great fortune and desirous of one day overrunning the Palace. So, the King appointed his sons to maintain control over his unruly subjects. The eldest son, Prince Economy, saw to it that the people worked their fullest share so that the harvests would be plentiful and would fill the Royal Treasury. The second son, Prince Law, dealt swiftly with those who disobeyed the King's commands.

There was also the homely eldest daughter, Welfare, who provided food and shelter to those unable to produce their own. She gave sparingly, however, for she feared that all the subjects might desert the vineyards and workshops if she gave too much. Education, a comely and seductive Princess, taught the children to perform all the various tasks that might be useful to the Crown. She was the Queen's favorite; did not her teaching show that the King was a just ruler and wanted only the best for his subjects? And to those who worked the very hardest, learning well to speak the language of the realm — for the people spoke harsh and barbaric tongues — and who swore their fealty to the Crown, this fair princess promised entry to her exalted boudoir — the University. Education usually gave her fullest favors only to those of Royal lineage, though she oft-times bared her enticing breast to those among the common people who showed their loyalty. And many of the youth were seduced. For, having entered the mistress' chambers, they need never return to toil in the fields. Indeed, they were rewarded instead with a life inside the Palace. Some became household servants — how much better than to labor in a dank workshop! Others were entrusted with even more important duties, usually the prerogative of the Royal Family itself, such as counting the crown jewels or acting as guardians of the Royal Libraries.

But still there was strife. The people yearned to be free — to labor for themselves, to speak their own language, and to keep their children. They asked not to have the Palace for themselves but only to partake of the fruits of their own labors. The King was fearful. He knew full well the ancient fable of the camel that begged to warm its nose inside the tent. Before the desert night was out, the camel occupied the tent and its master shivered in the cold.

Then he struck upon a plan. A daughter had been born to Education from a careless tryst inside the University. Bilingual Education was her name. Perhaps she could teach the children better to perform their tasks. Being illegitimate, she knew the people's language. And if the people could see the good intentions of the King, they surely would cease their demands for freedom. More of their children might be invited to the University and come to be employed in the Palace and thus to serve the Kingdom. They certainly would not object to that! Nor would Education ever allow a peasant tongue in her University (except perhaps in a moment of intense but fleeting passion). But Bilingual Education would speak the language of the people as she taught their children the Royal Tongue. What a marvelous opportunity for them! A truly ingenious plan. Why, even Welfare and Prince Economy would approve because their own tasks would be make lighter.

When the people first set eyes on youthful Bilingual Education, they were delighted. Here was a Peasant Princess who would teach the children in their own tongue. And, instructing them in the ways of the people, she would tell them of the King's insidiousness and teach them to be free. Those that wished could also learn the Royal Tongue so that they might be able to speak with the offspring of the King and live in harmony. The children would become leaders of the people rather than mere servants of the King. Taken by the people's enthusiasm, youthful Bilingual Education spoke also of freedom and opportunity and self-determination — ideas that all the Royal Family also cherished for themselves. A new day had dawned for the people.

Alas! It was not to be. Learning of the naive and subversive actions of the Princess, the King immediately sent his brother, the Duke of Bureaucracy, together with Prince Law to firmly instruct his wayward granddaughter. She must be told how such a plan was unthinkable and unrealistic. Her uncle, Prince Economy, who must be groomed one day to take the throne, would have a four-fold burden if the people were to determine their own tasks. Then, too, who would make the Queen her baubles if their subjects' children could not be made to serve within the Palace? "Unless you do my bidding," said the King, "I will not allow you to teach my subjects."

And Bilingual Education, yearning to be legitimate like her mother, obeyed the King's command.

*　　*　　*

For more than a decade, bilingual education has held forth the promise of equal educational opportunity for the children of linguistic minorities. Drawing on the experience of the Dade County schools and spurred by the intensification of the civil rights movement in the middle sixties, national and state legislatures have passed a variety of laws that provide for some level of instruction in the native language of such children. Several judicial decisions as well have supported special programs for non-English-speaking children.

Like the king in the fairy tale, however, all these laws and judicial rulings have been very careful to ensure not only that the level of opportunity be held to a reasonable minimum but also that the programs be carried out in conformity with the established philosophies and goals of the larger educational system. Thus, the majority of the statutes impose strong limitations on the use of the children's mother tongue in the classroom by requiring that at least part, and in most cases at least one-half, of the instruction be in English. An additional requirement that tends to ensure that a substantial amount of English is spoken in the classroom is that bilingual classrooms have a linguistic balance, i.e., half of the children are to be native English speakers. These requirements follow directly from the ideas that "limited English speakers" suffer from a linguistic handicap and that the primary purpose of bilingual education is the teaching of English. For example, the California Education Code states that:

> The inability to speak, read and comprehend English presents a formidable obstacle to classroom learning and participation which can be removed only by instruction and training in the pupils' domi-nant language. (Sec. 5761, p. 128)

The obstacle to be removed, it must be noted, is not the inability of the school to teach in a non-native language, but the inability of the child to speak, read, and comprehend English. The Code also asserts that:

> . . . a primary goal of such programs is, as effectively and efficiently as possible, to develop in each child fluency in English so that he may then be enrolled in the regular program in which English is the language of instruction. (Sec. 5761, p. 128)

The celebrated *Lau* v. *Nichols* decision of 1974, hailed by many as a landmark ruling in favor of equal educational opportunity through bilingual education, was nothing of the sort. This decision was not based on education as a fundamental right nor on constitutional grounds of equal protection. In an earlier action in *San Antonio Independent School District* v. *Rodriguez*, the Supreme Court found that education is not a fundamental right at all; in *Lau* it avoided the issue of equal protection by basing its decision on a provision of the Civil Rights Act rather than on the Constitution. The law gives the Department of Health, Education, and Welfare (HEW) the right to promulgate regulations in the implementation of the Act. Thus, the May 25th Memorandum required that districts receiving Federal funds take affirmative steps to rectify the "language deficiency" in order to open their instructional programs to national origin minority-group children, among other things. On the basis of this Memorandum, the Court decided that non-English-speaking children could not obtain equal educational opportunity through placement in a regular all-English curriculum. The sentiment of the Court was expressed in the concurring opinion written by the Chief Justice. It would be possible to conform to the law by instituting appropriate English-as-a-Second-Language (ESL) programs. It is important to note that the Court decision applied only to districts that are assisted by Federal monies. Enforcement is a cumbersome process involving the ultimate withdrawal of Federal funds, and it allows districts a great deal of latitude in the steps that they may take to remedy the lack of equal educational opportunity. *Lau* in no way mandates bilingual education nor makes it a basic right. Although it is true that HEW's Office for Civil Rights, in interpreting and enforcing the decision, has insisted on some sort of bilingual education for minimal compliance with the law, the rulings of the Office for Civil Rights are in the form of administrative regulations. While the regulations have the force of law, with a shift in the political winds the situation could just as easily be changed.

Given the explicit intent of the courts and legislatures that the primary goal of bilingual programs is to ensure that linguistic-minority children learn English, it seems amply clear that bilingual education is conceived as compensatory in nature, extending and incorporating ESL instruction. Rather than being a new concept in the meaningful education of minority children, it is merely a more sophisticated ESL methodology, a way to hold closed the floodgates of discontent and to more efficiently transform these children into the desired mold.

This unrelenting insistence on shaping the non-Anglo child to fit the Procrustean bed of English and Anglo values cannot be based on the conviction that only in this way will the child be able to attain a meaningful education. There is too much experience and too much evidence to the contrary. For example, hundreds of thousands of Chicano children learn English within a year of entering school; yet, next to Native Americans, Chicanos continue to occupy the lowest rung on the educational ladder. Studies of linguistic-minority children in various national and cultural settings point overwhelmingly to the conclusion that instruction in the vernacular is far superior to that in a non-native tongue and that the negative effects of instruction in a weaker language are far-reaching and long-lasting. These harmful effects are not restricted to the educational sphere. As has been pointed out elsewhere (Hernández, 1973), education in the non-native language for children of minorities that are socially, economically, and politically subordinate can and does have disastrous consequences not only for the children but for their families and their communities. Children suffer serious emotional damage engendered by the devaluation of their language and culture, frequently resulting in alienation between parent and child and a rejection by the child of the community and its ideals. These cleavages within families and entire communities can be traced directly to the doorstep of the Anglo-dominated and -oriented educational system. The resulting deleterious effects on the larger society are immeasurable.

Bilingual education has not changed this situation; if anything, it has exacerbated and accelerated the pernicious deculturation process. Because of bilingual education programs, Chicano children and their parents are less inclined to question the efficacy of the school since children can now learn basic subjects while not being held back for a lack of knowledge of English. The school no longer seems to be such a threatening institution, and the introduction to English becomes much less traumatic than in the blunt-edged, ESL-only programs. Children now are raped with the fine-honed blade of bilingual education and natural second-language acquisition methodologies. English is acquired rapidly and efficiently, Anglo values are inexorably inculcated, and the child's home language, the unlikely instrument of acculturation, is discarded and left to deteriorate.

The social and cultural ideals of the people are not only not reinforced, but they are also subverted and undermined in the name of educating children to become useful American citizens. Their own values are seen as inimical to the interests of the majority society. Heller (1966) states this position clearly when she writes:

> The kind of socialization that the Mexican-American children gener-
> ally receive at home is not conducive to the development of the
> capacities needed for advancement in a dynamic industrialized soci-
> ety. This type of upbringing creates stumbling blocks to future ad-
> vancement by stressing values that hinder mobility — family ties,
> honor, masculinity, and living in the present — and by neglecting
> values that are conducive to it — achievement, independence, and
> deferred gratification. (pp. 33-34)

This view is neither dated nor isolated, which Carter (1970) emphasizes:

> The vast majority of educators interviewed . . . and most of the
> relevant literature argue that Mexican American children are cultur-
> ally deprived or disadvantaged, that their home environment does
> not provide the skills, personality characteristics, or experiences
> necessary for a child's success in school. This view provides most
> schoolmen with plausible explanation for the failure of Mexican
> Americans in school. (p. 35)

Must we be constantly reminded that the principal and overriding function of the school is to pass on and perpetuate the dominant sociocultural values? Each individual must be assigned an appropriate social role, a role that is essentially defined by economic forces within the society:

> The local socio-economic system affects the sorting and sieving
> process. Although schooling is idealized as the way to rise in the
> status system, the local society, if it is to be maintained, requires that
> children be prepared to occupy the particular slots that the commun-
> ity has available for different categories of its population. (Carter,
> 1970, pp. 14-15)

Tracking systems, IQ scores, the election of class officers, or the school-teacher who assigns Anglo pupils as group leaders because "the Mexican children need to learn to follow directions" all function to determine who will be the leaders and who will be the followers.

The democratization of the American school system has its foundation in the need to expand the level of schooling to feed the ever more complex and technological economy. Carnoy (1974) states this point succinctly:

Those who have the qualities most desired by the economy and society — verbal ability, awareness of time, and the internalized responsiveness to extrinsic rather than intrinsic rewards — perform best in school. (p. 8)

The virtues of hard work, thrift, and delayed gratification that are among the highest ideals transmitted through the schools are also the characteristics that are of the greatest value to the economic structure.

These values, so closely identified with the dominant Anglo-American society, can best be taught through the medium of English. The use of a non-English language for education dilutes that teaching and threatens to introduce ideas and values that are foreign and that challenge the established order. Community responsibility and sharing are less than useful to a hierarchical economic system; autonomy and self-determination are absolutely inimical to entrenched political power. These are the forbidden fruits that were fleetingly and so tantalizingly offered by Bilingual Education and that were so swiftly proscribed by our fairy tale monarch. Bilingual Education cannot be our faithful lover; she must be a harlot like her mother, prostituting herself to the vested interests of the dominant society.

There are many lawmakers, educators, and linguists who support bilingual education reluctantly and only as long as it serves directly to inculcate the ideals of the majority society. Efforts to provide meaningful education to minority children are only made within these narrow constraints, with the result that they are ineffective unless the children accept and adapt to the values of the school. When those half-hearted and ethnocentrically oriented efforts fail, as they surely must, not only will it demonstrate that linguistically and culturally appropriate educational programs do not work, but it will also give credence once more to the idea that the causes of the failure lie in the socio-economic positions, the cultural backgrounds, or even the racial characteristics of minorities.

This seemingly harsh indictment of the American educational system of which bilingual education is an integral part is certainly not intended to impute ill-will to those individuals who sincerely believe that bilingual education can alleviate some of the major damage that is visited upon minority children by an all-English school system. Rather, it is intended to show that we cannot expect to address the problems of an inferior education for linguistic minorities or to approach the ideal of equal and free participation by all in the national society by focusing myopically on the educational process itself. Too often we find ourselves arguing the merits of alternate days versus alternate periods in the two languages, of partial or full bilingualism, or of transitional versus maintenance models. We debate various approaches to ESL, whether the local variety of the native lan-

guage should be used, and whether it is harmful to allow code alternation
by the children. We also divert our attention from the more fundamental
questions that deal with the role of education in our society and the place
that we are willing to give to cultural and linguistic diversity.

Current philosophies and practices in bilingual education are faithful
reflections of the ideals of the wider society. When programs are proposed
that attempt to teach children according to community norms, using the
native language for all phases of instruction, the quick result is severe legal
action. A case in point is Berkeley, California's *Casa de la Raza* (1974). The
basic idea of this school was that use of the student's home culture and
language within an instructional program that used culturally relevant
strategies would foster personal growth and academic advancement. Cru-
cially, decisions were to be made by the community although the school
was administratively part of the Berkeley Unified School District. Opposition to this concept came quickly from bureaucrats within the school
system and the Federal government who charged that control by a linguistic community involved reverse racism and was thus illegal. As long as the
traditional principles of the system are not upset, a new technique may gain
active support. A truly novel approach that challenges the precepts of an
existing philosophy will invariably be suppressed. The acceptance and
encouragement of bilingual education programs by the bureaucracy is
prima facie evidence of their innocuousness to the existing system and
their ineffectiveness in producing significant change.

A truly effective bilingual education can only be possible in a national
context in which bilingualism and cultural diversity are themselves viable
and dynamic ways of life and in which non-English native tongues can
flourish and serve the people in all activities. Today, lack of knowledge of
English is seen as a deficiency that must be treated as temporary and that
will be corrected by bilingual education in the schools. An urgent priority
should be given to initiating basic changes in this system in such a way that
the maintenance of linguistic and cultural traditions by non-English-
speaking peoples is regarded as a fundamental right. From voting to
judicial proceedings and from telephone service to credit applications, the
right to use one's native language must be asserted and must be held
inalienable. Participation in local and regional government must be
opened to all regardless of language.

It is obvious that the accomplishment of such modest goals is a distant
vision. Furthermore, it should be clear that obtaining a true equal educational opportunity for linguistic-minority children is only possible in an
environment in which a broad range of linguistic rights are recognized. A
national climate that claims that the only true Americanism is adherence to
Anglo traditions and values and that demands the assimilation of those who

differ cannot possibly be committed to a pluralistic model of education. We deceive ourselves if we believe that bilingual education can achieve educational quality or linguistic and cultural maintenance without concomitant, radical change in the allocation of language rights and other minority rights in this country. More importantly, we must recognize that such change can only occur in conjunction with the attainment of a substantial amount of political and economic power by the groups concerned. In large part, the assimilationist philosophies and reformist practices in bilingual education today are a consequence of the limited power that has been wielded by linguistic minorities for many generations. The very limitations on that power are reflected in the weaknesses of bilingual education and its basic inability to promote change.

*   *   *

Then one day the people left the fields and workshops in despair. "Why should we work and sweat throughout our lives," they asked, "only to provide food and fine clothing for Queen America?"

The young people all nodded their agreement. Their labor was long and hard, but most of the harvest went to fill the Royal Granaries.

The Elders, who had too long held their counsel, exhorted the people, saying, "Do not patronize the merchants for they swear allegiance to the King and it is they, not us, who rule our Sacred Councils for their profit."

On hearing this, the people were angered even more. "Let us be free," they shouted. "We will not work and we will not buy our wares from the King's merchants."

And so the Elders sent a message to the King that solemnly declared, "We do not shun toil, nor do we covet the merchants their shops. But for our sweat we must receive just wages and the King must return to us our Sacred Councils where we may speak our own tongue, conduct our own affairs, and educate our own children."

In the Royal Chambers there was great fear and anguish and the King demanded of Prince Law that those responsible be imprisoned. But soon the dungeons were full and the Prince reported to the King that the people still refused to work and to patronize the Royal shops. So to his rebellious subjects the King sent an emissary — someone who could speak their own crude tongue — and demanded, "Return to your homes and desist from this sedition. You should be grateful for my benificence. I give you food and shelter and even send the Bilingual Princess to teach your children. I order you to cease these unlawful acts on pain of more imprisonment."

The people were silent. They knew their actions were unlawful only by the King's decree. If they did not demand their right they could never be free. And so they spoke:

"Basta. Ya nos has cansado la paciencia. A menos que el rey nos dé nuestros derechos, seguirá la huelga."*

But the messenger of the King did not understand.

REFERENCES

California Education Code. *The Bilingual Education Act of 1972.* §Sec. 5761. Chapter 5.7.

Carnoy, Martin. *Education as Cultural Imperialism.* New York: David McKay Co., 1974.

Carter, Thomas P. *Mexican Americans in School: A History of Educational Neglect.* New York: College Entrance Examination Board, 1970.

Heller, Celia S. *Mexican-American Youth: Forgotten Youth at the Crossroads.* New York: Random House, 1966.

Hernández-Chávez, Eduardo. "The Home Language of Chicanos as a Medium of Instruction," *Claremont Reading Conference Thirty Seventh Yearbook, 1973,* ed. Malcolm P. Douglass. Claremont: Claremont Graduate School, 1973 pp. 28-36.

Lau v. Nichols, 414 U.S., 563 (1974).

San Antonio Independent School District v. *Rodriguez.* 93 S. Ct. 1278 (1973).

Study Commission of Undergraduate Education and the Education of Teachers. *Casa de la Raza: Separatism or Segregation, Chicanos in Public Education.* Hayward: Southwest Network, 1974.

---

*"Enough. We have lost all patience. Unless the King gives us our rights, our strike will continue."

PART THREE

Social Factors in Bilingual Education

Three Social Factors Involved in Language and Bilingual Education Programs

Peg Griffin

Separate developments in the fields of education and linguistics have considerable importance for bilingual education. Educators are increasingly interested in community involvement. Linguists are increasingly concerned with language in the context of its social use. Three aspects of this concern and their importance to bilingual/bicultural education (BBE) programs are discussed. The need of BBE programs to know how the two languages are used and evaluated in the community requires the methodology used in *the sociology of language*. The need to know how each language is used to serve the purposes of specific social interactional situations requires information from *an ethnography of speaking*. Finally, the need to know how subtle aspects of meaning are accomplished in the two language systems necessitates a study of *the pragmatics of natural languages*. Community development is mandatory in these studies because much of the information and the rules for getting this information are specific to the local situation. Furthermore, there is much basic and applied work that needs to be done that needs the cooperation of many people.

SEPARATE DEVELOPMENTS in the fields of education and linguistics have produced a state in both fields that is profitable for bilingual education. Each field has experienced a re-emergence of interest in wider concerns: for educators, the key term is community involvement; for linguists, the key phrase is language in the context of its social use. In this paper I discuss three aspects of this concern in linguistics as it affects bilingual education: the sociology of language, the ethnography of speaking, and pragmatics. Each aspect is intrinsically related to the communities that have bilingual/bicultural education (BBE) programs. In the first three sections of this paper, I discuss each aspect separately and include notes on its implications in a BBE setting. In the final section, I discuss how the social aspects of language and the community intersect with bilingual materials development. Throughout, there are references to the work prepared by the Center for Applied Linguistics (CAL) in conjunction with the San Francisco Citizens' Task Force as a response to the *Lau* v. *Nichols* decision (1975).

Sociology of Language

The first aspect concerns the *sociology of language*, a term used to refer to the view of language systems as social institutions. The types of information sought are:

1. What are the roles and resources of each language internationally, nationally, regionally, and locally? That is, when and for what purposes are the relevant languages used; and what material, personnel, and institutional support is available for each language?

2. What are the attitudes toward each language and toward its use in various situations?

3. What predictions can be made about the stability of these factors over time?

Information based on the above considerations can be used to make basic decisions about whether to undertake a BBE program in a particular locality. For example, this information is crucial in the San Francisco situation in three cases:

1. In the San Francisco Spanish-speaking community, decisions must be made about how the distinct varieties of Spanish shall be treated in curriculum and materials. To reach these decisions, information about the language varieties must be provided in teacher education programs. If one particular variety is viewed as more appropriate for school than another variety, decisions must then be made about which variety will be used in texts and tests and about what steps children should take to learn a variety that is uncommon in their out-of-school environment.

2. The Filipino community in San Francisco speaks several distinct languages, one of which has been declared a national language in the Philippines. The local decision-makers in San Francisco must weigh the effect of the institutional support and availability of materials in the national language against the number of students in San Francisco from each of the language groups.

3. Korean and Samoan populations are growing in San Francisco. Local decision-makers must determine whether this is a continuing trend for

which full maintenance BBE programs should be prepared, or if it is a temporary bulge in the demographic curves for which alternative approaches such as a few multi-age BBE classrooms or a transitional BBE program should be used.

Work on the sociology of language, reported by Fishman (1974) and Paulston (1974), reviews and integrates much of the recent theory and its application to BBE programs. Similar "macro" social factors must be investigated in the early stages of BBE program planning. The evaluation plans for BBE programs should include a consideration of the responsiveness of the program to changes in these social factors. From the cases discussed above, it is evident that the results of such investigations are also useful in curriculum and materials development, in assessment components, and in staff development.

Some of the relevant information can be gathered centrally by a Federal agency and shared by programs across the country, but other parts of the information must be gathered locally. The option of centrally developing an instrument to gather the local information may not be feasible because language and culture groups may differ as to what is permissible information to give and what are permissible ways of asking for information. Standardizing the questions cannot guarantee that the results would be uniform because of the variety of interpretations of the questions from the various populations. With these factors in mind, local BBE programs must be prepared to accomplish some of the data gathering. Furthermore, local programs must make their needs known to national programs so that these needs will be addressed in a coordinated and efficient manner.

What are the consequences to a program of ignoring these factors? A program may lose or never gain the support of the various segments of the community. The program may fail the students by limiting their options for mobility in their education and/or their future work. Financial support for subsequent BBE programs may be more difficult to enlist if an earlier program runs into difficulty by ignoring factors related to the sociology of language. Community involvement in BBE programs is necessary not only for political and idealistic reasons but also for academic and administrative matters.

Ethnography of Speaking

The second aspect of social factors concerns the *ethnography of speaking*. The types of information sought are descriptions of those elements that characterize speech events in a given community. Who talks to whom, how, about what, when, where, and for what purposes? Are there particular speech events or evaluations of speech that are specific to a given community? Are certain kinds of speaking encouraged and other kinds forbidden in certain social roles? Are there certain key parts of the communication event that determine all or much of the ethnography of speaking? The basic dimensions of this aspect of social factors have been discussed by Gumperz and Hymes (1964), Hymes (1974b), and Bauman and Sherzer (1974).

An awareness of the ethnography of speaking is useful in two areas to bilingual/bicultural programs: the first is traditional, and the second is an extension of, or perhaps a particularization of, the traditional:

1. In the first area, the information base is an ethnography of speaking of each of the languages separately insofar as they are represented separately in the community. The separate (and comparative) information is necessary for the preparation of adequate instructional and assessment materials for language proficiency. For example, whether teaching or testing a child's proficiency regarding, say, the "greeting routine" (e.g., in American English: "Hi. How are you?") one should be able to answer at least the following questions about both of the languages involved:

a. Are there rules concerning who should initiate the greeting? Do the routines depend on a formally static identification of status or on a more dynamic, interaction-determined relationship?

b. How many turns (i.e., how many times must or can each participant speak) are involved in the routine and how does it close?

c. Can the ostensible topic be covered in more substance later on in the conversation? How is it introduced?

d. What are the rules for subsequent turns?

e. What are the consequences of opting out of any turn?

For example, in Cebuano, a language spoken in the Visayan Islands in the Republic of the Philippines, the ostensible topic is "end point of trip," and this topic determines which of the conversants initiates the routine as long as one and only one participant is stationary. The topic also determines the number of turns and its closing rules. The routine has disjunctive sets of rules and is different from the routine for telephone and written communication. A particularly intricate subset of rules determines whether the initiating question will inquire ostensibly about the beginning or destination of the trip. A materials writer or test developer who thinks that the routines in American English and Cebuano differ only in that one asks "how are you" and the other asks "where are you going" is not going to prepare materials that are adequate.

Traditional ethnographies of speaking of each language in a BBE setting can also provide necessary background information for teacher education programs. To plan curricula sequences in any subject matter, it is necessary to understand the relationship among the elements of the ethnography of speaking and between these elements and other parts of the cultural system. Work by Philips (1976) illustrates the important and relevant findings that an ethnography of speaking can provide to educational planners. She shows there is a need to modify the informal questioning routine often used in first grade. However, even though this area is the most traditional and has been considered important for more than a decade, there is an inadequate information base; and nowhere to my knowledge has the information from an ethnography of speaking been fully applied in a BBE program.

2. The second area of usefulness of ethnography of speaking is that it provides a way to look at BBE programs. Evaluations comparing the relative effectiveness of differing models, materials, or instructional methods are of limited value and validity unless a clear description and understanding of the BBE program can ensure that the controlled differences are the only significant differences or at least that they are the only differences that have a causative relationship to the specific outcomes examined. A monograph by Engle (1974) explores the problems in using evaluations from BBE programs to plan new programs. Although the emphasis is on the lack of control of variables in design, it is clear that the problem runs deeper. In any investigation it is necessary to believe that the variables under consideration exhaust the list of those thought to be crucial and that these variables have equal amounts of independent identity. Educational research (particularly including reading and language arts research) reveals a paucity of such reasoning (Davis, 1971, Sections I and II). The examination of one school setting by Cicourel et al. (1974) underlines the difficulty in understanding and describing the variables in educational programs (Cazden, 1976).

An ethnography of speaking of a BBE program can provide the description and understanding necessary to argue for the validity of a quantitative evaluation and to use evaluations for program planning purposes. Part of our work on the San Francisco project involved revamping the organizational chart to: (a) increase the status of the BBE program-head relative to others in the school system, (b) clarify the relation between the roles of BBE staff as members of an educational system and as members of language and culture groups, and (c) formalize the permanent role of the community in the BBE program. Is this strange work for an organization of applied linguists? Not if an examination of unusable evaluations based on inadequate assessment of student language and academic proficiency revealed the need for reorganization. This need was emphasized by statements about (and observations of) troubles in the communication efforts of BBE staff members and community groups. What we did, in effect, was manipulate the framework so that it would allow necessary and desired changes in the ethnography of speaking in the BBE program.

Poor communication or lack of communication is often claimed to be a major problem: the ethnography of speaking provides a framework for examining who needs to talk to whom, about what, and when, and how this can be facilitated. When we consider two of the dimensions needed to describe the participants alone, the complexity of the communication problem is clear:

a. There are students, teachers, support staff, counselors, administrators, parents, other community members, and outsiders from a variety of academic specialties.

b. There are monolinguals in one language, monolinguals in the other, and varying types and degrees of bilinguals, as well as a range of people on a mono- to bicultural scale.

Perhaps the solution need not be complex; the problem is, however, and arriving at the solution is bound to be complex as well. Simple solutions have not worked. For example, to increase parent involvement, a pre-school program distributed a silverware set, piece by piece, to parents who attended meetings and conferences but there was not much of a real improvement in communication. In another case, an elementary BBE program mandated a relaxed atmosphere in classrooms to resolve a conflict between "traditional" and "progressive" teachers, which also did not work. The first attempted solution concentrated on one factor needed for communication — having the participants present. The second concentrated on another factor — having a clear message. Both attempts ignored the complexity of communication events that an ethnography of speaking can reveal. While both were perfectly clear actions, neither had a lasting effect on the development of a sound educational program, and not coincidentally, neither had a positive effect on the quality or quantity of communication.

As far as I know, there has been no publication of an ethnography of speaking in a BBE program. There are some studies in progress and some planned concerning BBE classroom interactions (some including the home),[1] but none look at the total program. Our work in San Francisco can be used as data to focus on those parts of the ethnography of speaking involving "outsiders." It is important to understand how communication is accomplished with outsiders because there are so many "outside" fields that can contribute to the progress of bilingual education. Three aspects of the CAL-San Francisco interaction are noteworthy:

1. Much of the inter- and intra-group discussion centered on evaluations of the ways in which speaking and writing are accomplished. Most of the

---

[1] For information contact Pedro Pedraza (Columbia Teachers College), Courtney Cazden (Harvard School of Education).

evaluation was negative; little specific change was suggested. Members of both groups indicated that they felt they had capitulated to the other as the work progressed. Some substantive issues were not treated in depth because the participants avoided them, focusing instead on issues of expression.

2. A change occurred in specific terms used during the course of the communication events. For example, "research survey" was replaced by "needs assessment"; "multilingual" was replaced by "bilingual"; and "TESOL" was replaced by "developmental English." Not all of these changes were equivalent. In the last instance, TESOL changing to developmental English, the term-change also indicates a concept change, and this fact is commented on in the final report. In the first two instances, a concept change did not occur. The term "bilingual" came to do the work that both terms do in other situations — contextual support provided the distinction when it was required. However, the terms "needs assessment" and "research survey" proved less malleable — an investigation that is called a "needs assessment" carries with it the framework and methodology of the field of education whereas a "research survey" is an interdisciplinary notion whose characteristics are determined by different fields and different problems at different times. This term-change was accompanied by a general avoidance of the difficult topic of the role of researchers in communities.

3. Various members of the "outside" group shared certain characteristics with members of the inside group. The most crucial characteristic seemed to be ethnic identity; i.e., some members of our team were Filipino, some were Spanish-speaking, and some were Chinese. The occasions, topics, and outcomes of interactions that involved these more or less "inside" outsiders differed in a great many ways from interactions with Anglo members of our team. It is difficult to determine which are the significant differences. In some instances more goals were met when our team members shared characteristics with the program people, but in other instances this was not the case.

An ethnography of speaking can bring about an understanding of these kinds of problems in interactions between those involved in BBE programs. Applications of such research might bring more substance to the notions "community involvement" and "academic field input" and smooth over the rough spots in the hard work required to implement successful BBE programs.

Pragmatics

The third aspect concerns *pragmatics*. Information is sought about aspects of the language system that are related to its use in a social context.

Morris (1938) distinguished syntax (the study of the relations among language forms) and semantics (the study of the relation between language forms and their referents) from pragmatics (the study of the relations of language forms and their users). Recent advances in the study of syntax have emphasized formalisms that give the appearance that, when understood, language will be seen as a system of mathematical truth and beauty. Those who study pragmatics would not necessarily disagree with this statement but would rather determine the function served by the system that can be so formally described. Data for this type of investigation includes information on how forms are used in social context. There is an overlap between pragmatics and the ethnography of speaking. Differences exist in the approaches of each field and at least in their intermediate goals: pragmatics starts with a language structure (or set of structures) and is responsible for establishing rules to account for its privileges of occurrence, including the distribution of usage in social contexts. The ethnography of speaking starts with a societal event and is responsible for establishing the rules to account for those structures that have privileges of occurrence in that social context. Although the approaches are different, both fields have advanced arguments to claim that the data must come in units larger than the sentence.

Pragmatics asks the following questions: What parts of the language system are responsive to who is doing the *talking*, who is being *addressed*, who is *listening*, and *why* the speech event is happening? How is it that several different surface utterances can serve similar purposes? What is "told" in utterances that is not stated outright, i.e., what must be true about the beliefs, knowledge, and attitudes of the speakers involved for a discourse to take place? Answers to these pragmatic questions can be useful to BBE programs in areas such as the following:

1. Teacher training programs can assist teachers to add to their repertoire of utterances in the second language in areas most needed in a school setting. At a BBE workshop at the Advisory and Learning Exchange in Washington, D.C., teachers discussed the particular problems involved in dealing with children whose dominant language is the teacher's second language. A young male teacher, a native Spanish-speaker, felt that his English repertoire for directives[2] (giving orders and requests) was so limited that many of the native English-speaking children restricted their explorations when they were with him and on some occasions reacted with fright. The teacher's repertoire was limited to utterances most common in situations of urgency and highly marked for status advantage to the

---

[2]See work in this area by Heringer (1971), and Lakoff (1972).

speaker. He said things such as, "Sit down, John," but had difficulty saying things such as "Would you like to sit here, John?" Both of those utterances function to get John to sit down but the first is more urgent and conveys the idea that the speaker is powerful. Research conducted by Montes (1978) indicated that native English-speaking children are cognizant of variation in directive utterances in at least two dimensions: the degree of urgency and the status relationship of the speaker and addressee. The teacher used English in a wider variety of situations than those for which he had an available repertoire. The children, knowing about urgency and status, could see this teacher as frightening. The teacher needed to increase his proficiency in his second language in two ways: to focus on a particular area ("weak" directives) and to add a way to identify goals for study that were of immediate relevance to his work with children. The language proficiency part of a teacher education program that guides teachers to such awareness and provides for the requisite learning is radically different in design and implementation than that offered by most language courses. Obviously, there are also implications for evaluating a teacher's language proficiency that differ radically from most that are current. In most courses, basic grammatical structures are tested and taught. There is little regard for increasing the teacher's ability to function with the language in the class-room setting.

2. Planning for and evaluating academic subject-matter learning in the second language should attend to the pragmatic aspects of the language. Two illustrative points follow.

First, some fairly frequent structures that can appear in instructional materials call for a detailed familiarity with the second language if one is to understand the point. For example, in a structure like (a) below, the infinitive (italics) is not important in the same way that it is in (b). The second part of (a) and (c) are equivalent in meaning, while the second part of (b) and (d) are far from equivalent:

    a. After working hard and saving throughout the winter, the colonists were upset *to learn* that a tax had been added to the price of tea.

    b. Since they did not believe in starting wars, the citizens were glad *to learn* that the enemy started the war.

    c. . . . the colonists were upset that a tax had been added to the price of tea.

    d. . . . the citizens were glad that the enemy started the war.

Since structures such as these are present in instructional and assessment materials, many questions need to be investigated about whether they are problematic for second-language students, and if so, when these problems arise. There are anecdotal reports of difficulty, but there has been no controlled investigation. However, evaluations of the success or failure of programs that espouse the learning of academic subject matter in the second language may be confounded by the amount of material that contains pragmatically complex structures.

The second illustrative point concerns not the comprehension of the second-language structure when used but the eventual representation of the structure (in memory). There are a series of structures in English that invite other meanings that aren't stated outright. A review by Harris (1975) considers the psychological import of such structures to theories of memory and comprehension. Implied thoughts are usually treated by the native speaker as if they were stated as fact. For example, statements like the following can often be treated equivalently:

    a. The children were not required to go to school.
    b. The children were not able to go to school.
    c. The children did not go to school.

Whereas adult native speakers recognize factors of context or syntactic structures that might deny the implication in the case of utterances like (a) and (b), children tend to accept implied propositions as facts more often than do adults. What second-language speakers do has not been investigated. There are several possible problems for learning theory with respect to second-language students:

    a. Second-language students may draw implications and treat them as fact moreso than is warranted and may end up with incorrect or contradictory sets of facts about subject matter taught in the second language.

    b. Second-language students may draw fewer implications, treat these as facts, and end up with less exposure to, or reinforcement in, the subject matter taught in the second language than do the students for whom the language of instruction is their first language.

    c. The problem may occur in both directions depending on the language structures or processes, and/or on the student's developmental level, and/or on the type and degree of contextual support.

Neither of these illustrative points should be taken to mean that subject matter should not be taught in the second language. On the contrary, the difficulties should be investigated and BBE programs should develop approaches to control them. The presentation here concentrates on what may be termed the receptive aspects of the second language, but in fact, the issue is not so limited. I had an experience with a productive aspect of difficulty with pragmatic implications a few years ago. I was reading manuscripts for children's stories written in English by previously unpublished authors with Spanish-speaking backgrounds. Several stories were about Benito Juarez, and three of them mentioned that, as a child, Juarez would talk to his sheep about his problems. The amazing aspect of the writing is that all three added the sentence, "But the sheep didn't answer." My suspicion is that each author felt that there was an implication that both parties talked and that they had to cancel this implication that sheep could talk by adding the above sentence. I don't know if that is due to the variety of English that all three shared, or to an influence from Spanish, or if each felt that it was a necessary aspect of writing for children. What I do know is that the sentence in question would be corrected or edited out by teachers or editors who speak English as a first or only language.

3. Pragmatic aspects of language are also important to the working of BBE programs that bring together children and adults of two different language and culture groups. There are elements in utterances that first-language speakers use to identify and, often, to evaluate the speaker. Second-language speakers may misrepresent themselves or mis-evaluate a speaker. Montes and I conducted an experiment (1975) with male and female first-language speakers and with female second-language speakers. We investigated five pairs of structures of English that seemed similar in that one member of each pair was "weaker" than the other. We also conducted a forced choice test to see if our subjects would be consistent in using this strong/weak difference and another task using a series of semantic differential scales to see how the subjects would evaluate speakers they heard using the strong/weak structures in scenarios. We observed differences and similarities where we expected them for the pairs of structures, the two tasks, and the sex of the subject. However, for the second-language subjects, our results were confusing: they didn't act like first-language women or men, and they often evaluated on a basis that was consistent but different from the first-language subjects. The second-language speakers' idea of what constituted more opinionated, aggressive, overly assertive language use differed from those of the first-language subjects. I do not claim that the evidence of this experiment transfers directly to interactions among teachers or among teachers and children and parents. I do suggest, however, that if difficulty arises in such interactions, it may be useful to see if second-language speakers evaluate minute aspects of the language system differently than native speakers. Teachers in a BBE program may have difficulty working in a group to plan a curriculum if half of them evaluate a given utterance as "wishy-washy" and the other half evaluate it as "opinionated." Although recognizing the problem does not solve it, recognizing it can at least provide direction for trial solutions.

Conclusion

BBE programs need to take into account how the two languages are used and evaluated in the community (*the sociology of language*), and they need to be aware of how each language is used to serve the purposes of specific social interactional situations, including the implementation of the BBE program itself *(the ethnography of speaking)*. BBE programs also need to know how subtle aspects of meaning, particularly those aspects important to oral and written instruction, are accomplished in the two language systems *(the pragmatics of natural language)*. Much of this information must be generated by local BBE programs with effective community involvement for three reasons: (1) much of the information is specific to the local situation, (2) many of the rules for getting accurate information in an efficient and pleasant way are specific to the local situation, and (3) there is so much basic and applied work that needs to be done (not only answering questions but also formulating new ones) that the cooperation of many people is needed.

A BBE curriculum and materials development project can give an impetus to such local work by BBE program staff, teachers, and community. Consider, for example, that all three of these social aspects of language can be seen as parts of the academic content areas called social science, and language arts. Working with questions arising from these three aspects also involves concepts and skills commonly found under the curriculum area labeled natural science. A curriculum and materials project can locate specific concepts and skills in all these academic fields that could be learned by students while studying and investigating the social aspects of language. The curriculum and materials project can prepare documents that set out reasonable prioritized goals and guides for teachers and community members. The goals would include, at the beginning, ways to obtain the necessary information and, at the end, ways to utilize the information in BBE program planning, teacher education, student assessment, and student learning objectives where appropriate. At various points, working with researchers or having the BBE program staff act as researchers will be necessary to this endeavor.

The difficult problems of transferring findings from relevant fields to educational applications will be circumvented if some of the findings come from the setting itself. Will researchers be willing to let community educational needs influence their identification of problems to work on? Hymes (1974a) notes:

> The treatment of linguistic structure has been closely linked to other interests, such as logic, rhetoric, poetics, philosophy, theology — in short with the uses of language recognized and valued by the societies . . . (p. 6)

The question, then, is whether our society recognizes and values the educational use of language. Bilingual education seems to be a natural "other interest" for linguists at this time in the history of linguistics when the social aspects of language are the focus of much linguistic research.

REFERENCES

A Master Plan for Bilingual-Bicultural Education in the San Francisco Unified School District in Response to the Supreme Court Decision in the Case of Lau vs. Nichols. Arlington: Center for Applied Linguistics, 1975.

Bauman, Richard, and Joel Sherzer, eds. Explorations in the Ethnography of Speaking. London: Cambridge University Press, 1974.

Cazden, Courtney B. Review of "If School Is a Performance, How Do We Change the Script," Contemporary Psychology, XXI, No. 2 (February, 1976), 125-126.

Cicourel, Aaron V. et al. Language Use and School Performance. New York: Academic Press, 1974.

Davis, Frederick B., ed. The Literature of Research in Reading with Emphasis on Models; Final Report. New Brunswick: Rutgers University, Graduate School of Education, 1971, Section I, pp. 1-1 to 1-23, and Section II, pp. 2-1 to 2-18.

Engle, Patricia Lee. The Use of Vernacular Languages in Education. Arlington: Center for Applied Linguistics, 1974.

Fishman, Joshua A. "A Sociology of Bilingual Education." Final Report to the Division of Foreign Studies, Department of Health, Education, and Welfare, United States Office of Education, Contract No. OECO-73-0588, 1974.

Gumperz, John J., and Dell Hymes, eds. "The Ethnography of Communication," American Anthropologist (Special Publication), LXVI, No. 6, Part 2 (December, 1964).

Harris, Richard. "The Psychology of Pragmatic Implication." Unpublished PhD dissertation, Kansas State University, 1975.

Hymes, Dell. "Introduction: Traditions and Paradigms," Studies in the History of Linguistics: Traditions and Paradigms, ed. Dell Hymes. Bloomington: Indiana University Press, 1974a, pp. 1-38.

_____. Foundations in Sociolinguistics; An Ethnographic Approach. Philadelphia: University of Pennsylvania Press, 1974b.

Herringer, James T. Some Grammatical Correlates of Felicity Conditions and Presuppositions. Dissertation. Ohio State University Working Paper, No. 11. Columbus: Ohio State University, Linguistics Department, 1971.

Lakoff, George. Hedges: A Study in Meaning Criteria and the Logic of Fuzzy Concepts. Papers from the 8th Regional Meeting, Chicago Linguistic Society. Chicago: Chicago Linguistic Society, 1972.

Montes, Rosa. "Extending a Concept: Functioning Directively," Final Report to the Carnegie Corporation, eds. Peg Griffin, and Roger Shuy. Arlington: Center for Applied Linguistics, 1978, Chapter V.

_____, and Peg Griffin. "Being Asserted At," Proceedings From NWAVE V, eds. Ralph W. Fasold, and Roger W. Shuy. Washington: Georgetown University Press, 1975.

Morris, Charles W. Foundations of the Theory of Signs. Chicago: University of Chicago Press, 1938.

Paulston, Christina Bratt. Implications of Language Learning for Language Planning: Concerns in Bilingual Education. Arlington: Center for Applied Linguistics, 1974.

Philips, Susan U. "Some Sources of Cultural Variability in the Regulation of Talk," Language in Society, V, No. 1 (April, 1976), 81-95.

Ethnographic Monitoring

Dell Hymes

The contributions of ethnography in the planning, conduct, evaluation, and justification of bilingual programs are essential to the success of bilingual education. In order to "start where the child is," initial, systematic knowledge of the child's verbal repertoire in relation to the verbal repertoire of the community is essential in planning the program. Ethnographic monitoring involves the required feedback to program directors and staff in the conduct and evaluation of programs. Regular community participation in the guidance of programs and ethnography performed by a member of the community are highly desirable. Schools have served to maintain social stratification by determining the acceptable linguistic norms *for* the community. Bilingual education challenges this by adhering to the goal of overcoming linguistic inequality. Consequently, pressures may arise to do away with bilingual education. Ethnographic information and research will be needed to counter these pressures.

I WANT TO consider the contribution of ethnography to bilingual education, and to argue, indeed, that ethnography is essential to the success of bilingual education.

One contribution of ethnography has to do with the planning of programs and the need for knowledge of the initial state of affairs. This contribution of ethnography (initial knowledge) is perhaps familiar, though neglected. There are two other kinds of contributions as well. One has to do with the conduct of programs, the need to recognize and understand patterns and meanings that may emerge during the course of a program, perhaps outside the classroom. The other has to do with the evaluation and justification of programs, and ultimately, the evaluation and justification of bilingual education itself. The second and third contributions can be thought of as *ethnographic monitoring*, the one of an on-going operation, the other of effects and consequences. Attention should be paid to both.

Ethnography might be thought of as something purely descriptive and objective, done by someone who comes from outside. This is not the view I hold. Ethnography must be descriptive and objective, yes, but not only that. It must be conscious of values and goals; it must relate description to analysis and objectivity to critical evaluation. Bilingual education involves social change in the light of certain goals. As a matter of law, it is defined in terms of the goal of equality of educational opportunity. As a matter of social change, it involves much more — personal goals and commitments, what people consider their life chances and identities to be, what they want them to become. Not everyone may agree on the goals of change, or how much and what kind of change is desirable. An ethnographer must come to understand the values involved and the validity of those values to those who hold them, as well as come to understand his/her own attitudes (perhaps attitudes that emerge in the course of his or her work) and the reasons for them. Only explicit concern with values, in short, will allow ethnography to overcome hidden sources of bias. To be truly useful, ethnography must relate what is described to goals. It may be that certain goals and certain situations are not compatible, or that certain goals and certain means are not, or that an unwitting inconsistency exists among goals or means. Ethnography is an essential way of discovering what the case is, and social programs that ignore it are blind; but ethnography that ignores values and goals is sterile.

Ethnography might be thought of as something done by someone from without, a hired professional. It does require training and talent; not just anyone can do it. But of all forms of scientific knowledge, ethnography is the most open, the most compatible with a democratic way of life, the least likely to produce a world in which experts control knowledge at the expense of those who are studied. The skills of ethnography consist of the enhancements of skills all normal persons employ in everyday life; its discoveries can usually be conveyed in forms of language that non-specialists can read. It comes to know more of a way of life than those that live it are consciously aware of, but most take crucial account of what they consciously, and unconsciously, know. A crucial ingredient of ethnography is what in a sense is already known to members of a community, what they must know, consciously and unconsciously, in order to be normal members of the community. As a discipline, ethnography adds a body of concepts and techniques that directs attention and relates observations more systematically than community members would normally have occasion to do, that provides for making explicit relationships and patterns that members leave implicit, and that provides for interpreting patterns in the light of a comparative knowledge of other ways of life to which a community member would not usually have access. Ethnography, in short, is a disciplined way of looking, asking, recording, reflecting, comparing, and reporting. It mediates between an understanding of what members of a given community know and do, and an accumulated comparative understanding of what members of communities generally have known and done.

A member of a given community, then, need not be merely a source of data, an object at the other end of a scientific instrument. He/she already possesses some of the local knowledge and has access to knowledge that is essential to successful ethnography; he/she may have a talent for sifting and synthesizing it, a special insight into some part of it. What the member needs is the other part of disciplined ethnography, the comparative insight distilled over the decades. This can come in a variety of idioms and does not require a graduate degree. Indeed, one might argue that an educational system devoted to a democratic way of life would provide this other part to every student, as a right and as a basis for citizenship. Not to do so is to withhold from citizens the best that we have to offer for the understanding of social experience and for coming to terms with it or changing it.

When I refer to ethnography, then, I assume that the person doing the ethnography may be from the community in question. Indeed, I think it is highly desirable that this be the case in a large proportion of cases (Hymes, 1974a; Hymes, 1972).

The contribution of ethnography to initial knowledge may be familiar. Still, when I suggested ethnography to the director of a language program in a large city, the response was, "What would you want to know?" The only elaboration of the answer was that the people in the community would not want it to be known that so many of them were illiterate.

Such a response suggests that the idea of sociolinguistic description, of ethnography of speaking, has not gone very far beyond academic halls. Indeed, it has not gone very far within them, so far as educational settings are concerned. One repeatedly cites Philips' study (1972, 1974) of the relation between Madras, Oregon classrooms and the Warm Springs Indian reservation culture, not only because it is good but also because it remains unique.

Most educators would agree with the principle that teaching should start where the child is. Few appear to recognize that to do so requires knowledge of the community from which the child comes. Many teachers would agree with the Office for Civil Rights that formal tests do not adequately show the abilities and needs of children. These teachers may not recognize that their own observations may be skewed, confounding impressions of intellectual ability with impressions of voice and visual appearance. Observation needs to be systematic across a range of settings and activities: in class, on the playground, and at home. The interdependence between specific settings and a display of abilities and skills is coming to be recognized as a crucial focus for research.

To start where the child is, then, one needs systematic knowledge of the *verbal repertoire* of the child in relation to that of his/her community: the range of varieties of language, the circumstances, purposes, and meanings of their use. These can differ from one community or district to another, and local knowledge is needed. One needs to know the role of speaking, hearing, writing, and reading, in a given language variety and what it means to do each of these activities. These can differ from one place to another, too, and local knowledge again is needed. One needs to know, in short, the locally relevant *ways of speaking* (using "speaking" as a shorthand expression for all modes of language use). The organization of language use in a classroom is but part of a systematic whole, from the vantage point of the student; and from that vantage point, classroom norms may take on a meaning not intended or comprehended by school personnel (Hymes, 1974b).

It is common to think of a choice of one language or another, one variety or style or another, one genre or another, a mode or occasion of use of language, as appropriate or inappropriate, right or wrong. Certainly teachers in classrooms often seem to think in this way. An essential ethnographic point is to remember that a choice may have to do with elements in a system of signs. The language used has to do with more than right and wrong. It is not only the elements within a language that are to be understood as signs, as uniting form and meaning or as showing their status by contrast with other signs. Every choice within a way of speaking — of language, variety, style, genre, mode, occasion — conveys meaning through contrast with other choices not made quite in addition to the meaning conveyed by what is written or said. The same is true for the use of language; Goffman (1956) has called it deference (what one conveys about one's attitude toward oneself). Too often one thinks that one particular choice represents order, anything else, a lack of order. This assumption can keep one from discovering the true order that is present, the system of sociolinguistic signs implicit in students' communicative conduct. One may wish to change that conduct — to change that system. One has to recognize it, be able to interpret accurately what is communicated, in order to know what one wishes to change. (This is an example of the relation between the descriptive and critical aspects of ethnography.)

The point applies both to rules of language and to rules of the use of language. Let me say a little more about the latter first in order to highlight their importance.

A teacher or curriculum may make an assumption — about the role of language in learning, about the etiquette of speaking, listening, writing, reading, about getting and giving information, getting and giving attention in talk — that is at variance with what students experience elsewhere. Variance in itself of course is simply a fact. Whether or not it is a problem depends on the situation. If a classroom pattern is accepted and respected by all concerned, it may succeed, at least as success is defined by those concerned. (Their goals of course may not include equality or social change.) The pattern may also stamp what is learned in the classroom as appropriate only in similar settings.

Schools have long been aware of cultural differences, and in recent years have attempted to address them, rather than punish them. Too often the differences of which the school is aware, of which even the community is aware, are only the most visible, "high" culture symbols and the most stereotyped conventions. What may be slighted is the "invisible" culture (to use Philips' title), the culture of everyday etiquette and interaction, and its expression of rights and duties, values and aspirations, through norms of communication. Classrooms may respect religious belief and national custom, yet profane an implicit ceremonial order having to do with relations between persons. One can honor cultural pride on the walls of a room yet inhibit learning within them.

One may find children fitting classroom expectations, but in a way that defeats the purpose of their being there. Some Anglo teachers in Philadelphia schools have been delighted to have Spanish-speaking children in their classes because the children are so well behaved — that is, quiet. The reason for the quietness is that the children do not understand what is being said. When they do understand (after being placed in a bilingual classroom, for example), they participate actively. The equation of being good with being quiet implies a further equation with being dumb (both senses of the word). Communities, of course, may differ in the meanings and normal occasions of silence, something that needs to be known in an individual case.

Knowledge of the local repertoire of varieties of language is obviously essential. In terms of the descriptive contribution of ethnography, a salient concern is the local meaning and interpretation of the joint use of both Spanish and English forms. Of course, instances of the occurrence of elements of one language in the context of another may be quite *ad hoc*, due to the familiarity or the forgetting of particular words. But some may consider mixing of any sort reprehensible, and especially if it is extensive. Others may recognize in extensive mixing a special style of speech, appropriate to certain people and situations. They may find not a failure to keep languages apart but rather a skill in mingling them, one that has to be learned. Someone who knows Spanish and knows English may not know how to mingle them in the special style. From one standpoint, then, error and confusion are something to be stamped out; from another, a skill with social meaning to be enjoyed.

The significance of mixing cannot be judged without knowledge of the community and individual norms, but the knowledge is not an end to the matter. The temptation of descriptive ethnography is to let understanding imply acceptance, but ethnography can be used critically. In a given case, a community may not have been conscious of some aspects of its pattern of language use, and it might wish to reject some part when brought to its attention. Or a community may decide that a change of pattern is desirable, even necessary. Or it may decide to accept and value a pattern previously little noted. Whatever the case, the goals of bilingual education should be informed by ethnography but set by those affected. The most difficult issue may be to analyze and assess information bearing on choice of *linguistic norm* and on its implementation.

It is clear that there is an issue. There have been classrooms in which the native speakers of Spanish were seated in the back of the Spanish class and the Anglo students in front. There is a school in West Chester, Pennsylvania, whose Spanish-speaking Colombian teachers are certain that their Spanish-speaking Puerto Rican students need to be taught correct (Colombian-flavored) Spanish, ignoring a demonstration that the students are able to read newspapers published in Madrid. In both cases, a different classroom norm would yield different results.

There well may be a genuine problem of inadequacy of competence in certain cases. Puerto Rican children raised in New York City may be disadvantaged in schools in Puerto Rico. Children growing up in a particular community may not acquire the full range of varieties and levels of Spanish, especially if Spanish has been part of a stable multilingual situation as a language of the home rather than of education. Ethnography can help discover the facts of local situations in this regard. Whatever the facts, difficult matters of analysis and assessment remain. At this point the critical, comparative use of ethnographic knowledge becomes essential.

Let me address the issue of linguistic norms — of which to use, accept, and reject. Some leaders in bilingual education have been heard to say there might be a danger of perpetuating through Spanish the failures of schools conducted in English. We are indeed familiar with the kinds of misperception and misconception of ability that can be fostered by prejudicial attitudes towards varieties of English different from the variety assumed in the classroom. Is the problem of attaining equality then simply one of such differences? Could the problem be solved by eliminating the differences, either by stamping out all but the preferred norm, or by substituting or adding one common norm in the repertoires of everyone?

I think that such an approach fails, and fails necessarily, in the United States, if the problem is indeed defined as one of eliminating linguistically-defined inequality. If every user of English in the United States used certifiably standard English, in recognizably middle-class ways, little would change except for the cultural impoverishment, the loss of diversity, and interest in American ways of life. Fault would continue to be found. People who do not use double negatives may be found redundant in their adjectives. People who do not misuse tenses can be faulted for their use of adverbs and conjunctions.

Variability and evaluation of usage are indeed universal in human life, but the issue here is not one of individual differences — of the variation in personal ability inevitable in any group. If such were the case, it would be a matter of talent; as it stands, it is a matter of shibboleths. If linguistic discrimination is a culturally deep-seated way of maintaining social distinctions, then discrimination is likely to continue. If not through English against other languages, then through one dialect of English against others, or one style of standard English against others. What Barth (1969) has shown for ethnic boundaries holds for class boundaries as well: even slight and infrequent features will serve as boundary markers, if there must be boundaries.

One can further suggest that the United States is culturally organized to produce continually the appearance of a "falling rate of correctness," of a "law of increasing illiteracy." There is not only the constant reproduction of linguistic inferiority, but also the constant renewal of markers of it. There is also the constant projection of decline. This last one draws on a disposition to interpret change in language (itself inevitable) as inevitably for the worse. From this standpoint, necessary distinctions are always being lost, never gained; etymology condemns vitality. Intelligibility is so often found wanting that one must infer that for the vast majority of people, talk is nothing more than a verbal blind man's bluff.

It is a curious thing that a country whose civic ideology has been so committed to "progress" should so despair of language. I suspect two complementary attitudes and interests to be at work: a widespread popular distrust of verbal skill and an elite's definition of verbal skill as something only it can have and so control. It is perhaps an interaction between these two forces that produces a phenomenon such as a President careful to explain to an audience that he didn't know a word he used and had to look it up in a dictionary, while expecting to be trusted to manage a vast bureaucracy that lives and breathes with the manufacture and manipulation of esoteric discourse.

The role of language in the maintenance of cultural hegemony in the United States has been little explored. The main point — and this brings us back to the role of schools — is that the United States would seem to have a culture in which discrimination on the basis of language is endemic. To achieve equality within a given language, it would never be enough to change the way people speak. One would have to change what the way people speak is taken to mean.

In this regard, one can hardly avoid the thought that a latent function of schools has been to define a certain proportion of people as inferior, even to convince them that they are so, and to do this *on the seemingly neutral ground of language*. Language seems a neutral ground, so long as one can maintain that there is just one proper norm, and that the schools do their duty if they provide everyone access to that norm. The language of the norm is necessary, and everyone has a chance to acquire it (so one can imagine the reasoning). Any inequality of outcome cannot be the fault of the school or system, but must be fair and reflect differences in ability, effort, or desire on the part of students. If it is pointed out that some students begin unequally, relative to the norm assumed in the school, the responsibility is assigned to the student or student's community, for lack of proper language or even a virtual lack of language at all.

Centers to stimulate verbal communication in infants in disadvantaged homes are even now being newly established. From what I have said, you can see that questions about such centers would arise. What are the norms of communication, including use of language, in such families? What is the evidence that they are inadequate? Are they judged to be inadequate intrinsically, or inadequate in relation to the assumptions made in local schools as to the role of language? Is the set of assumptions made in local schools the only possible set? Is the difference between schools and homes a difference between normalcy and impoverishment, or a difference between two ways of doing things, two ways of speaking, each normal in its own setting? Is the program of such a center to change the culture of the home something we would call cultural imperialism if it were reported from the Soviet Union? Is change of the culture of the homes the only option? Could the differences be tolerated, or the schools change? These questions are not rhetorical. Reasonable people might arrive at different answers, given different situations. The essential thing is that such questions be asked. Given the many differences among societies in the role of language in child-raising, yet the unfailing success of children in acquiring language, together with the norms of use appropriate to their society, it is doubtful that any viable community needs a program of verbal stimulation for its children for its own successful continuation. A program, of course, may be a way of changing the community or of diverting the children from it.

Bilingual education challenges the very fabric of schooling insofar as it adheres to the goal of overcoming linguistic inequality, by changing what happens in schools themselves. But if linguistic discrimination is a culturally deep-seated way of maintaining social distinctions deeply embedded in educational institutions, is bilingual education likely to escape its influence? I have suggested that the form of attention to language in schools serves to maintain social stratification, and as long as the society requires such stratification, it is likely to find ways to reproduce it linguistically. The society is defined as one of opportunity, yet the relative distribution of wealth and class position hardly changes year after year, decade after decade; language plays some part in accomplishing and legitimizing that result. Is success for bilingual education then to mean that the accusation, "That's not Spanish," will be heard as widely as the accusation, "That's not English?" Or that children who know varieties of Spanish other than the norm adopted for a classroom will bear the stigma of not knowing *two* languages? (One hears of teachers saying to a child, "I thought your problem was that your language was Spanish instead of English; now I find out that you have no language at all.")

The issue of linguistic norms is inescapable within the level of an established standard itself, because of the distinctness of Cuban, Puerto Rican, Mexican, and other national standards represented in the United States. It is inescapable as well with regard to the relation between national and regional standards, on the one hand, and the other components of the verbal repertoires of Spanish speakers in this country. The issue of norms involves the verbal repertoire as a whole. What is the desired role of each component of the repertoire, and what is the attitude toward each? As I have indicated, ethnography can assist in obtaining the initial knowledge needed to determine the present state of affairs. Clearly, ethnography is needed instead of questionnaires and surveys. What to make of the knowledge provided by ethnography is a matter for the bilingual community to decide. Perhaps in a given case it may be decided that an insistence on standard Spanish is necessary in order to maintain the language. It is also entirely possible that some may decide to reject bilingual education and Spanish as necessary ingredients of, say, Puerto Rican identity, spurred in their decision perhaps by elitist decisions as to the norm within Spanish (see Language Policy Task Force, 1978).

Let me make clear that I do not mean to imply that all evaluation of language and usage is merely social bias. The point is that social bias infects evaluation. It is not the case that "anything goes," but it is also not the case that there is a single, homogeneous, unquestionable norm. The existence of a norm is a social fact, but not a fact beyond critical analysis in the light of knowledge of other norms, of the effects of the norm in question as it is implemented, of alternative relations between linguistic norms and ways of life.

There are normative criteria that apply to languages and their use, e.g., criteria of clarity, elegance, pithiness, musicality, simplicity, and vigor. The difficulty is that people differ in the criteria to which they give most weight, even within the same community, let alone between communities. People may differ in what they count as satisfying a norm on whose importance they agree. Much of the history of language policy and attitude, much of the history of linguistic research itself, can be related to alternate attitudes towards the existence and character of two broad classes of norm, "standard" and "vernacular." In general, social bias affects willingness to recognize the presence and legitimacy of a norm in the first place and the interpretation placed upon meeting or failing to meet it. Is adherence to a "standard" elegance or pretentiousness? Is it logical regularity or empty form? Is adherence to a "vernacular" revitalizing or corrupting? Natural or uncouth? Is it an expression of the spirit of the folk or of the spawn of the uneducated?

Differences in pronunciation are stigmatized as stupidity the world over; absence of features of grammar is taken as absence of logic; propriety of diction identifed with virtue. Such interpretations of the speech of others are frequently arbitrary. The association between a feature of language and a feature of intelligence or character is generally not inherent and universal, but local, secondary, and projected.

Within one's own linguistic tradition, one may be on surer ground in assessing the speech of those who share it, but it is ground that cannot be made more secure than the tradition itself. One can judge others (and oneself) in relation to known norms but not withhold the norms themselves from scrutiny, if their consequences cause them to come into question. Despite their pervasiveness and familiarity, the norms may be secondary and projective. We may honor them because through them we have experienced so much that is inseparable from our own naming and knowing of life: satisfactions and illuminations even that mastery of a norm may sometimes permit. Even so, we have to accept that similar experiences may occur in relation to norms we can hardly recognize as such. There must be norms, if there is to be mastery, whether of interactional wit or composed art. But the norms themselves are not fundamental, I think. What is fundamental is that which the norms make possible, the functions served in creative, resourceful, adaptive, and expressive uses of language. Many norms can serve those functions, and a given norm can be made into an enemy of them.

We want to ask, then, not if the norm is observed but what is accomplished through observance of the norm? Is it desirable to spend a term insisting that a child be perfect in a minor grammatical feature, if the result is to teach that child that the norm of which the feature is a part is a torture chamber? Or if the child is inhibited from ever attempting to use that norm resourcefully?

We recognize that there are universal capacities for the structures and functions of language shared by all normal human beings; that a degree of individual variation in ability is inescapable; that a degree of normative stability is essential to the possibility of reliable communication and expressive mastery; that mastery of features may facilitate their resourceful use, but that the same features, treated as shibboleths, may inhibit resourceful use of language. The functions of language are fundamental, the forms instrumental. Quite literally, the letter killeth, but the spirit giveth life.

The goals of a community of course may not be to encourage creative and resourceful use of language. The goals may be to ensure that persons can be placed by the way they speak and write. Or to ensure that persons can perform useful work, can read instructions, newspapers, and other communications from those who direct things. (It is perhaps instructive that our society defines reading, a receptive ability, as its main concern, not the productive ability to write.) Insofar as a community both says and means that resourceful, creative use of language is a goal for all its citizens, then questions of norms, and questions of pedagogy too, must be decided in favor of an emphasis on function as primary, form as instrumental. This is not to ignore the one in favor of the other but to recognize which of the two will bring the other in its train.

If this view is accepted, then the task of ethnography is both indispensable and difficult. It is not enough to discover what varieties of language are in use, when and where and by whom, what features of language vary according to what parameters. One has to discover what varieties of language, features of language, are being used *for*, and to what effect. Is the choice of one norm over another the choice as well of certain functional possibilities as against others? Let me cite the circumstances of many Native American communities, which have acquired English but not the literary glories that English departments like to cite, while having lost rich literary traditions of their own. These communities have English instead of some Native American language, insofar as it is a question of language alone. They have been impoverished insofar as it is a question of the functions of language.

The issues and choices are difficult. I only hope to have shown that the knowledge one needs in order to deal with them is ethnographic in nature. This is true, not only with regard to initial knowledge, but with regard to the monitoring of on-going programs and of outcomes.

Whatever the strategy of a program, those who direct it obviously benefit from feedback during its course. Test scores and other classroom results may give some indication of the progress of students. Even with regard to what is learned alone, observation is desirable as well. Students may show abilities in peer-group interaction and other settings that do not appear on tests. Insofar as the program is concerned with the general development of the students, and with the success of bilingualism itself, ethnographic observation is essential. A central question will be: what does it come to mean to succeed, or to fail, in the program? What does it come to mean to do well or poorly?

Perhaps some of the meaning will have been clarified through the assignment of students to locations in the classroom or to other groupings. Studies by Rist (1970), McDermott (1974) and others have shown the importance for success and failure, and for social meaning of success and failure, of teacher-assigned groupings.

Some of the meaning of the program to its students, and to the community from which they come to school, will emerge in interaction outside of school. Peer-group discussions and judgments, family discussions and judgments, community perception of the purposes and consequences of the program, need to be known and taken into account. While the program is teaching language, it will also be creating social definitions and judgments. These definitions and judgments may be as important to success for bilingualism in the country as formal instruction.

A great deal can be accomplished by establishing regular community participation in the guidance of the program. Still, no one is a perfect or even adequate ethnographer of him/herself, if engaged in observation, comparison, and inference only *ad hoc*. It would be a valuable element of the monitoring of a program during its operation to have one or more persons formally responsible for ethnographic observation and inquiry. What groupings emerge in classrooms, playgrounds, or elsewhere? Does use of language change outside of class during the course of the program, and if so, in what ways? Does conversation about language change? What is said about the program, about those who succeed better than others, about those who do less well? Even more meaningful is discovery of what is *presupposed* in what is said — what comes to be taken as shared assumption in terms of which specific remarks are to be understood, e.g., that a student who does well is a teacher's pet, that a student who does poorly is stupid, that only students from a certain class or neighborhood or kind of family do well, or do poorly.

Ethnographic monitoring need not be conceived as an isolated task. The staff of the program and representatives of the community could participate valuably, if one or a few people were responsible for coordinating information, for providing initial orientation as to the kinds of observation needed, and, indeed, for listening to learn the kinds of observation that might not have been initially thought of. A much higher degree of validity might be possible through cooperation. Since the purpose of the ethnography is to aid the program, its result must be communicated to the participants in the program in any case. It is far better to have the communication as an ongoing process throughout the program. An additional benefit may be to share ethnographic skills that participants in the program will be able to use in other circumstances.

The greatest value of cooperative ethnographic monitoring is that the participants in the program will have the firmest grasp possible of the working of the program, of its successes and failures, strengths and weaknesses, in relation to their hopes for it. They will not be in the position of being confronted by an outside evaluator's charts and tables, and told a rating for their program, with nothing to say, or nothing, at least, that such an evaluator feels required to heed. The participants will not have been bystanders. They will have concrete knowledge of the process of the program, and be able to address the processes that have produced whatever statistics and graphs a formal evaluation process may yield. An evaluation in terms of gross numbers can only guess at what produced the numbers, and indeed, can only guess as to whether its numbers were obtained with measures appropriate to what is being evaluated. The participants in cooperative ethnography may benefit from having their cumulative observations and interpretations compared with independently obtained measures. Both kinds of information could be combined to provide a deeper understanding. But if measures are to mean anything, especially in relation to bilingual education as a process of social change, the ethnography is essential.

All this is the more important, if we look ahead, and think of the monitoring and assessment of individual programs as contributing to judgments likely to be made a few years from now as to the success or failure of bilingual education as a national policy.

A few years from now the charge is likely to be made that bilingual education has failed. Money was spent, little was accomplished — it is easy enough to predict what will be said if bilingual classrooms join busing and poverty programs as targets of resentment.

The political strength of those who support bilingual education may be great enough to offset the pressure of those who will make such charges, once the first wave of support and funding has crested. And much can be said to deflate the prejudice that may lie behind such charges. From the standpoint of what is known about languages and their uses, it is clear that bilingualism can be an entirely taken-for-granted aspect of a society, something entirely within the normal capacity of individuals. The list of flourishing bilingual, even multilingual, situations throughout the world is long indeed. The evidence that human beings can readily acquire a range of varieties of language is so clear that the question must be, not, is it possible, but where it does not happen, what prevents it?

Arguments from suspicion of bilingualism in general, then, can be won. Arguments from the situation of bilingualism in the United States may be more difficult. Arguments will likely raise two issues: educational success, and political consequences. As to educational success, it can be pointed out that a few years is hardly enough to overcome the consequences of generations of effort to impose monolingualism in schools. And insofar as successful programs require research, there has been little accumulated knowledge on which to build. Most linguists have been as blind to the importance of the linguistic diversity of the country as anyone. They too have proceeded as if knowledge of English alone would be sufficient. Far too few scholars of other disciplines have been helpful. Only in recent years has any substantial number of anthropologists thought ethnographic research in their own country legitimate. As we know, bilingualism has been made a vital issue through social, political, and legal processes. These have led the way. Research, by and large, has only begun to follow. Insofar as successful programs require accurate initial knowledge of the situations in which they operate, and appropriate methods for assessing the communicative competence of students, they have had little on which to draw. Bilingual education may be accused of having failed before it has been fairly tried, if to be fairly tried means to have the support of the kinds of knowledge and methods indicated.

In this regard, the ethnographic monitoring of programs can be of great importance. The circumstances and characteristics of successful results can be documented in ways that carry conviction. Unsuccessful efforts can be interpreted in the light of the conditions found with success. Attempts to argue that bilingual education as a whole has been a failure in the United States can be countered by getting down to cases and knowing well what the cases are. To do this requires confidence in the kind of knowledge that ethnography provides, a willingness to accept the legitimacy of the conclusions arrived at by cooperative ethnographic observations and analysis, if such conclusions differ from formal tests and measurements. I think we frequently accept the legitimacy of understandings of our own that are ethnographic in nature, as against statistics that run counter to our personal knowledge. I think we should do so; to do so is essential to a democratic way of life. But it is necessary to admit that we do; only by admitting that we do can we proceed to go beyond impressions and attain the validity of which an ethnographic approach is capable.

Some will argue against the political consequences of bilingual education, claiming that it is divisive. There is a general answer to this, of course; the social meaning of languages is not inherent in them, but a consequence of the uses to which they are put. Where languages are symbols of division, it is because of social forces that divide and pit people against each other along lines that coincide with language boundaries. Difference of languages is hardly necessary; a single sound will suffice, as the Biblical example of the killing of those who said *shibboleth* instead of *sibboleth* indicates. The greatest internal conflict in the history of the United States, the Civil War, was not fought in terms of language boundaries. On the other hand, there are many areas in which multiplicity of language is in no way a part of social mobilization and conflict. In sum, small differences can become symbols of hostility and large differences can be accepted and ignored. The causes are outside of language.

To be sure, a given language policy may favor some interests as against others. Bilingualism may be experienced as a burden by people who have been able to assume that theirs was the only language that counted, that their convenience and the public interest were the same. But to argue that bilingualism is divisive is really to argue that it makes visible what one had preferred to ignore, an unequal distribution of rights and benefits. It is common to call "political" and "divisive" the raising of an issue that one had been able to ignore, and to ignore the political and oppressive implications of ignoring it. In this regard, the ethnographic monitoring of programs can also be of great importance. The ethnographic approach can go beyond tests and surveys to document and interpret the social meaning of success and failure to bilingual education.

It may be that some years from now those who work for bilingual education will not themselves be of one mind about its role. One view of the relation between such movements and general social processes is that they represent a phase of the interdependence between an expanding world economy and locally exploited groups. It may not be presently clear to what extent the movement for bilingual education is a recognition of sheer educational necessity, an expression of a phase in the relation between a minority group and forces dominant in the society, an expression of a growing commitment to the ideal of a multilingual/multicultural society. It may be that some sectors of the Spanish-speaking community will argue for intensive English training as a preferable route to economic opportunity while others argue for Spanish maintenance programs on the grounds of cultural identity. Class differences may appear in this regard.

My own belief is that a multilingual society is something to be desired and maintained, but it is for others to decide their own interests. Whatever the ultimate policies decided upon, the wisdom of those choices will be greatly enhanced if ethnographic monitoring has been an integral part of bilingual education.

REFERENCES

Barth, Frederick. "Ethnic Groups and Boundaries," *The Social Organization of Culture Difference,* ed. Frederick Barth. Boston: Little, Brown & Co., 1969.

Goffman, Erving. "The Nature of Deference and Demeanor," *American Anthropologist,* LVIII (June, 1956), 473-502.

Hymes, Dell. "Introduction," *Functions of Language in the Classroom,* eds. Courtney B. Cazden, Vera P. John, and Dell Hymes. New York: Teachers College Press, 1972, pp. xi-lvii.

——————————, ed. *Reinventing Anthropology.* New York: Vintage Press, 1974a.

——————————. "Ways of Speaking," *Explorations in the Ethnography of Speaking,* eds. Richard Bauman, and Joel Sherzer. New York: Cambridge University Press, 1974b, pp. 433-451.

Language Policy Task Force. "Language Policy and the Puerto Rican Community," *Bilingual Review* (February, 1978). (An earlier version was circulated as "Toward a Language Policy for Puerto Ricans in the United States," by E. Gonzalez Atiles, P. Pedraza, and A. C. Zentella.)

McDermott, Ray P. "Achieving School Failure: An Anthropological Approach to Literary and Social Stratification," *Education and Cultural Process: Toward an Anthropology of Education,* ed. George D. Spindler. New York: Holt, Rinehart and Winston, 1974, pp. 82-118.

Philips, Susan U. "Participant Structures and Communicative Competence: Warm Springs Children in Community and Classroom," *Functions of Language in the Classroom,* eds. Courtney B. Cazden, Vera P. John, and Dell Hymes. New York: Teachers College Press, 1972, pp. 370-394.

——————————. "The Invisible Culture." Unpublished PhD dissertation, The University of Pennsylvania, 1974.

Rist, Ray C. "Student Social Class and Teacher Expectations: The Self-Fulfilling Prophecy in Ghetto Education," *Harvard Educational Review,* XL (August, 1970), 411-451.

On Bilingualism and Biculturalism in Education

Muriel Saville-Troike

The affective component of bilingual education is discussed in this paper from the standpoint of the development of biculturalism. The various English programs of ENL (English as a Native Language), EAL (English as an Auxiliary Language), EFL (English as a Foreign Language), and ESL (English as a Second Language) are contrasted primarily on the basis of the different cultural emphases in each. The differences between *enculturation* and *acculturation,* and *assimilation* and *biculturalism* are explored. *"Dinomia"* is suggested as a term to describe the situation when "two or more cultural systems . . . are used by the same people under different conditions." The discussion concludes with a statement calling for desperately needed research in the areas of students' proficiency in both languages, cultural appropriateness of curriculum materials, and the attitudes of students and parents toward themselves and the group.

$\mathbf{D}$ISCUSSIONS OF bilingual education in the United States frequently emphasize the difference between two distinct dimensions, domains or components — the *cognitive* and the *affective*. While such a dichotomy may not be valid for all purposes, it is nevertheless a useful distinction to make when considering the rule of first- and second-language development in the education of students who are native speakers of Spanish.[1]

Most proponents of bilingual education argue that the use of the native language is essential in at least initial subject-matter instruction if there is to be uninterrupted cognitive development and that it contributes to such

---

[1] Although this paper focuses on students who are native speakers of Spanish, I do not wish to imply that the same principles would not apply to speakers of other languages, nor that I am accepting a one-way or compensatory view of bilingual/bicultural education.

affective factors as positive self and group identity. It is also generally
agreed that the acquisition of the national language (here, English) is
essentially and obviously related to content learning. The term *bicultural* is
often used in combination with the term *bilingual* to stress the view that
more than language learning is involved in bilingual programs. Such a
usage implies that formal recognition is given to aspects of the student's
traditional culture within the instructional program to ensure that the
student has the opportunity to learn about it and to enhance the student's
feeling of acceptance within the school context. However, the relation of
second-language learning to the development of biculturalism is a question
that so far has received little attention. It is to this issue that the following
discussion is primarily addressed.

To what extent is learning a second *culture* related to learning a second
language? Historically, the pragmatic answer to this question has been
somewhat imperialistic in nature and intent. English teachers around the
world have generally carried the cultural baggage of England and North
America with them: pronunciation drills set in restaurants in New York or
London; illustrations of Englishmen or Anglo-Americans shaking hands,
doffing hats, and wearing suits and dresses from Bond Street and Macy's;
and reading selections chosen from Hemingway and Thomas Hardy. It has
been considered axiomatic that because language is an integral component
of culture, only the culture of the speech community from which the
language is derived (in the case of English, both North America and
England) is appropriate content for its expression, and that teachers must
transmit that content to those who are learning the language.

Similarly, when the focus is explicitly on inculcating a second culture,
teaching the language of that culture has been considered a primary and
necessary means to that end. This practice has been shown clearly in
American history by the language and educational policies adopted toward
Native Americans. In the 1880's, for instance, the Commissioner of Indian
Affairs reported:

> The first step to be taken toward civilization, toward teaching the
> Indian and mischief and folly of continuing in their barbarous prac-
> tices, is to teach him the English language . . . we must remove the
> stumbling-blocks of hereditary customs and manners, and of those
> language is one of the most important. (Atkin, 1887)

More recently, learning English in Puerto Rico was explicitly equated
with accepting American cultural dominance.

> Since the United States is a major nation of the world, Porto Rico
> [*sic*] can well get the pace from a growing and ascending nation and

learn the expression of the ways of a great people. (Cremer, 1932, p. 338)

Even today, it is probably fair to say that most of the foreign-language teaching efforts of such official agencies as the International Communication Agency, the British Council, the Goethe Institute, and the Alliance Française are much more concerned with spreading the influence of their respective cultures than with teaching their languages in and of themselves.

This same belief in the intrinsic relation between a language and the culture of the speech community from which it historically derives forms the basis for one of the principal arguments raised against bilingual education in the United States: the language of the United States is English. To speak anything else is considered un-American, and to teach another language is viewed as culturally divisive and contrary to the goals of national unity.

The exclusive identification of English with British and American culture has been seriously challenged in recent decades by countries such as Nigeria and India, which have long used English for their own national purposes and have developed native literatures in English for the expression of their own cultures. In addition, a number of countries that have taught English primarily as a means of access to technical knowledge have insisted on limiting its initial use strictly to expressing only the immediate needs of students in the schools. Most consistent in this practice, perhaps, has been the People's Republic of China. Members of the delegation of linguists and English teachers from China that visited the United States in 1973 emphasized the importance of teaching English in their country and showed great interest in our developments in language teaching theory and methodology. But they were firm in regarding American instructional material as inappropriate because of the cultural content that accompanies it. English is wanted and needed in China as a tool for learning about external technological and scientific developments, but the teaching of English, like that of all subjects, is first required to contribute to the larger goals of the society.

As these examples illustrate, there is no intrinsic reason that the structures and vocabulary of one language cannot be used by many diverse speech communities to express their respective cultures. Thus, although language is unquestionably an integral part of culture, the supposedly necessary relation between learning a language and learning the traditional culture associated with that language is now being seriously questioned from a number of perspectives.

The differences in the relationship between English and the culture in which it is used constitute the essential basis for identifying four distinct settings for learning and teaching the language: (1) ENL (English as a Native Language), (2) EAL (English as an Auxiliary Language), (3) EFL (English as a Foreign Language), and (4) ESL (English as a Second Language). It is ESL that forms part of bilingual education in the United States.

In learning English as a *native* language, it is both part of the native culture that is being acquired in the process of children's enculturation and a primary medium for the transmission of other aspects of that culture from one generation to the next, such as values, beliefs, and rules for social behavior. If speakers remain in contact with their native culture, their native language proficiency expands to include expression of the new concepts they develop, the new domains in which they function, and the new role-relationships in which they participate. This intrinsic relationship of language to culture is so natural as to operate at an unconscious level for most native speakers, furthered by informal means more than by formal education, and by family and peers more than by professional educators.

Learning English as an *auxiliary* language usually occurs in a country where no single indigenous native language is accepted or developed sufficiently for it to serve all official purposes, or where the national language of a country does not have widespread distribution in the world and English is used as a *lingua franca* internally or for international contacts and access to advanced technical knowledge. In each case, English generally serves directly as a medium of communication only in some of the more public and formal domains of the culture, and it is seldom used for the enculturation of children, for communication with close friends and family (except where they may lack a common language), or for religious or artistic purposes. In the domains where EAL is used, it is at least partly expressive of the culture of the speech community that has adopted it and not of the British or American cultures from which it was originally borrowed. Native English speakers from America working in Nigeria, India, or the Philippines sometimes find their rules of usage inappropriate; if they wish to communicate effectively in the EAL of those speech communities, they must learn the new systems of culture and the rules for appropriate behavior that are expressed in its structures and that govern its use. Speakers of ENL and EAL may sometimes fail to communicate with one another, even when using the same language forms, because they do not understand the differential relationship of English to their respective cultures. (While EAL is usually learned in formal educational contexts, no language teaching materials yet developed have contrasted its cultural content and function to that of ENL.) The communicative conflicts that occur are seldom recognized as such because of the unconscious level at which the respective relationships operate, and each side may attribute them to the rudeness or difficult nature of the other. Although very unfortunate international consequences may result, neither individual nor group feelings of identity are likely to be threatened.

Learning English as a *foreign* language also occurs in countries where ENL is not widespread and in formal rather than informal educational contexts, but its relationship to culture is quite different. The primary focus of EFL is on learning its phonology, syntax, and vocabulary; its cultural content is either neutral and universal (if its function is primarily to be as a technical medium), or else consists of information about the native speakers. While it is expected that English phonological and grammatical rules will be internalized, there is no requirement that English beliefs, values, dress, and other non-linguistic rules of cultural behavior be similarly drilled and practiced (though a passive knowledge may be required). EFL is not tied to the expression of the native culture; both motivation and rewards for learning are, in general, mainly academic or economic in nature, as is the function of EFL for its speakers.

Learning English as a *second* language takes place in countries such as the United States where English is the language of the dominant culture and where proficiency in English is essential for a full educational, political, and economic participation in the larger society. ESL involves learning much more than English phonology, syntax, and vocabulary, for it must be able to serve most of the same functions as English does for the native speaker: medium of instruction, expression of concepts and feelings, and participation in expanding social domains and role-relationships. Unlike EAL and EFL, therefore, ESL also requires that its speakers be able to function according to the rules of the dominant culture. While the native of a culture acquires these rules quite naturally and unconsciously in the process of *enculturation*, the process for students acquiring a second culture is *acculturation*, the addition of a second set of rules for behavior that may co-exist beside the first, replace it, or modify it. One possible result of this acculturation process is loss of the native culture or the merger of cultures until they are indistinguishable, called *assimilation*. Perhaps one of the most important contributions of the movement for bilingual education in the United States has been the valuation of another possible result of acculturation: the selective maintenance and use of both cultural systems, or *biculturalism*.

The nature and extent of students' cultural competence is therefore just as important as their linguistic competence for determining appropriate level and content for instruction in bilingual/bicultural education.[2] It is

---

[2]For suggestions on how the cultural competence of students can be identified and described, see the article by Dell Hymes, "Ethnographic Monitoring" in this volume.

now beginning to be recognized that students who enroll in Spanish/English bilingual programs in the United States have varying degrees of oral proficiency in the two languages of instruction (Spanish monolingual, Spanish dominant, balanced bilingual, English dominant, and English monolingual) and that they may or may not already be literate in Spanish. There is no reason to assume, however, that the Spanish-dominant students have acquired the culture of such Spanish-speaking countries as Mexico or Spain in the process of acquiring Spanish as their native language. They indeed have acquired a culture, but it might well be the beliefs, values, and rules for appropriate behavior common to the dominant American society. In this case, becoming bicultural would involve learning about their *ancestral* cultural heritage, which is analogous to learning about the culture of the British or the Americans when studying EFL; it need never be internalized.

Most probably, except for students who have immigrated directly from Spanish-dominant countries, Spanish-speaking students in the United States will have been enculturated into the minority subculture of a bilingual community. It is important that bilingual educators recognize the validity of these students' culture; comments have been made that students who have not acquired the culture of the dominant American society or the culture of the dominant society of a Spanish-speaking country have no culture at all. Such comments are often made by the same people who feel that students who do not speak a standard variety of English or Spanish, or who code-switch between them, are "alingual." These views are based on ignorance and misunderstanding of the nature of language and culture, and are potentially as damaging to students' self-concept and identity as those that forbid the use of their native language at school.

While recognizing and accepting that the culture that students bring to school is important, the same reasons exist for learning the dominant American culture as for learning English: it is necessary for full participation in the larger American society. The comparison with adding a second language is a useful analogy to continue because adding a second culture has many of the same implications for both theory and methodology.

First, to understand and facilitate learning, educators should know what is being acquired and how it compares with their students' native cultural systems. Unfortunately, cultural rules often have been recognized only in their breach and when the consequences have been dramatic or traumatic enough to the second-culture learner to be of note — a kind of error analysis. More humane, if it can escape cultural stereotyping (i.e., present vs. future orientation and passive vs. active coping styles), would be a contrastive analysis to facilitate the identification of potential cultural conflicts for students and the development of instructional means and materials to teach these points. (This concept and a proposed model for implementing it were presented by Lado in 1957, and related interesting and practical ideas were developed by Seelye in 1974.)

Also to be explored are analogous questions on interference. What influence does the native culture have on the acquisition of a second? To what extent is its nature and degree influenced by the age of the students, by attitudes, and by learning contexts? Is there a continuum of compound to coordinate biculturalism? Under what circumstances does learning a second culture require modifications in the first, and under what circumstances can acculturation be a purely additive process?

Analogies can also be drawn with questions of culture domains and culture choice and can be applied to questions of the appropriate usage of behavioral rules and to switching between alternative cultural systems. The minority culture first learned by many Spanish-speakers in the United States is comparable to the "Low" (L) variety of a language as it is described by Ferguson (1964) in his concept of *diglossia,* and the dominant American culture is comparable to the "High" (H) variety of a national language. Just as with Ferguson's L and H language varieties, the L culture is generally learned by children at home, and the H culture is learned at school. The H culture has more prestige in the society than the L, and most importantly for educational applications, there is a specialization of function for H and L. I propose that this relationship and distribution be called *dinomia* as it relates to varieties of culture, which translates roughly from Greek as "two systems of laws."

The concept of diglossia introduced by Ferguson is restricted to the complementary use of two or more linguistic systems by the same speakers in a single speech community.[3] To continue the analogy, the concept of dinomia is restricted to *two or more cultural systems that are used by the same people under different conditions, one of which is the dominant cultural system of the larger society and the other subordinate and less prestigious cultural varieties from within that same society.*

This concept has importance for teacher training and curriculum development because it recognizes the nature and viability of students' native cultures while providing for identification of the aspects of the dominant culture that need to be acquired for appropriate situations and for prediction of potential areas of cultural interference, conflicts, or overlap. All

---

[3]The term *speech community* is sometimes used to designate units of different size and scope. It is used here in the sense of a larger social unit whose members have in common many attitudes, values, and rules for both linguistic and nonverbal behavior. Perhaps most importantly, its members share a sense of common identity (often equated with national boundaries, such as "American"), even though many subgroup identities may be recognized (e.g., Native American, Mexican-American, Afro-American, and Anglo-American).

instruction that relates to developing and reinforcing positive feelings of
individual and group identity should be based on such recognition and
understanding.

The concept of dinomia also may prove useful to those concerned with
improving equal educational opportunity for minority-group students by
serving as an analytic device for guiding research on one of the major
unresolved problems in their education: the lack of consonance between
the culture of lower socio-economic groups and that of the school or that
which is taught in the school, no matter what the language of instruction.
Whether students are from a lower class Spanish-speaking background,
from the inner city, or from the "hollers" of Appalachia, it is well known
that they are likely to have greater difficulty in school than if they are from a
middle class urban background. This complex factor, frequently labeled
"low SES background," currently lacks explanatory power and needs to be
explored more fully in order to identify the specific cultural variables that
lead to inequality in educational achievement.

Some of the larger questions of the nature of the relationship of language and culture learning to social and cultural setting that I have dealt
with here have important implications for examining the goals, objectives,
and methods of bilingual programs. Of critical importance in all planning
and evaluation, for example, are understanding of students' prior experiences; awareness of the attitudes of students, parents, staff, and the wider
community toward the languages and cultures of home and school; and
knowledge of the feasibility of theoretically possible alternatives for instruction. As a specific example, a valid selection for evaluation of cultural
appropriateness in classroom materials and activities is entirely dependent
on knowledge of not only the students' language skills, important as that is,
but also of the relationship of their linguistic experiences to conceptual
development and to individual and group values, feelings, identity, and
aspirations. To assume specific cultural experiences and rules of behavior
as invariable coordinates of specific linguistic skills is an oversimplification
of the relationship of language and culture that ignores a primary tenet of
bilingual education: to accept students (linguistically and culturally as well
as cognitively) as they are and to build in a positive way on their prior
experiences. This phrase is repeated so often and so automatically in
education as to be in danger of becoming a mindless platitude, but if we
give adequate thought to its complex meaning and implications, we will
realize how much needs to be learned about students and the importance of
doing so if bilingual/bicultural education is to fulfill its promise.

In this area of bilingualism and biculturalism, much more should also be
said about such topics as cultural prerequisites to language learning and
curriculum planning based on contrastive ethnographic and

communicative miscue analysis, and the importance of culture-specific presuppositions and pragmatics. These topics, however, must await further development of our own experience and expertise. For the present, there is a great need to explore all these topics in depth and to carry out extensive research as the basis for improving curriculum planning and developing more effective teaching strategies in bilingual/bicultural education.

REFERENCES

Atkins, J. D. C. Annual Report of the Commissioner of Indian Affairs, September 21, 1887. *House Executive Document* No. 1, 50th Congress, 1st Session, Serial 2542, pp. 19-21.

Cremer, Henry. "Spanish and English in Porto [sic] Rico," *School and Society*, XXXVI (September 10, 1932), 338.

Ferguson, Charles A. "Diglossia," *Language in Culture and Society: A Reader in Linguistics and Anthropology*, ed. Dell Hymes. New York: Harper and Row, 1964, pp. 429-439.

Lado, Robert. *Linguistics Across Cultures: Applied Linguistics for Language Teachers.* Ann Arbor: University of Michigan Press, 1957.

Seelye, H. Ned. *Teaching Culture: Strategies for Foreign Language Educators.* Skokie: National Textbook Co., 1974.

PART FOUR

Language and
Content in
Bilingual Education

Language Acquisition and Language Learning in the Late-Entry Bilingual Education Program

Stephen D. Krashen

This paper discusses the critical learning age and compares language acquisition before and after adolescence. Before age 10, all children acquire at least one language without overt language teaching from adults. Around age 12, cognitive development (Piaget's formal operations) involves a meta-awareness of thoughts and behavior and contributes to psychological feelings of vulnerability, self-consciousness, and reluctance in revealing self, which may disturb the language acquisition potential. The hypothesis presented is that adults utilize both a consciously learned system and a subconsciously acquired system in the production of second language syntax. The conscious grammar is utilized as a monitor that inspects and alters the utterance before it is actually spoken. Some theoretical and practical implications of this theory for the late-entry bilingual subject-matter classroom are discussed, and specific recommendations for classroom activities that promote language acquisition and learning are made.

THIS PAPER examines contributions that the school can make to encourage bilingualism in the adolescent years (grades 7 to 12). Although this age group is extremely interesting, it has been neglected in language acquisition and language-learning studies, which have dealt primarily with much younger or older subjects. The adolescent years are a turning point linguistically as well as socially and cognitively, and these changes are very uncomfortable for many young people. This paper considers some of these changes and their causes and relationships to one another, concentrating on the obstacles these changes place in the way of the adolescent's progress toward bilingualism.

Language Acquisition Before Adolescence

The time around puberty is thought to be the close of a critical period for language acquisition. Either first- or second-language acquisition seems to proceed much more easily in children. A fair amount about this process has been learned, and it will be useful to review some of the major findings of child language research here.

First, language acquisition in children appears to be a powerful drive. In the absence of brain damage or strong external social factors that prevent the child from interacting with native speakers of a language, acquisition is inevitable. Some children may proceed at a slightly faster rate, but practically all children eventually master at least one variety of their mother tongue. Also, for children below age 10 or so, complete mastery of a second language is very common when sufficient involvement with native speakers is possible.

A second important finding is that language acquisition in children does not require overt language teaching from adults. For first-language acquisition, studies have shown that parents do not pay attention to grammatical correctness but focus instead on whether the message is true or false (Brown *et al.*, 1973), nor do children's grammatically correct utterances do a significantly better job of getting a message across (Brown and Hanlon, 1970). For children acquiring a second language, current research indicates that when the child is in an environment rich in the target language, extra language classes do not significantly increase proficiency (Fathman, 1975; Hale and Budar, 1970).

Some things adults do may be of help, however. Several studies have shown that adults often simplify their speech to children acquiring both first and second languages (Snow, 1972; Cazden, 1972; Wagner-Gough and Hatch, 1975). This simplification may speed up the acquisition process because it allows the child to concentrate on just that portion of the language that is relevant to linguistic development, which appears to be sufficient for language acquisition. This relevant input, or "intake" (Corder, 1967), may be a very small part of the total amount of language the child hears (Friedlander *et al.*, 1972).

Successful acquisition can also occur without any overt speech on the part of the child. Lenneberg (1962) describes a case of congenital anarthria in an eight year old boy who never spoke but who could understand spoken English quite well.

Language acquisition is also characterized by certain universal principles that researchers believe apply to children acquiring any first language: that is, there are universal strategies in the human brain that all acquirers utilize (Slobin, 1973; Ervin-Tripp, 1973). Their application results in the remarkable uniformity seen in the stages of first- and second-language acquisition for a given language. Recent research has revealed striking similarities between children acquiring English as a first language and those acquiring English as a second language (Klima and Bellugi, 1966; Milton, 1974; Gillis, 1975; Brown, 1973; Dulay and Burt, 1972, 1974; Cancino *et al.*, 1975). Hatch and Wagner-Gough (1975) also conclude that similar strategies are employed by both first- and second-language acquirers.

Of particular interest is how well children within the critical age period acquire a second language in the bilingual education situation. Results of second-language testing in programs in which "majority language" children are immersed in a second language are similar: via subject matter alone and, in most cases, using just the teacher as a source of primary linguistic data, children make excellent progress in second-language acquisition in bilingual programs, acquiring enough of the target language to follow the academic curriculum via the second language. After several years, the children's proficiency approaches that of native speakers of the target language (Lambert and Tucker, 1972; Swain, 1974; Cohen, 1975; Bruck *et al.*, 1974). Such reports are very encouraging because they indicate that there is no real linguistic barrier to bilingualism in this age group. This performance, however, does not equal what some children accomplish in a non-academic situation, e.g., the playground. Although some individual variation exists (Hatch and Wagner-Gough, 1975), many immigrant children appear to be indistinguishable from the local children in terms of target language competence in less than a year. Amount of exposure does not seem to be the main factor here, as students in bilingual programs do not achieve the native level even after many years (Bruck *et al.*, 1974). What is apparently crucial in achieving perfection is contact with peers who speak the target language, which is largely absent in bilingual programs involving the non-dominant, second, or foreign language (Selinker *et al.*, 1975).

The Close of the Critical Period

The close of the critical period occurs between age 10 and 15. The most obvious manifestation of this event is the foreign accent, rare in immigrants who arrive in their new country before age 10 and nearly always present in those arriving after age 15 (Seliger *et al.*, 1975). There has been much speculation as to what occurs at this age to cause such a change, and opinions have differed as to how the acquisition process is affected. Some researchers maintain that children and adults have the same language acquisition capacities (Macnamara, 1975), although much second-language teaching methodology implicitly claims that children and adults differ in language acquisition.

Lenneberg (1967) presented the first clear hypothesis for the critical age period and suggested that neurological factors, namely the close of the development of cerebral dominance, were responsible for the child-adult differences. Many subsequent studies place this event much earlier and disassociate it from the close of the critical age period for language acquisition (Krashen, 1973, 1975c).

A more recent suggestion is that cognitive development, namely, Piaget's formal operations, may be responsible (Inhelder and Piaget, 1958). This hypothesis was independently formulated by Rosansky (1975) and Krashen (1975b). Also, Schumann (1975) and others suggest that psychological and social factors play an important role in child-adult differences. The author's current view is that these latter two positions are both correct and are intimately related.

During formal operations, which commences around age 12, children (or now adolescents) become capable of abstract thought and can have an extensive meta-awareness of thoughts and behavior. Concrete operational children can also deal with abstractions, but only those based in the concrete; that is, they can deduce an abstract principle from concrete data. Formal thinkers, on the other hand, can relate two abstract concepts and arrive at a higher level of abstraction. In Elkind's terms formal thinkers can "take his mental constructions as objects and reason about them" (1970, p. 66). A direct consequence of this ability to think abstractly is the conscious grammar that adult second-language users possess and use in performance (Krashen, 1975a). While concrete operational children may have some meta-awareness of their linguistic behavior, it is probably nowhere near as extensive as the older learner's and is not put to extensive use in linguistic performance.

Formal operations also seem to contribute to the profound psychological changes children experience as they pass into adolesence. Elkind (1970) suggests that often-observed feelings of vulnerability, self-consciousness, and the general reluctance adolescents show in revealing themselves relate to this new ability to reason about mental constructions. According to Elkind, new formal thinkers are fully aware for the first time of the mental lives of other people and of the possibility that other people are thinking about them. Their self-consciousness is further increased because of the physical/biological changes they are experiencing, and they eventually conclude that others are concentrating on them and what they consider to be their inadequacies.

Such feelings may disturb the language acquisition potential. Just how this happens cannot be precisely specified, but a plausible theory is that self-conscious adolescents tend to avoid placing themselves in language acquisition situations for fear of making an error. This fear could result in an inability to acquire through a failure to interact with primary linguistic data and/or the use of first-language structures and phonological rules that the language user feels to be correct in all linguistic circumstances.

Another indirect effect of formal operations that may inhibit language acquisition is the adolescent's new feelings of nationalism and group pride. Inhelder and Piaget (1958) note that formal thought is necessary to grasp the concept of a nation as a collective reality, and various studies confirm that ethnic stereotypes and social class attitudes become stable during adolescence (Wilson, 1963). Consistent attitudes toward linguistic groups also develop at this time (Labov, 1970; Lambert *et al.*, 1966).

Unfavorable attitudes toward the group speaking the target language is one of several factors that Schumann (1975) cites as causing social distance to occur between the adult learner and the speakers of the target language. As in the case of adolescent self-consciousness, this attitude can inhibit acquisition without directly affecting the operation of the language acquisition device. One can still maintain, as Macnamara (1975) does, that the adult has complete access to the universal strategies children use in language acquisition. Psychological change in the acquirer, catalyzed or initiated by formal operations, prevents the acquirer from using these capacities completely by keeping the acquirer at a distance from primary linguistic data.

Formal operations thus has a profound effect on language acquisition. It provides the adult with a conscious linguistic system and causes barriers to exist between the adult and speakers of the target language. The failure of older adults to acquire second languages naturally and completely indicates that these effects are lasting.

Adult Second Language Performance

The hypothesis has been discussed elsewhere that the adult uses both a consciously learned system and a subconsciously acquired system in second-language syntactic production (Krashen, 1976). Utterances in a second language are initiated by the acquired system, that is, by linguistic competence gained in ways similar to those used by children in language acquisition. The conscious grammar is utilized as a monitor, inspecting and altering the utterance just before it is actually spoken. The monitor, or consciously learned competence, is internalized somewhat differently from acquired language. While feedback does not seem to be of value for acquisition, it may be very helpful in learning because error correction provides a means for learners to adjust their hypotheses about the target language. Thus, although speaking, or actual language production, is not crucial for the acquisition of linguistic competence, it is quite useful for learning because it exposes the learner's errors for correction. Error correction or detection, in addition, appears to be built in to nearly all standard methods of adult second-language teaching (Krashen and Seliger, 1975).

Error correction is thus directed solely at the monitor and appears to be most useful in those aspects of grammar that the monitor can best handle. Although learners may have conceptions of a wide variety of linguistic phenomena, certain aspects of grammar are more easily handled by the monitor than others, and it is here that error correction is most useful. Specifically, the monitor is most adept at altering and adding morphology. Dušková (1969) notes that morphological errors are, in general, self-correctable and not influenced by the learner's first language, indicating that morphology is influenced by the monitor in performance. The monitor has trouble, however, in dealing with word order and with movement transformations, which suggests that this domain is difficult to teach and learn but is acquired when mastered (see Krashen, forthcoming, for more detailed argumentation).

Advanced second-language performers utilize their acquired knowledge of the second language to initiate utterances — this fact is evidenced by comparing errors made by groups of adult English-as-a-Second-Language (ESL) students when conditions allow monitoring (e.g., written grammar tests) with errors made when conditions do not allow monitoring (e.g., oral tests in which no self-corrections are allowed). Under monitor-free conditions, adult morphology errors are surprisingly similar in terms of order of difficulty to errors made by younger acquirers (Bailey et al., 1974). When more response time is allowed, this similarity decreases and subjects agree with each other much less, a manifestation of the idiosyncratic monitor in operation (Larsen Freeman, 1975).

Less advanced second-language performers, and those who have little chance for interacting with primary linguistic data of the target language (those in foreign-language as opposed to second-language learning situations), may use certain features of the first language in producing early utterances before much acquisition has taken place. Specifically, in such performers the effect of the first language is felt most strongly in word order and in the direct translation of word-for-word phrases (LoCoco, 1975; Dušková, 1969). The second-language order and movement rules gradually replace these first language rules in the successful acquirer. As mentioned above, morphology is largely immune from first-language influence — in the early stages it is inserted by the monitor, and in later stages it is eventually acquired by the advanced student.

There appears to be individual variation among adults as to dependence on monitoring. Some adults seem to monitor whenever they can and may also overdo it (i.e., they correct utterances that are already well-formed, not trusting their feel for the target language). At the other extreme, some adults do not appear to utilize a monitor at all and seem to be immune to error correction (Krashen, 1975a).

The most successful adult acquirers appear to be integratively motivated, that is, they identify with native speakers of the target language (Gardner and Lambert, 1972). The indirect effects of formal operations, however, act to inhibit this sort of motivation. The best learners or monitor users are probably the best formal thinkers, which gives an intuitively satisfying picture of the most proficient adult second-language performers. They are people who are sympathetic with native speakers of the second language and who have the kind of intelligence that lends itself to learning grammar.

Bilingual Education, Acquisition, and Learning

The above sections indicate that second-language acquisition in late-entry bilingual education is a different and more complicated problem than in early-entry programs. Many children begin formal operations and enter biological puberty in the eighth and ninth grades and experience the often anguishing side effects of these events for the next few years. Because these cognitive and affective changes affect the school situation in many ways, specific recommendations for classroom activities that most effectively and painlessly promote bilingualism in the school situation are needed.

Perhaps the most basic issue is the extent to which the subject-matter classroom and/or the standard foreign- or second-language classroom should be utilized in acquiring and learning the second language (or in some cases the second dialect). In younger children, as discussed above, learning subject matter via the second language appears to be sufficient for promoting skills in the second language. Because of their new cognitive and affective state, however, many adolescents may need or desire supplementation — conscious rules to be used as a monitor — and a suitable environment for the most effective presentation of input for acquisition.

Promoting Language Acquisition

According to the model given above, full and complete acquisition is possible in the child, while acquisition in the adult tends to be incomplete. The adult potential for full acquisition is blocked by affective factors, catalyzed by formal operations, that prevent full utilization of primary linguistic data. The adolescent is between these two stages and may have a large acquisition potential, dependent on psychological factors. The integratively motivated adolescent may in fact be able to acquire quite well. In a study by Seliger *et al.* (1975) of the self-report of second-language proficiency among immigrants, it was found that those who arrived in their new country before age 10 inevitably reported native-like proficiency in the second language, and those who arrived after age 15 nearly always did not. The 10 to 15 year group, however, was evenly divided — about one-half reported that they felt native speakers of the second language thought they were also native speakers while half did not or were not sure. In addition, the successful acquirers reported significantly more close friends who spoke the second language and, in the case of immigrants to the United States, said they felt "more American." Although successful acquisition may have caused more integrative feelings, it is possible that integrative motivation was the causative factor. Consistent with this possibility is evidence that degree of integrative motivation correlates directly with performance on tests that tap only acquired rather than learned competence (Krashen, 1975a).

It can be concluded, then, that the student relating to or identifying with speakers of the target language or dialect will acquire more and that many adolescents have a good acquisition potential.

There are, in addition, important linguistic factors that bear on the question of how acquisition can be promoted in the bilingual situation. As mentioned above, simplified input probably facilitates language acquisition, which may be difficult to achieve in the late-entry bilingual subject-matter classroom for several reasons. First, Wagner-Gough and Hatch (1975) point out that adults have a tendency to use syntactically and semantically complicated language in interacting with older acquirers. Some examples (Hatch and Wagner-Gough, 1975) illustrate this point:

Paul, a five year old acquirer of English as a second language in the United States studied by Hatch's student Huang, engaged in conversations similar to this one:

Observer	Paul
Paul, are you writing?	Yeah.
What are you doing?	I'm write.
Paul, are you writing?	Yeah.
What are you doing?	I'm writing.
What's the baby doing?	Baby cry.
Is the baby crying?	Yeah.
What's the baby doing?	Baby is crying.

On the other hand, Butterworth's subject, Ricardo, a 13 year old ESL student, did not have the benefit of such rule isolation but had to hear language that was syntactically and semantically very complex:

Observer	**Ricardo**
In Colombia, do they (lobsters) have claws?	Claws?
Claws. Do they have . . . the lobster, do they have claws?	Octopus?
No. The lobsters. Do the lobsters have hands?	Huh?

Questions asked of Ricardo during his first month in the United States included:

> Would you sit down here?
> Did you ever have any trouble with your ears?
> What do we mean by question mark?

Wagner-Gough and Hatch (1975) conclude that while young ESL acquirers hear "a limited body of graded language data" (dialogues focused on the here and now with heavy use of commands, noun phrase location, and noun phrase identification structures at early stages), the older learner/acquirer is asked to supply answers to obscure questions, deal with why-questions, and talk about activities displaced in time.

This tendency is compounded in the late-entry classroom by the presentation of relatively complex subject matter. In addition, simplified reading material for the subject-matter classroom may not be available. Finally, a wide range of target language or dialect abilities can be expected: some students may have used the language at home since infancy and may, at worst, face only a second dialect problem; others, even those who identify themselves as members of a linguistic group, may have little proficiency in the language. Simplified input, therefore, may not be appropriate for all students.

As discussed previously, complex input does not make language acquisition impossible. It does, however, add something to the acquirer's task — the primary linguistic data that can be utilized must be separated from that which cannot. With simplified input, a larger percentage of the heard language will be understandable and useful for acquisition.

What is the responsibility of the subject-matter teacher in encouraging acquisition? If acquisition in the adolescent is similar to acquisition in the child, the teacher's main responsibility is simply to provide meaningful primary linguistic data. (For suggestions, see Cazden, 1978). Error correction will be of value only for monitor users, which may not include all late-entry students.

One primary function of the language classroom in bilingual education could be to provide a supplementary source of appropriate primary linguistic data when one of the above-mentioned problems arises in the subject-matter classroom. Experienced teachers have implicitly recognized that the language classroom can be a source of language acquisition as well as language learning (Krashen, 1976). This implicit realization is the basis for contextualized practices and methods that stress active involvement of the student in real language-use situations.

The explicit goal of the language classroom is, of course, to increase language learning, or in terms of the model, to develop the monitor. The optimal use of the language classroom in the late-entry bilingual education program occurs when activities are structured so that pre-formal acquirers can profit (acquire) and cognitively more advanced students can both acquire and learn simultaneously. This goal can be accomplished with some changes in emphasis in normal language-teaching practice. Specific suggestions are made below along with a review of the essential characteristics of formal second-language instruction.

Promoting Language Acquisition and Language Learning

Perhaps the most fundamental dichotomy in approaches to formal language teaching and learning is deductive versus inductive rule presentation. Traditional definitions of these terms involve the sequencing of rules and practice. In deductive language teaching grammatical principles are presented first, with exercises or practice following. Here, the role of practice is thought to be a means of internalizing the presented rule. In inductive language teaching the exercises are presented first, during which the student is expected to determine the generalization. The rule may be presented explicitly at the end of the exercise to check whether the student's mental representation corresponds to the teacher's conception of the rule. Certain methods utilize primarily deductive presentation (grammar-translation, cognitive-code) while others can be analyzed as inductive (audio-lingual, Silent Way). Some current research suggests that individual differences exist among learners, some attaining more success with deductive presentation and some with inductive presentation (Krashen et al., 1974; Hartnett, 1975). Deductive learners, in fact, may be those with left cerebral hemisphere preference and may have a more digital, sequential, analytic cognitive style, while inductive learners may excel in right hemisphere, part-to-whole, relational abilities (Hartnett, 1975; Krashen et al., 1974). Researchers in the area of cerebral dominance have suggested that cultural as well as individual differences may exist in "hemisphericity," or hemisphere preference. TenHouten and Kaplan (1973) suggest that in Western cultures where the left hemisphere mode of thought predominates, subdominant or oppressed groups develop a preference for right hemisphere thought. It has been suggested that the optimal rule-presentation choice for any classroom in which explicit rule presentation is possible is deductive, or rule first (Krashen et al., 1974).

This choice will satisfy both deductive and inductive learners if the exercise is such that inductive rule learning is possible from it.

Krashen and Seliger (1975) suggest that another universal of formal language instruction for adults is rule isolation, or the presentation of just one new grammatical principle at a time in exercises. As noted above, this feature may also be present in optimal linguistic environments for acquisition. Thus, the presentation of linguistic material designed for inductive learning may also serve as optimal intake for acquistion. This method is very efficient for the late-entry bilingual-education language classroom because an effective contextualized presentation of novel linguistic material can serve the cognitively advanced students as both an acquisition source and as an inductive rule-learning exercise. A brief, explicit summary of the new rule before the activity would benefit deductive learners and could be ignored by inductive learners and concrete (non-formal) students who presumably only acquire. There is no reason why this explanation could not be in the student's first language. The pure acquirer could benefit from such a classroom because it would provide the supplementary source of simple primary linguistic data needed for additional acquisition.

Error correction, of use to learning but not to acquisition, may be employed in the classroom but in such a way that pure acquirers can ignore it (as children apparently ignore the error correction inherent in expansions — Cazden, 1965) and that the self-conscious adolescent will not be embarrassed by it. Gentle correction for monitor users within the domain of the monitor (morphology) may, in fact, be quite useful.

Conceptions of language testing and student achievement might need some modification in dealing with this special situation. If the premise is accepted that the student has little conscious control over language acquisition and if at least some students in a supplementary language class are not learners, testing cannot be utilized in the regular manner. For these students, research shows that providing a suitable linguistic environment for acquistion has been successful. Similarly, tests on those aspects of linguistic structure that are normally acquired for monitor users (certain word order and movement rules) reflect on the quality and quantity of input and the acquirer's orientation, rather than on the student's diligence and intelligence. In view of the formal thinker's unusual affective state at this age, the testing of conscious language learning might be deemphasized as well.

Specific implementation of these proposals is certainly possible within existing methodologies, but it appears that no one language teaching system currently in use is sufficiently inclusive. Elements of Asher's Total Physical Response system and Gattegno's Silent Way may be useful (Asher, 1969; Stevick, 1974).

REFERENCES

Asher, James T. "The Total Physical Response Approach to Second Language Learning," *Modern Language Journal,* LIII (January, 1969), 3-17.

Bailey, Nathalie, Carolyn Madden, and Stephen D. Krashen. "Is There a 'Natural Sequence' in Adult Second Language Learning?" *Language Learning,* XXIV (December, 1974), 235-243.

Brown, Roger William. *A First Language; the Early Stages.* Cambridge: Harvard University Press, 1973.

Brown, R., Courtney B. Cazden, and U. Bellugi. "The Child's Grammar From I to III," *Studies of Child Language Development,* eds. Charles A. Ferguson, and Dan I. Slobin. New York: Holt, Rinehart, & Winston, 1973, pp. 295-333.

Brown, R., and C. Hanlon. "Derivational Complexity and Order of Acquisition in Child Speech," *Cognition and the Development of Language,* ed. John R. Hayes. New York: Wiley, 1970, pp. 11-53.

Bruck, Margaret, Wallace E. Lambert, and G. Richard Tucker. "Bilingual Schooling Through the Elementary Grades: The St. Lambert Project at Grade Seven," *Language Learning,* XXIV (December, 1974), 183-204.

Cancino, Herlinda, Ellen J. Rosansky, and John H. Schumann. "The Acquisition of the English Auxiliary by Native Spanish Speakers," *TESOL Quarterly,* IX (December, 1975), 421-430.

Cazden, Courtney B. *Child Language and Education.* New York: Holt, Rinehart, and Winston, 1972.

_____. "Curriculum/Language Contexts for Bilingual Education," *Language Development in a Bilingual Setting.* Los Angeles: National Dissemination and Assessment Center, 1978, pp. 129-138.

_____. "Environmental Assistance to the Child's Acquisition of Grammar." Unpublished PhD dissertation, Harvard University, 1965.

Cohen, A. "Progress Report on the Culver City Spanish Immersion Program: The Third and Fourth Years," UCLA Working Papers in *TESL,* IX (1975), 47-52.

Corder, S. P. "The Significance of Learner's Errors," *International Review of Applied Linguistics (IRAL),* V (November, 1967), 161-170.

Dulay, Heidi, and Marina K. Burt. "Goofing: An Indicator of Children's Second Language Learning Strategies," *Language Learning,* XXII (December, 1972), 235-252.

_____, and _____. "Natural Sequences in Child Second Language Acquisition," *Language Learning,* XXIV (June, 1974), 37-53.

Dušková, Libuše. "On Sources of Errors in Foreign Language Learning," *International Review of Applied Linguistics (IRAL),* VII (February, 1969), 11-36.

Elkind, David. *Children and Adolescents: Interpretive Essays on Jean Piaget.* New York: Oxford Press, 1970.

Ervin-Tripp, Susan Moore. "Some Strategies for the First Two Years," *Language Acquisition and Communicative Choice,* ed. Anwar S. Dil. Stanford: Stanford University Press, 1973, pp. 204-238.

Fathman, Ann. "The Relationship Between Age and Second Language Productive Ability," *Language Learning,* XXV (December, 1975), 245-253.

Friedlander, Bernard Z., Antoinette C. Jacobs, Barbara B. Davis, and Harriet Wetstone. "Time-Sampling Analysis of Infants' Natural Language Environments in the Home," *Child Development,* XLIII (September, 1972), 730-740.

Gardner, Robert C., and Wallace E. Lambert. *Attitudes and Motivation in Second-Language Learning,* Rowley: Newbury House, 1972.

Gillis, M. "The Acquisition of the English Verbal System by Two Japanese Children." Unpublished MA thesis, McGill University, 1975.

Hale, Thomas M., and Eva C. Budar, "Are TESOL Classes the Only Answer?" *Modern Language Journal,* LIV (November, 1970), 487-492.

Hartnett, D. "The Relation of Cognitive Style and Hemispheric Preference to Deductive and Inductive Second Language Learning." Unpublished MA thesis, TESL Department, UCLA, 1975.

Hatch, Evelyn, and Judy Wagner-Gough. "Second Language Acquisition," *An Introduction to the Teaching of English as a Second Language,* eds. M. Celce-Murcia, and L. McIntosh. Los Angeles: UCLA, TESL Department (Pre-publication version), 1975, pp. 70-99.

Klima, E., and U. Bellugi. "Syntactic Regularities in the Speech of Children," *Psycholinguistic Papers: The Proceedings of the 1966 Edinburgh Conference,* eds. John Lyons, and R. J. Wales. Edinburgh: Edinburgh University Press, 1966, pp. 183-208.

Krashen, Stephen D. "A Model of Adult Second Language Performance." Paper presented at the Winter meeting of the Linguistic Society of America, San Francisco, 1975a.

_____. "The Critical Period Hypothesis and its Possible Bases," *Developmental Psycholinguistics and Communication Disorders*, eds. R. Rieber, and D. Aaronson. New York: New York Academy of Sciences, 1975b, pp. 211-224.

_____. "The Development of Cerebral Dominance and Language Learning: More New Evidence," *Developmental Psycholinguistics: Theory and Applications*, ed. D. Dato. Washington: Georgetown University Roundtable on Languages and Linguistics, 1975c, pp. 179-192.

_____. "Formal and Informal Linguistic Environments in Language Acquisition and Language Learning," *TESOL Quarterly*, X (1976), 157-168.

_____. "Lateralization, Language, and the Critical Period: Some New Evidence," *Language Learning*, XXIII (June, 1973), 63-74.

_____. "Sources of Error and the Development of Proficiency in Adult Second Language Performance," forthcoming.

_____, and Herbert W. Seliger. "The Essential Contributions of Formal Instruction in Adult Second Language Learning," *TESOL Quarterly*, IX (June, 1975), 173-183.

_____, H. Seliger, and D. Hartnett. "Two Studies in Adult Second Language Learning," *Kritikon Litterarum*, II, No. 2 (1974), 220-228.

Labov, William. *The Study of Nonstandard English*. Urbana: National Council of Teachers of English, 1970.

Lambert, Wallace E., and G. Richard Tucker. *The Bilingual Education of Children: The St. Lambert Experience*. Rowley: Newbury House, 1972.

_____, Hannah Frankel, and G. Richard Tucker. "Judging Personality Through Speech: A French-Canadian Example," *The Journal of Communication*, XVI (December, 1966), 305-321.

Larsen Freeman, Diane E. "The Acquisition of Grammatical Morphemes by Adult ESL Students," *TESOL Quarterly*, IX (December, 1975), 409-419.

Lenneberg, Eric H. *Biological Foundations of Language*. New York: Wiley, 1967.

_____. "Understanding Language Without Ability to Speak: A Case Report," *Journal of Abnormal Social Psychology*, LXV (1962), 419-425.

LoCoco, V. "An Analysis of Spanish and German Learner's Errors," *Working Papers on Bilingualism*, VII (1975), 96-124.

Macnamara, J. "Comparison Between First and Second Language Learning," *Working Papers on Bilingualism*, VII (1975), 71-95. (Also to appear in *Die Neuren Sprachen*.)

Milton, John P. "The Development of Negation in English by a Second Language Learner," *TESOL Quarterly*, VIII (June, 1974), 137-143.

Parsons, Anne, and Stanley Milgram, trans. *The Growth of Logical Thinking from Childhood to Adolescence*, by Bärbel Inhelder, and Jean Piaget. New York: Basic Books, 1958.

Rosansky, E. "The Critical Period for the Acquisition of Language: Some Cognitive and Developmental Considerations," *Working Papers on Bilingualism*, VI (1975), 93-100.

Schumann, J. "Second Language Acquisition: The Pidginization Hypothesis." Unpublished PhD dissertation, Harvard University, 1975.

Seliger, H., Stephen D. Krashen, and P. Ladefoged. "Maturational Constraints in the Acquisition of Second Language Accent," *Language Sciences*, XXXVI (1975), 20-22.

Selinker, Larry, Merrill Swain, and Guy Dumas. "The Interlanguage Hypothesis Extended to Children," *Language Learning*, XXV (June, 1975), 139-152.

Slobin, Dan I. "Cognitive Prerequisites for the Development of Grammar," *Studies of Child Language Development*, eds. Charles A. Ferguson, and Dan I. Slobin. New York: Holt, Rinehart and Winston, 1973, pp. 175-208.

Snow, Catherine E. "Mother's Speech to Children Learning Language," *Child Development*, XLIII (June, 1972), 549-565.

Stevick, Earl W. "Review of Caleb Gattegno: The Silent Way," *TESOL Quarterly*, VIII (September, 1974), 305-314.

Swain, M. "French Immersion Programs Across Canada: Research Findings," *Canadian Modern Language Review*, XXXI (1974), 117-129.

TenHouten, Warren D., and Charles D. Kaplan. *Science and its Mirror Image: A Theory of Inquiry*. New York: Harper and Row, 1973.

Wagner-Gough, Judy, and Evelyn Hatch. "The Importance of Input Data in Second Language Acquisition Studies," *Language Learning*, XXV (December, 1975), 297-308.

Wilson, W. Cody. "The Development of Ethnic Attitudes in Adolescence." *Studies in Adolescence*, ed. Robert E. Grinder. New York: Macmillan, 1963, pp. 262-274.

This paper describes a partial French immersion program in Canada beginning in grade 8. All such programs share two factors: (1) all participants are highly motivated students who speak the majority language and belong to the dominant culture, and (2) participation is voluntary. Three basic questions are explored in this paper: do students learn subject matter well in the second language, do students learn French better than those not in similar programs, and what special problems arise for teachers in the area of error correction? Subject matter is learned in the second language, although certain subject areas are learned better in French than others. In general, students in this program learn French better than students studying French only as a second language. Forms of teachers' corrections are explored from the standpoint of implicit versus explicit corrections, and one finding is that the correction of content errors takes precedence over the correction of linguistic errors. Areas of future research are suggested.

Second Language and Content Learning: A Canadian Bilingual Education Program at the Secondary Grade Levels

Merrill Swain

RECENTLY IN Canada there has been a considerable growth of innovative instructional programs for English-speaking students designed to develop a high level of proficiency in French. Developing proficiency in the second language, however, is not to be achieved at the expense of native language development, subject-matter learning, cognitive development, or social-emotional development (Swain, 1974; Stern *et al.*, 1976).

One type of program that appears to be compatible with these goals is that of total or partial French immersion whereby French is used as the medium of instruction for all or part of the curriculum during one or more years of schooling. Many French immersion programs presently in operation in Canada start in Kindergarten or Grade 1 (Barik and Swain, 1975, 1976; Bruck *et al.*, 1974; Edwards and Smythe, 1975; Lambert and Tucker, 1972). A few programs, however, begin at higher grade levels (Edwards and Smythe, 1976; Genesee *et al.*, 1977). The program discussed in this paper is a partial immersion program that begins in Grade 8 and that has been in operation since September, 1971. It was initiated by the Peel County Board of Education (Ontario).

Although no two French immersion programs are identical, it is important to remember that all share two characteristics. First, the programs involve students who already speak the majority language and belong to the dominant culture; hence, their identity is not endangered by second-language immersion program participation. Second, participation in an immersion program is voluntary. These characteristics, along with others outlined by Cohen and Swain (1976), are important to consider when discussing the applicability of the immersion model to minority-group students.

Let us now turn to a brief description of the Peel County partial immersion program. In Grade 8, approximately 70% of the curriculum is taught in French and 30% in English. The subjects taught in French are French, mathematics, history, geography, science, and art. Music, English, physical education, and home economics/industrial arts are taught in English. In Grades 9 and 10, approximately 40% of the curriculum is taught in French and 60% in English. French is used as the medium of instruction for the teaching of history, geography, and French; and English is employed for the teaching of mathematics, science, English, and other course options. Prior to entering the immersion program, the students have had only one year of French as a Second Language (FSL) instruction — 20-minute periods daily, intensified to 60-minute periods during the last two months of their Grade 7 year.

To date, most teachers associated with the French component of the program have been native speakers of French who have taught either FSL classes to English-speaking students, or subject material to French-speaking students. The teachers find the lack of text materials appropriate to both the linguistic and cognitive levels of the students to be the major handicap in teaching. In Grade 8, much of the material used is prepared by the teachers themselves. At the later grade levels the teachers have made use of textbooks used in Francophone classes, but they still find that much adaptation is needed as is the preparation of additional supplementary material.

The students in the program come from middle- to upper-middle-class homes and live in a basically unilingual English-speaking suburban community near Toronto. For the first several years of the program, students were selected on the basis of above-average IQ and generally high academic ability as well as expressed student interest in, and parental approval of the program. Recently, the program has been opened up to admit all students who choose to enter.

An evaluation of the program has been undertaken each year since it began in 1971 by following the initial group of students and the succeeding two groups of students who enrolled in 1972 and 1973 as they progress through the program. A detailed description of the annual evaluations — the composition of the comparison groups, the tests used, the statistical analyses employed, and the results — have been reported elsewhere (Barik and Swain, 1976; Barik et al., 1976). Only those findings related to the general question of whether a second language and subject material can be learned together will be summarized here.

Before we summarize these findings, two related questions need to be examined. First, how well do students achieve in subjects taught in a second language when compared to a similar group of students taught in their native language? Stated differently, are the students able to learn subject material taught in a second language? Second, do students taught in the second language attain a higher level of proficiency in that language than those studying the second language as a subject only?

Let us consider the second question first. In general, we have found that students in the partial immersion program are considerably ahead in French proficiency of their peers who have had only 20-minute daily periods of FSL instruction. Proficiency was measured through tests of comprehension, speaking, reading, writing, and vocabulary knowledge. Only two exceptions to the general superiority of the immersion groups[1] were noted: (1) in pronunciation, where the immersion and comparison groups obtained similar scores at the end of Grade 9, and (2) in writing, where on one subsection of the test (requiring students to make appropriate morphological changes to words in a sentence), the immersion and comparison groups obtained similar scores at the end of Grade 10.

As a further check on the achievement of immersion students by the end of Grade 10, the same French reading and listening tests that were administered to the Grade 10 immersion students were also administered to a selected group of FSL students from Grades 12 and 13 who were judged to be the best students in French by their French teacher.[2] The Grade 10 immersion students scored higher than the Grade 12 students and about the same as the Grade 13 students, thus performing as well in French

---

[1]Three results are based on the testing of three groups at the Grade 8 level, two groups at the Grade 9 level, and one group at the Grade 10 level.
[2]The Grade 12 and 13 students had had FSL instruction each year beginning in Grade 7.

reading and listening as the best FSL students who were two to three grades ahead of them.

Let us now turn to the findings related to the learning of content material taught in a second language. In this program Grade 8 immersion students were taught science in French. On a standardized science test administered in English, the Grade 8 immersion students did as well as their comparison group, which had been instructed in English, at the beginning of the year but not as well at the end of the year. This finding was interpreted as revealing a slight negative effect of the immersion program on the attainment of general science concepts. In a mathematics test administered in English, although taught in French in Grade 8, one group of immersion students (Cohort 1) performed as well as its English-educated comparison group, another immersion group (Cohort 2) scored better than its comparison group, and a third immersion group (Cohort 3) did not perform as well as its comparison group when account was taken of initial differences between the two groups in level of mathematical achievement, age, and IQ.

In history and geography, taught in French to the immersion students throughout the program (Grades 8 through 10), a comparison of the French immersion and English-educated groups is not possible because the same tests were not administered to both groups. However, on tests devised by the teachers, the immersion students performed satisfactorily.

In summary, these results suggest that the teaching of content subjects in a second language in later grade levels improves second-language skills considerably. In addition, the subject material itself is learned, as indicated by the immersion students' scores on achievement tests when compared with the scores of their comparison groups — native English-speaking students taught in English.

Up to this point we have discussed the effects on *learning* when subject material is taught via a second language. But how is *teaching* itself affected? Does being concerned both with second-language teaching and content teaching create unique instructional problems? Intuitively, it seems that special problems must be created. For example, if a student's response during a geography lesson contains both a linguistic and content error, should the teacher correct the linguistic error and ignore the content error, correct the content error and ignore the linguistic error, or attempt to correct both? It is unlikely that situations involving these choices arise frequently when students are taught subject material in their native language. Such situations are probably more likely to occur in second- or foreign-language classes where communicative competence is the goal.

These questions led us into the classroom to see how teachers actually responded to linguistic and/or content errors made by the students during a subject lesson. We recorded a Grade 8 science lesson, geography lesson, and mathematics lesson, and a Grade 9 geography lesson. Three different teachers were involved. Although our goal is ultimately to determine if any strategy or combination of strategies is more effective than another (as judged by student performance), we are still a long way from that goal. However, we have now identified some methods that teachers use when teaching content material in a second language. Preliminary and tentative though they are, some findings are presented below.

The *form* of the teachers' corrective reaction was noted first. The transcripts indicate that in many cases the corrective reaction is no different in form from a non-corrective reaction. For example, if the student makes a linguistic error, the teacher may repeat the student's response but with some modification that corrects the error and presumably draws the student's attention to it. Then, without waiting for the student to repeat the correct form, the teacher proceeds with the lesson as in Examples 1 and 2 below. It was found, however, that the teachers follow the same procedure even when the students have not made an error, as in Example 3.

Example 1: S: **Mets le objet dans le prouvet.**

T: **Dans l'éprouvette. Je mets l'objet dans l'éprouvette.** *Je mets l'objet dans l'eau. Je mets l'objet dans le cylindre. Bien.*

Example 2: T: *Pourquoi est-ce qu'il n'y a pas de vignes dans l'Isle de Prince Edouard?*

S: **Parce qu'il boucoup de pleut.**

T: **Parce qu'il y a beaucoup de pluie.** *Le climat n'est pas très chaud. Pas assez chaud.*

Example 3: S: *Il n'y a pas beaucoup de forêts.*

T: *Pas beaucoup de forêts, oui. Mais est-ce qu'il y en avait?*[3]

The immediate effect on the students is not clear. Over a period of time the students' linguistic performance does improve, but in the short run it appears that many of the corrections have little effect because similar errors are repeated again and again. Whether the specific error that is being corrected is not perceived as a correction by students because of its similarity in form to non-corrective verbal reaction or because of the global manner in which the correction is made is not clear.

The question is then raised of what is meant by a correction. Perhaps it is useful to draw a distinction between an implicit and an explicit correction. An implicit correction is one where the teacher corrects[4] the students but

---

[3]Students' errors and teachers' corrections are in boldface italics.

[4]It may be that the teacher does not intend that the response functions as a correction. Yet, because the teacher's response provides a correct model for the student's incorrect utterance, it is implicitly, at least, a correction.

does not stop to check whether the students have perceived that an error has been made or that they are able to correct it. This behavior corresponds to that of adults in first-language acquisition studies where it has been shown that adults rarely explicitly instruct the young child how to say something correctly, but rather often repeat and expand the child's utterance (Brown and Bellugi, 1964). An explicit correction, on the other hand, is one where the teacher corrects the error and in some way verifies that the students are aware of it and can correct it.

In general, corrections related to linguistic errors made by the students during a content lesson tended to be implicit in nature, whereas corrections related to content errors tended to be explicit in nature. This observation corresponds to Brown and Hanlon's (1970) finding that adults tend to correct errors in child speech related to the truth value of the statement rather than to its linguistic form.

Considering all the errors made by the students during the four recorded lessons, it was found that of the errors in content (i.e., when the student's statement was either inaccurate, inappropriate, unclear, or incomplete), approximately 90% were corrected either explicitly or implicitly. Of the linguistic errors (i.e., errors in vocabulary usage, syntax, and morphology), approximately 40% were corrected either explicitly or implicitly. In addition, the teacher often corrected errors in pronunciation. Calculating a percentage of pronunciation errors, however, was virtually impossible because, in general, the pronunciation of students was non-native, thus making anything said by the teacher equivalent to an implicit correction of pronunciation.

Those pronunciation errors the teachers choose to explicitly correct, and when, is an area that deserves further attention. In fact, those linguistic errors the teachers choose to explicitly correct, and when, is a question of general interest yet to be examined. Perhaps teachers correct explicitly only those linguistic errors that affect communication, those that have been taught in the French class, those that they find "annoying," or those that occur when the content is considered relatively unimportant or adequately mastered.[5]

Krashen (1978) states that:

> Error correction is thus directed solely at the monitor and appears to be most useful in those aspects of grammar that the monitor can best handle. . . . Specifically, the monitor is most adept at altering and

---

[5]A technique that might be useful to identify the most likely hypotheses would be to tape a lesson and then listen to the tape immediately after the class so that the teacher could comment on why an error was or was not corrected.

adding morphology. . . . The monitor has trouble, however, in dealing with word order and with movement transformations . . . (p. 105)

It is interesting to note, therefore, that of the morphological errors made by the students, approximately 35% were corrected, primarily implicitly; whereas of the word-order errors, approximately 80% were corrected, again primarily implicitly. However, approximately 15 times as many morphological errors than word-order errors were made by the students.

When an utterance contained both linguistic and content errors, the content error was never ignored. On the other hand, approximately 35% of the time the linguistic error was ignored while the content error was corrected. Both types of errors were corrected approximately 50% of the time.

These results suggest that correction of content errors takes precedence over the correction of linguistic errors when subject matter is taught, but by no means is language teaching left entirely to the period set aside for second-language instruction, although explicit language instruction is relatively infrequent.

In conclusion, the results suggest that learning both a second language and content material at the same time in school is not incompatible. In fact, it may be the most effective means of learning a second language if the way in which a first language is learned is taken as a model. We need, however, to devote more attention to at least two issues. First, it must be determined which teaching strategies are most effective in attaining the goal of learning both a second language and content material. Second, it must be determined if specific subjects are more suitable than others (e.g., history versus science) for developing second-language competence.

REFERENCES

Barik, Henri C., and Merrill Swain. "A Canadian Experiment in Bilingual Education: The Peel Study," *Foreign Language Annals*, IX (October, 1976), 465-479.

_____, and _____. "English-French Bilingual Education in the Early Grades: The Elgin Study Through Grade Four," *The Modern Language Journal*, LX (January-February, 1976), 3-17.

_____, and _____. "Three-Year Evaluation of a Large Scale Early Grade French Immersion Program: The Ottawa Study," *Language Learning*, XXV (June, 1975), 1-30.

_____, _____, and Vincent A. Gaudino. "A Canadian Experiment in Bilingual Schooling in the Senior Grades: The Peel Study Through Grade Ten," *Revue Internationale De Psychologie Appliquee (International Review of Applied Psychology)*, XXV (October, 1976), 99-113.

Brown, Roger, and Ursula Bellugi. "Three Processes in the Child's Acquisition of Syntax," *Harvard Educational Review*, XXXIV (Spring, 1964), 133-151.

_____, and C. Hanlon. "Derivational Complexity and Order of Acquisition in Child Speech," *Cognition and the Development of Language*, ed. John R. Hayes. New York: Wiley, 1970, pp. 155-207.

Bruck, Margaret, Wallace E. Lambert, and G. Richard Tucker. "Bilingual Schooling Through the Elementary Grades: The St. Lambert Project at Grade Seven," *Language Learning,* XXIV (December, 1974), 183-204.

Cohen, Andrew D., and Merrill Swain. "Bilingual Education: The 'Immersion' Model in the North American Context," *TESOL Quarterly,* X (March, 1976), 45-53.

Edwards, H. P., and F. Smythe. "Alternatives to Early Immersion Programs for the Acquisition of French as a Second Language," *Proceedings of the Research Conference on Immersion Education for the Majority Child,* eds. Merrill Swain, and Margaret Bruck. *Canadian Modern Language Review,* XXXII, No. 5 (1976), 524-533.

——————————, and ——————————. *Evaluation of Second Language Programs: 1974-75 Annual Report, Ottawa Roman Catholic School Board.* Report submitted to the Ontario Ministry of Education, 1975. (Mimeographed.)

Genesee, F., E. Polich, and M. Stanley. "An Experimental French Immersion Program at the Secondary School Level — 1969 to 1974," *Canadian Modern Language Review,* XXXIII (1977), 318-332.

Krashen, Stephen D. "Language Acquisition and Language Learning in the Late-Entry Bilingual Education Program," *Language Development in a Bilingual Setting.* Los Angeles: National Dissemination and Assessment Center, 1978, pp. 100-112.

Lambert, Wallace E., and G. Richard Tucker. *The Bilingual Education of Children: The St. Lambert Experiment.* Rowley: Newbury House, 1972.

Stern, Hans H., Merrill Swain, L. D. McLean, R. J. Friedman, B. Harley, and S. Lapkin. *Three Approaches to Teaching French: Evaluation and Overview of Studies Related to the Federally-Funded Extensions of the Second Language Learning (French) Programs in the Carleton-Ottawa School Boards.* Toronto: Ontario Institute for Studies in Education, 1976.

Swain, Merrill. "French Immersion Programs Across Canada: Research Findings," *Canadian Modern Language Review,* XXXI, No. 2 (1974), 117-129.

The Development of Curriculum in L1 and L2 in a Maintenance Bilingual Program

Gustavo González

Early bilingual programs were primarily known as second-language (e.g., ESL) programs, and prior to their introduction, no second-language instruction existed; students were expected to learn on their own. This paper maintains that bilingual curriculum is needed from K-12 if maintenance is to be continued. Because programs in existence now are primarily designed for the early grade levels, it is suggested that parallel content areas in both the first and second languages are needed throughout the K-12 grade continuum. In addition, the same content areas might be presented in different levels of grammatical complexity in both the first and second languages. The question of whether various Chicano dialect forms should be introduced in the curriculum is also discussed. This paper suggests that during the presentation of content areas the only skill required should be that of communication and that no language corrections should be made.

THE ADVENT of national legislation providing for bilingual education programs brought in its wake an immediate focus on the educational needs of children of limited-English-speaking ability. School districts that had previously denied the existence of linguistically different children within their confines suddenly discovered that they had a sizable population of such children. In response to this discovery, districts established programs purporting to address the educational needs of the linguistically different groups. The haste with which these early programs were organized and implemented allowed little time for reflection on what the ultimate goals of bilingual/bicultural education should be, how these goals could best be achieved, and what components could provide the core for accomplishing the stated goals.

Indeed, the first bilingual programs funded under Title VII of the Elementary and Secondary Education Act of 1965 were little more than English-as-a-Second-Language (ESL) programs. The primary purpose of these early attempts (and still the goal of many programs today) was to teach the child English as quickly as possible. Rather than attempting to strengthen the child's first language, these programs encouraged the use of the first language only as a bridge to English. For example, although the threat of physical punishment no longer prevented Spanish language dominant children from speaking Spanish in the schools, it was quite clear that Spanish occupied a position subordinate to that of English.

The prevailing atmosphere perhaps was best summed up by Dr. Gloria Zamora of the University of Texas, San Antonio. In testimony before the Subcommittee on Education, Committee on Labor and Public Welfare (1973), she stated:

> What I discovered in my early years of teaching predominantly Spanish-speaking children of my own ethnic group, was that they were expected to conform to an institution and a curriculum that was not geared to, nor willing to, "Begin with each child where he is" and to "Move him from the known to the unknown." The fact that he was a Spanish speaker made no difference. It soon became apparent to me that my mission was to help him assimilate into Mainstream America at the expense of his language and culture — indeed at the expense of his very being.

With the passage of time and the acquisition of experience and wisdom, the linguistic minority community began to demand more of bilingual education programs. Instead of accepting this type of program as a remedial effort designed to bring the Chicano child's English language skills up to par, Chicanos began to see in the bilingual/bicultural program a viable means of maintaining, strengthening, and in some instances, recapturing their language and culture. Evidence of this movement emerged in the regulations issued under the new Bilingual Education Act proposed in 1973. Whereas the original regulations focused on growth and achievement in English, the new regulations began to require some proof of growth in the first language as well. The first language (at least officially) had begun to assume a status equal to that of English. Lawmakers at the national level had finally realized that children do not have to give up their first language to acquire a second; the concept of maintenance bilingual/bicultural education programs had achieved a new respectability.

The term maintenance bilingual program as used in this paper refers to those programs that have as their goals: (1) to encourage, extend, and maintain the native language of the students, and (2) to help the students become completely fluent in the second language — English. Unfortunately, maintenance bilingual/bicultural programs have progressed little beyond the concept stage. Several factors have contributed to this sad state of affairs. It is the intent of this paper to examine one of these: the lack of curriculum in first and second languages at all levels, from kindergarten through twelfth grade.

The development of curriculum materials for bilingual programs on a national scale has received little attention. With very few exceptions, the needs of bilingual/bicultural programs are met through the importation of books and language programs from other areas (e.g., Mexico and Puerto Rico). Some districts are fortunate to have the resources to develop their own curriculum but none, to my knowledge, has developed a comprehensive curriculum for levels K-12 in all relevant content areas. The Dissemination and Assessment Center for Bilingual Education in Austin, Texas, has done a commendable job of disseminating curricular efforts throughout the country at minimal cost. But this effort is not enough. If maintenance bilingual programs are to become a reality, we must direct our energies toward producing quality materials in the first and second languages at the levels where none presently exist.

The situation to date leaves much to be desired. The great majority of Spanish/English bilingual programs are concentrated at the K-3 level; thus, the bulk of curriculum-development activity has been and continues to be at the lower end of the educational spectrum. The result of this situation, even under the best of circumstances, can only be a quasi-maintenance effort that is programmed to self-destruct at the end of the elementary school years. If children have not acquired enough English by then, they will be forced to return to the "sink or swim" atmosphere of monolingual instruction in English, which certainly is not in keeping with maintenance bilingual education.

The general lack of bilingual programs beyond the sixth grade results in a failure to meet the needs of increasingly large numbers of Chicanos. In addition to the graduates of K-3 programs, there is a significant number of recent immigrants from Mexico that would benefit from participation in an expanded maintenance Spanish/English bilingual program. These new arrivals invariably include students in the middle and upper grades. Presently, the system is not sufficiently prepared to meet the needs of these students; at best, only a weak ESL program is available in which it is hoped that the students will "pick up English as they go along." No attempt is made to meet the needs of the "total" person.

If maintenance bilingual/bicultural programs are to be successful in preserving the culture and language of the Chicano, opportunities to participate must be provided for the child at every level, from kindergarten

through twelfth grade and beyond. Failure to provide this positive reinforcement for the child's language and culture will result in a loss of interest
in school and possibly the child's dropping out altogether. The teachers
involved in such programs must be competent and must possess a positive
attitude toward the philosophy of maintenance bilingual education. Students would receive instruction in all content areas in both languages; their
exposure to ideas and concepts would be systematic and in keeping with
their preferred learning style. The first and second languages would not
only be languages to be learned as subject matter but would also serve as
communication tools.

The development of a strong, comprehensive curriculum is critical to the
existence of a K-12 maintenance bilingual/bicultural program. Thus, great
care must be exercised in this enterprise to ensure its relevance to the
Chicano community and to maximize the positive impact on the education
of the Chicano. At the very least, the curriculum at each level must cover
parallel concepts in both languages. If, for example, the math lesson at a
certain grade level is focusing on trigonometry, the same topic would be
available in the curriculum in both languages. The objective of this approach is to ensure that the student is not held back in concept development because language skills in the first or second language may not be
sufficiently developed to enable the student to handle the lesson.

Like curricula currently in use, bilingual curriculum should proceed
from the simple to the complex, from the concrete to the abstract, and from
the known to the unknown. Part of the child's learning experiences would
include the acquisition of new vocabulary in both the first and second
languages. Although this process would seem obvious, it doesn't always
appear that way to teachers engaged in bilingual/bicultural instruction.
The acquisition of new vocabulary seems normal and is readily accepted in
second-language classes but is viewed with some caution and curiosity
when it occurs as part of a content lesson. The question often arises, "If the
children do not possess the word for a new concept in Spanish, should it be
taught to them or should only the English word be taught?"

No child comes to school with a fully developed vocabulary in any
language. This aspect of language continues to grow and develop throughout life. For some reason, teachers sometimes expect Spanish-speaking
Chicano children to have a complete vocabulary in Spanish; they tend to
forget that the Chicano child's language ability is still growing. If the
Chicano child is not familiar with the vocabulary that accompanies a certain
concept, the terminology should be provided as part of the learning process. This principle applies equally well to concept learning in the first and
second languages.

A matter related to expectations in vocabulary development is that of the level of grammatical complexity of the first and second languages in the presentation of content material in the curriculum. Is there a need to control the degree of complexity of linguistic structures in Spanish and English? If so, on what basis will language structures be included or excluded? Unfortunately, the answers in this area are few and hard to come by. Language development in English and Spanish language dominant Chicano children has yet to receive the scrutiny it deserves. Research into the acquisition of grammatical structures has been conducted, but it was limited to children between two and six years of age (González, 1970). Spanish-language development beyond that age remains to be charted.

The learning of English as a first or second language by Chicanos is another area that remains to be explored extensively. The acquisition of English has been explored to some degree, but these investigations have been carried out on Anglo children and have concentrated on the very early stages of language. But as with Spanish, there is a lack of information in language development beyond the age of six. Without such scientific studies, our only guide to the appropriate level of linguistic complexity in content material is experience and intuition.

Because of this absence of basic linguistic information on which to structure the curriculum, the task must be approached from a different direction. One solution is to express the same idea or concept (in the first or second language) using linguistic constructions of varying complexity. Instead of utilizing one structure to present ideas and concepts, several different ones could be indicated. In some cases, the difference would lie in substituting a lexical item; in others, basic changes in linguistic structure would be affected. The advantages of such an approach are twofold: (1) it enables students possessing a wider range of language skills to participate in lessons in which major concepts are presented, and (2) the variety of ways of expressing the same thought serves as a type of language enrichment activity.

Of course, not all concepts would lend themselves equally well to this treatment. In some cases, the number of options possible would be quite limited. The primary goal is communication of the idea or concept; any means that the teacher can use to achieve this goal should be encouraged wholeheartedly.

The incorporation of this approach into content-area instruction could be accomplished in one of two ways. The first method involves actually indicating the different ways of expressing each major concept in the curriculum itself. The second and perhaps more realistic method is to provide training for teachers in the skill of devising alternative ways of expressing the same idea. This latter procedure has the added advantage of flexibility; it does not limit the teacher to a set of predetermined structures.

Those attempting to develop Spanish curriculum that is relevant to the Chicano eventually have to come to grips with the issue of dialect. The Chicano population of the southwestern United States speak a variety of Spanish that traditionally has been looked on with disfavor, even by Chicanos themselves. As Hernández-Chávez (1975) states:

> *Entre los mexicanos se dice de los chicanos que ni hablamos Español ni hablamos Inglés. Enfrentados con estos conceptos negativos, muchos chicanos también miramos nuestro vernáculo como un idioma ilegítimo, e indigno de ser escrito excepto en una forma "pura," concepto que queda indefinido.*[1] (p. 234)

With regard to curriculum development, then, to what extent should the Chicano dialect forms be incorporated in the lessons? Part of this question is resolved by the nature of the content area under consideration. Areas such as mathematics or science would be less subject to change even when viewed from the Chicano dialect perspective than would areas such as social studies. This latter area, in which the Chicano child and neighborhood become the focus of the curriculum, of necessity must reflect the child's reality, including the use of the child's own language variety.

A word of caution is in order at this point. Although the use of the child's Spanish dialect-variety is encouraged, this form should not be the only variety the child is exposed to. As the student progresses in language development and as horizons continues to expand, the student should be made aware of other varieties of Spanish such as the standard form. To deny the child this exposure is to limit communication skills and to hamper the ability to communicate in Spanish beyond the limits of the child's *barrio* or *colonia*. Just as the purpose of bilingual education is to maintain and develop skills in both languages, so should the goal in the Spanish-language component of a maintenance program be to add to the child's Spanish language skills by gradually exposing the child to the standard form of the language and by making the child aware of the social contexts in which each variety is appropriate. The basic idea, of course, is to *add* skills, not to replace one set of skills with another.

Needless to say, the overall effect of the curriculum will be much greater if the structures in the content area curriculum reinforce those structures introduced in the second-language component. Although this meshing occurs only rarely, there should be a concerted effort to accomplish this goal nonetheless.

---

[1]Mexicans say that we Chicanos speak neither Spanish nor English. Confronted by this negative attitude, many Chicanos perceive our vernacular as indeed an illegitimate language, unworthy of being written except in a "pure" (standard) form — a very indefinable situation indeed.

Since the goals of the content-area component differ in general from the goals of the second-language component, the expectations would also be different; that is, students would work toward refinement of language skills during the time set aside for that purpose. During the presentation of content areas, the only language skill required of the children would be communication. This arrangement allows the child to use the structures learned in a free conversation form, fully cognizant that the child will not be corrected. At the same time, it provides the teacher with the opportunity to help the child in areas of difficulty.

Maintenance bilingual programs, therefore, offer the best alternative if the needs of Chicanos at different grade levels are to be met. One important part of such an approach is the K-12 curriculum. Little information is available to guide curriculum writers as to the linguistic complexity of the language of the target group. Nevertheless, by providing alternative forms of the same information, maximum participation and comprehension can be ensured. While dialect forms should not be discouraged, the child should be exposed to other varieties, including the standard. Content material that uses structures introduced in the language component of the program should be presented as much as possible, thereby providing positive reinforcement for those structures.

In closing, I take exception to Fishman's (1974) view that partial bilingualism is preferred to full bilingualism as a goal. If we Chicanos were not caught in a gigantic struggle to maintain our language and culture, perhaps it would be easier to agree with Professor Fishman. However, to meet head-on this threat posed by the dominant society, it is necessary to work toward full bilingualism at all levels. Quoting Hernández-Chávez (1975) once again:

> . . . si tenemos la esperanza y la voluntad no sólo de conservar nuestra herencia lingüística sino también de insistir en que se les enseñe el español a nuestros hijos y que se utilice dicho idioma en todos los niveles de la educación como medio de instrucción, entonces nos es de lo más urgente establecer programas verdaderamente bilingües en todas las escuelas donde asisten estudiantes chicanos.[2] (p. 234)

Undoubtedly there is much at stake. The next few years should indicate to what extent we have been successful.

---

[2]If we have the hope and the willpower not only to conserve our linguistic heritage but also to insist that Spanish be taught to our children and used at all levels of education as the medium of instruction, then it is of the greatest urgency that we establish truly bilingual programs in all schools where Chicano students attend.

REFERENCES

Fishman, Joshua A. *A Sociology of Bilingual Education*. Final Report to the Division of Foreign Studies, Department of Health, Education, and Welfare, Office of Education, OECO-73-0588, September, 1974.

González, Gustavo. "The Acquisition of Spanish Grammar by Native Spanish Speakers." Unpublished PhD dissertation, The University of Texas at Austin, 1970.

Hernández-Chávez, Eduardo. "Consideraciones Sociolingüisticas en Materiales para la Educación Bilingüe," *Proceedings of the First Inter-American Conference on Bilingual Education,* eds. Rudolph C. Troike, and Nancy Modiano. Arlington: Center for Applied Linguistics, 1975, pp. 228-238.

Zamora, Gloria Rodríguez. Testimony before the Subcommittee on Education, Committee on Labor and Public Welfare, United States Senate, on Bills S. 2552 and S. 2553, October 31, 1973.

Curriculum/ Language Contexts for Bilingual Education

Courtney B. Cazden

In this paper a discussion of some of the variables involved in deciding how to combine two languages in a bilingual program focuses on teachers' patterns of language usage and curriculum subject areas. Bilingual English/Spanish-speaking teachers observed in two elementary school bilingual programs code-switched dramatically more frequently into English. Also, it was determined that English was the primary language of discipline and important messages. In addition, the use of L1 vs. L2 in teaching science and mathematics is explored, with the following observations: (1) science requires more language activities than mathematics since the latter is primarily a solitary, silent activity, (2) the vocabulary of mathematics is limited in size and meaning, and (3) the active role of students in the instructional dialogue in mathematics is restricted since the teacher does most of the talking. The implications of these variables for L1/L2 combinations in bilingual programs are discussed.

IN EACH bilingual education program a decision has to be made as to how two (or more) languages are to be combined. (See Jacobson, 1975, for one recent discussion.) Decisions about teacher language use should be conscious and considered; otherwise, as the small amount of observational data on language use in bilingual classrooms suggests, one language or the other will predominate in teacher talk — in perhaps unfortunate ways.

Phillips (1975) and Shultz (1975) have observed the patterns of teacher language use in primary grade bilingual program classrooms in the Los Angeles and Boston areas, respectively. (See Genishi, 1975, for a more extensive analysis of code-switching by kindergarten children.) Phillips listened to teacher/pupil talk during Spanish language lessons to native

English-speaking children (S) and English language lessons to native Spanish-speaking children (E). Although both teachers were bilingual, there was a dramatic difference in the frequency with which they code-switched from the language of instruction into the native language of the children:

S teachers switching to English — 140 switches
E teachers switching to Spanish —   2 switches

In the most extreme contrast, the first grade S teacher switched to English 64 times while teaching a class composed of 83% native English speakers, but the kindergarten E teacher did not once switch to Spanish while teaching a class composed of 95% native Spanish speakers. Perhaps what is surprising is not that the S teacher switched so often but that the E teacher switched so seldom.

Of the 142 teacher code-switches, 115 were manually recorded for content as well as language. Of these 115, 80 (70%) expressed disciplinary functions. Phillips concludes that "the contrast between the patterns of teacher code-switching during the language lesson may be signaling to students that English functions more efficiently than Spanish for 'important' messages in the classroom" (p. 57) and that there are differential expectations about language use in the two cases.

Shultz (1975) tape recorded classroom talk through wireless microphones worn by children in rotation. Although his analysis focused on code-switching by children, he also tabulated teacher speech picked up by the microphones:

> English was taught 70% of the time, and as such could also be seen as the important language. Arithmetic, science and English language arts were all taught in English, and the only subject which was actually taught in Spanish was Spanish language arts. However, even during the Spanish language arts lesson we observed, the teachers would frequently revert to English to give directions or to reprimand someone. Again, Spanish was set aside as being something special, and the only teaching which was done in Spanish was teaching about the language itself.

> The above description of language use by the teachers leaves one with the impression that English was the language which was considered to be somehow "natural," while Spanish was always used in a "marked" way. That is, someone was addressed in English, unless the person did not speak English very well; something was said in English, unless it could not be, as in a Spanish language arts lesson; Spanish was used only if it was absolutely necessary to do so. The "hidden agenda" of this classroom, then, was that it was advantageous to use English, and not advantageous to use Spanish. The teachers

did not communicate any of this explicitly to the students. The students were never told not to speak Spanish, or to speak English all the time, unless one language or the other was critical for a specific lesson. The communication of this strategy for language use was very subtle, and yet very real, because the message came across very clearly to the older students: English is the language to use. (p. 18)

Since there is no reason to believe that these observations are atypical, they suggest that a deliberate decision about teacher language use is needed. To the extent that a powerful implicit message is conveyed that English is the unmarked, more "natural" language, then a program is not truly bilingual. Although it may be impossible to avoid that message in the United States today, I assume that we want to support the use and maintenance of L1 (the child's native, or first, language) as strongly as possible. I assume also that in addition to supporting L1, one goal of a bilingual program is to help students acquire L2 (a second language).

Everything we know about language acquisition, as well as maintenance, argues for the power or *using* language, not learning *about* it. Paulson (1974) summarizes:

> There is general agreement that children's proficiency in their L(2) is directly related to the years it has been used as a medium of instruction in subject matters other than the language itself. (pp. 26-27)

Ervin-Tripp and Mitchell-Kernan characterize the difference between the two situations:

> The child's language faculty is engaged only when the child needs to communicate. Language could not be learned if children did not, at the beginning, construe meanings from context. In this view, natural language learning has as a basic and necessary feature the dependence of the learner on communication. When this is absent, as in most experimental and classroom learning of languages, one enrolls the learner in problem-solving activity, which may have quite different properties than natural language learning. (1977, p. 6)

In any curriculum subject area, there are likely to be particular benefits and particular problems associated with the use of L1 or L2 as the language of instruction. The purpose of this paper is to explore those benefits and problems through a contrast between two subjects, science and mathematics.

Science

How do we create environments (i.e., design curriculum) in which learners can communicate in L2 and thereby acquire it? It is particularly difficult to design curriculum for all learners at early stages in their L2 acquisition and for older children for whom the gap between communicative intent and communicative resources is temporarily so great. We must create environments that will successfully activate and support powerful cognitive capacities that produce universal success in L1 acquisition and equally dramatic success for many informal L2 learners outside of school. Fishman (1974) describes the informal contexts in which L2 is successfully learned:

> That millions of people become successfully bilingual without formal instruction does not imply that we can dismiss classrooms as a means for creating bilinguals. But it does imply that we should attempt to adapt to classroom use the contexts outside the classroom which successfully create bilingualism. The circumstances whereby second languages are acquired outside the classroom have been little studied. But two things seem clear. First, learners have an opportunity to hear and to practice the language in contexts in which nonverbal cues can help the learner decipher the meaning of verbal ones. Second, the verbal interactions in which the learner participates serve a communicative function. The learner speaks (and listens) in interactions in which it is necessary to communicate. If the teacher can create realistic communicative situations in which supporting nonverbal cues exist and in which emphasis is placed on the communicative function or purpose of the interaction, he will have gone far toward simulating the conditions under which successful language learning takes place outside the classroom. (p. 254)

This description also fits the simplified environment in which young children learn L1 (Macnamara, 1973).

The context of mutual activity is important for three reasons: (1) it activates human language-learning capacity because communication is necessary; (2) it is more likely that the focus of all participants is on meaning, not form; and (3) it facilitates language learning because the presence of concrete referents for some of the words makes communication possible even at the earliest stages.

Although it is undoubtedly true that even beginning L2 learners will cope somehow with talk about the non-present (in which nonverbal supports for communication are less available), it is still probable that ongoing activities are a helpful context for learning in the early stages for learners of all ages. To make this statement does not imply that the referential function of language is all important, or that labeling concrete objects and actions is a major part of that function. I only suggest that the act of attaching meaning to new sounds starts and is grounded somewhere, and that the activity one is actively engaged in for non-language-learning reasons should be preferable to the "pencils and door" of beginning language instruction drills.

How can we create environments for concerted human activity in school? This problem does not exist for young children in preschool and kindergarten programs, which may be one reason for the importance of kindergarten in the Canadian immersion programs. But for upper elementary and secondary students, school is sitting down and talking about, not doing together. Science can be a notable exception; science, that is, that involves active investigation by the learners with talk both during laboratory investigations and afterward when talking and arguing about the results.[1] As far as I know, there is no research evidence for the value of science activity as a curriculum context for L2 communication and learning. Only three related items can be cited — one hypothesis and two pieces of related research.

A research planning report for the National Institute of Education (NIE) on *Teaching as a Linguistic Process in a Cultural Setting* included a recommendation for research that would try to "specify the critical components or characteristics of natural communication situations that are necessary for the acquisition of communicative skills in a second language." One hypothesis that should be tested is that:

> . . . if the subject matter of a course is such that most activities in the course include manipulation of objects by children, instructions that are clearly demonstrable, clear referents for the nouns and verbs in classroom discourse — such as those in elementary science — children will learn both the concepts presented in the activities and second language structure . . . (Cazden *et al.*, 1974, p.22)

In suggesting that science be taught in L2, at least in the early stages of L2 acquisition, I am admittedly speaking as if the hypothesis had already been tested and confirmed.

Another research recommendation of the same NIE panel is to "explore science as a curriculum context for teaching children to use more context-independent speech":

> . . . One critical characteristic of science as an activity is the need for precise communication, for descriptions that convey what was done and what was found out so explicitly that an experiment can be replicated and the results compared. These characteristics of scientific communications are those of "context-independent" speech,

---

[1]Here I am drawing on recommendations of a group assembled to recommend priorities in research to NIE (Cazden *et al.*, 1974). The contributions of panel members Heidi Dulay and John Gumperz were especially helpful.

> which contrasts with most everyday talk that often depends on the
> listener's knowledge of fill-in relevant details . . .
> . . . The underlying assumption is that rules of language usage may
> be learned best by being used in natural communication contexts
> where they are required. Science lessons constitute one example of
> such contexts. Furthermore, the value neutrality of science content
> and scientific terminology may be an additional asset in facilitating
> classroom communications . . . (Cazden *et al.*, 1974, pp. 16-17)

Although this recommendation was conceived with reference to L1, it
could apply as well to communication in L2.

I am not familiar with secondary school science programs. At the
elementary level, however, there are at least two programs that are examples of a combination of laboratory activity and discussion. One is the
Science Curriculum Study (SCIS). It was the positive evaluation of the
effect of this program on fifth graders' referential communicative competence by Gumperz and Bowyer (1972) that encouraged the NIE panel in
the above recommendation. Another program, embodied only in a text for
teachers and not in particular materials, is *Teaching Elementary Science
through Investigation and Colloquim* (Lansdown *et al.*, 1971).

As in any curriculum area, however, there are special limitations and
potentialities when students receive instruction in their weaker language.
Collison (1974) analyzed the conceptual level of statements made by 12 to
14 year old students in Ghana in science discussions conducted in their
native language and in English, using a coding scheme developed by
Lansdown *et al.* (1971) that is derived from the Soviet psychologist Vygots-
ky's levels of conceptual thought. Collison found that in science discussions
conducted in L1, the students made more statements, their statements
were at more complex conceptual levels, and they more often reported
relationships among non-perceptual aspects of the scientific phenomena
being studied. Thus, while in some ways science may be a useful curriculum context for L2 acquisition, the students' understanding of scientific
concepts (or at least their ability to verbalize those concepts in class
discussions) may be more restricted than if instruction were in L1.

Mathematics[2]

Mathematics contrasts with science in many ways. First, mathematics is
a solitary and silent activity. Except when mathematicians talk about
mathematics, its use outside of the classroom is a private, intra-personal
matter. In short, mathematics is not basically interactional work; one may

---

[2]I am indebted to Dr. Pearla Nesher of the Universities of Haifa and Jerusalem for discussion
of ideas in this section.

have to translate the product of mathematical operations into another language — as in money transactions — but the operations themselves need not be communicable to anyone else. Mathematics, therefore, contrasts sharply with science, whose content will appear frequently in out-of-school life.

Second, the vocabulary of mathematics is limited in both size and meaning. In a "register of mathematics," discussed in a UNESCO publication (1974), there are terms rarely encountered in non-mathematical contexts — such as *exponent* — and other terms whose meanings in natural language have to be suppressed in favor of single, technical definitions — such as (in English) *set, even, root,* and *power.*

Not only is the vocabulary of mathematics restricted, but the role of students in classroom instructional dialogue is apt to be restricted as well. One study showed that, in a comparison with social studies teachers, mathematics teachers talked more often and their students volunteered less frequently (Aiken, 1972). Moreover, pupil responses in mathematics lessons are more apt to be "yes" or "no" or a number. In short, mathematics is probably not a curriculum context that will contribute much to L2 acquisition.

If the criteria for selecting a language of instruction for particular subject areas shifts from optimal stimulation for L2 acquisition to maximum achievement in that subject itself, other aspects of mathematics suggest continuation of instruction in L1 at least beyond the beginning stages of the learner's L2 acquisition. More than any other subject in formal education, mathematics is a sequential subject. What one is learning at any moment builds on what one has already learned — e.g., multiplication on addition — in a way that is not true in social studies or science. Continuity for the learner is essential. The mathematics teacher must be able to tap the student's prior knowledge and build on it. For the secondary student who has already studied mathematics in L1, e.g., in Mexico, the easiest way to achieve that continuity is to continue learning mathematics in L1, in this case in Spanish.

Mathematics is also the subject area in which success or failure is most obvious. If the student is studying mathematics in L2, the likelihood of error is increased, especially in oral classroom recitations. Moreover, when an error is made, neither the student nor the teacher can be sure whether the problem lies in the student's inadequate comprehension of L2 or of mathematics.

These characteristics of mathematics could lead to opposite recommendations for the language of instruction at different ages. For young children in kindergarten or grade 1 (just beginning education in formal mathematics) the restricted vocabulary and responses required in classroom lessons could be arguments for teaching in L2. Moreover, mathematics at that level is taught with a wide variety of manipulative materials — beans, abacus, or Cuisenaire rods — which could serve, like laboratory activities in science, as the non-verbal cues to support L2 acquisition. For secondary students, however, continuity takes precedence. At whatever point the language of instruction is changed, instructional time would have to be spent teaching the students the special "language of mathematics" in L2. Because the special words and construction in that register (e.g., "let X stand for . . . ") are limited in number, the translation task is not severe.

But a major difficulty would remain with word problems. They are difficult for all students, even in L1, because solving word problems can be considered a "bilingual" task. These problems require translation from natural (verbal) language into formal (mathematical) language, and like translation from one natural language to another, this type of translation rarely can be done successfully by a sequential word-by-word strategy. Different words may translate into a single mathematical expression, and conversely, the same word can assume various meanings depending on context. Nesher and Teubal (1975) discussed examples of both these difficulties:

> Example (1):
> Every day three buses *left* the station with 15 people each.
> John *bought* 3 notebooks. The cost of each one is 15 cents.
> Don *won* the lottery three times, $15 each time.
>
> All three story-problems are to be grasped as describing a situation whose formal expression is the equation:
> $$3 \times 15 = 45$$
> If the student is to grasp this relation, he must disregard the specific key words appearing in each case: "left," "bought," "won," etc., and he must concentrate on the type of relationship which underlies the specific verbal formulation.
>
> Example (2):
> (A) "five *more* than three"
> (B) "five is *more* than three"
> which, when translated into mathematical symbols look as follows:
> $$3 + 5$$
> $$5 > 3$$
> In this case the word "more" can assume various meanings depending on the syntactic context. It is not the grasping of the meaning of the isolated word "more," but also the grasping of the syntactic context, which counts here as well. (pp. 42-43)

In addition to these difficulties, there is a vocabulary burden in word problem prose — the *buses, station, people, notebooks,* and *lottery* of example (1) above. In word-problem applications of mathematical operations to real life, the vocabulary expands to express that life. It is not surprising, therefore, that even when mathematics instruction in L2 does not impair achievement in mathematics computation, it does impair achievement on tests of problems such as these (Macnamara, 1967). This finding is another argument for mathematics instruction in L1 until a good reading knowledge of L2 has been acquired in other contexts.

Conclusion

The discussion in this paper of relationships between particular curriculum contexts and language is only exploratory. Decisions about how to combine two languages into any bilingual education program will be made on the basis of local community values and interactional norms, and on the practical grounds of availability of teachers and texts. It is hoped that these remarks will be helpful in implementing those decisions in actual classroom instruction.

REFERENCES

Aiken, Lewis R., Jr. "Language Factors in Learning Mathematics," *Review of Educational Research (RER),* XLII (Summer, 1972), 359-385.

Cazden, Courtney B., *et al. Teaching as a Linguistic Process in a Cultural Setting.* NIE Conference on Studies in Teaching, No. 5. Washington: National Institute of Education, December, 1974.

Collison, G. Omani. "Concept Formation in a Second Language: A Study of Ghanaian School Children," *Harvard Educational Review,* XLIV (August, 1974), 441-457.

Ervin-Tripp, Susan, and Claudia Mitchell-Kernan, eds. *Child Discourse.* New York: Academic Press, 1977.

Fishman, Joshua A. *A Sociology of Bilingual Education.* Final Report to the Division of Foreign Studies, Department of Health, Education, and Welfare, Office of Education, OECO-73-0588, September, 1974.

Genishi, C. H. "Rules for Code-Switching in Young Spanish-English Speakers: An Exploratory Study of Language Socialization." Unpublished PhD dissertation, University of California, Berkeley, 1976.

Gumperz J. C., and J. Bowyer. "The Development of Communication Skills Through Everyday Reasoning: An Experiment Using the SCIS Program." Unpublished manuscript, 1972.

Jacobson, R. "The Dilemma of Bilingual Education Models: Duplication or Compartmentalization," *New Directions in Second Language Learning, Teaching and Bilingual Education,* eds. Marina K. Burt, and Heidi C. Dulay. Washington: TESOL, 1975, pp. 123-138.

Lansdown, Brenda, Paul E. Blackwood, and Paul F. Brandwein. *Teaching Elementary Science Through Investigation and Colloquim.* New York: Harcourt Brace Jovanovich, 1971.

Macnamara, John. "Nurseries, Streets and Classrooms: Some Comparisons and Deductions," *Modern Language Journal,* LVII (September-October, 1973), 250-254.

——————. "The Effects of Instruction in a Weaker Language," *Journal of Social Issues,* XXIII (April, 1967), 121-135.

Nesher, P., and E. Teubal. "Verbal Cues as an Interfering Factor in Verbal Problem Solving," *Educational Studies in Mathematics,* VI (1975), 41-51.

Paulson, C. B. *Implications of Language Learning Theory for Language Planning: Concerns in Bilingual Education*. Bilingual Education Series #1. Washington: Center for Applied Linguistics, 1974.

Phillips, J. M. "Code-Switching in Bilingual Classrooms." Unpublished MA thesis, California State University, Northridge, 1975.

Shultz, J. "Language Use in Bilingual Classrooms." Paper presented at the TESOL Annual Convention, Los Angeles, March, 1975.

UNESCO. *Interaction Between Linguistics and Mathematical Education*. Final Report of the symposium sponsored by UNESCO, CEDO, and ICMI, Nairobi, Kenya, September, 1974.

PART FIVE

Assessment in
Bilingual Education

Problems in the Assessment of the Effect of Language Education Policies in a Multilingual Society

A model is presented describing the complexity of any educational policy adopted in a multicultural society and delineating seven sets of factors that may have a bearing on or be affected by a bilingual program. In addition to the obvious educational factors, which in some situations may be relatively insignificant in deciding whether or not to establish bilingual programs or in evaluating such programs' successes, psychological, sociological, economic, political, religio/cultural, and linguistic considerations are explored. Not all factors will be of equal importance in each particular bilingual situation and each of the areas will require different kinds of measurement necessitating input from many different disciplines and the various communities involved.

Bernard Spolsky

Work IN testing in recent years has been marked by a search for scientifically valid tests (Spolsky, 1977). We have moved away from what might be labeled a pre-scientific period where testing was considered an art carried out by a few highly qualified teachers or testers who were presumed to be able to judge a student's ability but were not required to justify that judgment or be consistent in it. Such an approach was essentially elitist. In a more democratic framework, any method of establishing individual differences must be fully justifiable. The attacks on the reliability and validity of the pre-scientific tests can in these terms be seen as part of the move toward social justice, calling for the greatest care when judgments are made that affect the lives of individual citizens.

Testing in general and language testing in particular developed in a general intellectual climate which called for scientific precision in measurement. Language tests reached their present sophistication in a period of empiricism and behaviorism. Philosophically, they depend on a belief that it is possible not only to analyze and understand but also to measure human linguistic capacities. Unfortunately, one of the basic implications of this belief has been missed. In much work with human behavior and the measurement of human abilities, we seem to have expected a degree of certainty that we imagine exists in the study of the physical universe. In so doing, however, we are missing the point of the principle of uncertainty; and we are expecting a degree of certainty about an individual human being which no physical scientist would expect of predictions about an individual electron.

We have fallen into the trap, I suspect, of confusing the ability to make general predictions about groups with the ability to make specific predictions about individuals. We are not satisfied with understanding language proficiency; we want a technology that will measure any individual. And once we have these measurements, we use them as though they were certain, thus producing the same kinds of self-fulfilling prophecies for language proficiency as for I.Q. and the various methods of measuring it.

In the assessment of the effects of bilingual education programs, we run into this danger when we expect to find simple measures that will show the effect of a bilingual curriculum. To obtain measures of sufficient reliability, we often find it necessary to focus our attention on the most easily measurable items. There is a great temptation to oversimplify, to use for instance a simple vocabulary test to show what effect a program has had. Any such approach will, however, lead to a serious distortion of the complex truth involved: first, because of the inherent uncertainty in even the finest instrument we can devise, and secondly, because such an approach fails to recognize the multitude of factors leading to and affected by bilingual education programs. In the remainder of this paper, I would like to sketch briefly a model that we have developed for the description of bilingual education and suggest some of the ways in which it is applicable to the assessment of the effects of such programs.

A Model for the Description of Bilingual Education

The model (Spolsky, Green, and Read, 1976) is an attempt to map all the relevant factors on to a single integrated structure and to suggest some of the lines of interconnection. The model is based on a hexagonal figure. (For a later version, see Spolsky, in press a and b.) Each side of the hexagon represents a set of factors that may have a bearing on, or be affected by, the operation of a bilingual program in a particular situation. The six sets of factors are labeled psychological, sociological, economic, political, religio/cultural, and linguistic. Not all of the factors will be equally (or even at all) relevant in an individual case; but since our aim has been to make the model as universally applicable as possible, the full range of factors is presented with no special concern for their relative significance.

It is important to note that there are no dividing lines within the figure, to remind one of the fact that the various factors overlap and interact with

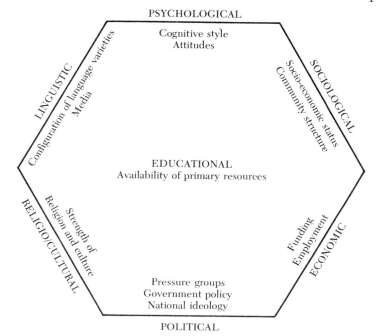

Figure 1a. THE SITUATIONAL LEVEL

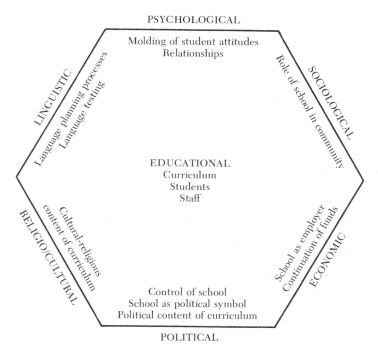

Figure 1b. THE OPERATIONAL LEVEL

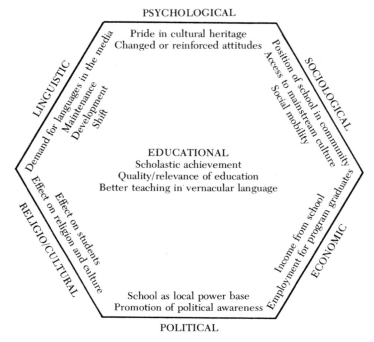

Figure 1c. THE LEVEL OF OUTCOMES.

one another in a manner that cannot be adequately represented without sacrificing the simplicity required. For this reason, too, there is a certain arbitrariness about placement of the categories in relation to each other around the figure. In the center of the figure, we locate a seventh set of factors, the educational ones. This is not done to assert the primacy of these factors. In fact, the main purpose is to show how relatively insignificant educational considerations may be, both in the decision whether or not to establish a bilingual program and in the evaluation of a program's "success" in reaching its goals. However, we are engaged in the study of an educational activity; and it is appropriate to place education in the middle as the focus of the figure, while the other factors circumscribe and shape it on all sides.

The three dimensions of the model may be thought of as ordering each of the factors in three major levels. The first level represents the total situation of a community before a bilingual program is introduced. *Community* here should be understood to include any relevant socio-educational entity, ranging from a village or neighborhood to a school district, a geographically focused ethnic group, province or region to a whole nation. The model is intended to be broad enough to deal with the consideration of bilingual education in any of these. This level then sets out the whole range of factors that should, ideally, be taken into account in deciding on the establishment of a bilingual program. The second level includes those factors that are more or less under the control of the people administering a bilingual program or that may be directly influenced by the operation of the program. The prime factor here is a central element of the whole model, the use of two languages as media of instruction and in particular, their distribution in the school curriculum. The first level represents factors that predate and are independent of a bilingual program, whereas the second deals with factors involved in the interaction of the school with the outside world upon the introduction of bilingual education. It thus includes the sources of the program's basic needs (funds, personnel, materials), the constraints within which the administrators have to work, the program's contribution to the community, and the potential reasons for the program's failure. The third level deals with the perceptions of those responsible for the program, perceptions such as the effects of the outcome on the individual participant and on the community at large. Included here are the goals of those who have planned the program, whether explicit or implicit. There is clearly the possibility that different participants might have different views of the outcome: the community might have one feeling, the educators another.

Linguistic Factors

In describing what is essentially language education policy, it is appropriate to consider first the linguistic factors. Various suggestions have been made for the description of a speech community, however small or large it is, and of its communicative networks (e.g., Fishman, 1971, 1972). The data which form the base for a sociolinguistic description necessarily include a statement of the languages and significant varieties spoken, the numbers of speakers of each, the domains in which each is used, and the modes employed (spoken or written). The description might focus on the complete community or the individual child. In any case, it will need to distinguish between the school and the people who comprise it (the administrators, the non-professional staff, the teachers, and the students), as well as the community outside the school. From this description will emerge a general configuration of languages within the community concerned. Usually, there will need to be some distinction between standardized and local varieties or languages; often, the complete pattern will form one version or another of diglossia. The description of the sociolinguistic situation will need to focus specifically on literacy in each of the varieties of language. Going beyond, it will describe the opportunities to hear or read each of the varieties in the public media: radio, television, newspapers, and books.

The first focus in this area of linguistic description is language use: in order to measure the situation, language testing and functional skills might be called for (Cooper, 1968). A second dimension of the linguistic situation is the state of standardization and development of each of the languages (Fishman, 1974). While the whole range of possibilities is clearly a continuum, there are two related but separate dimensions: the provision of access to advanced science and technology, and the provision of access to literacy and modern life. The description of the varieties in these terms will usually refer to the existence of dictionaries, grammars, established orthography, and provision for lexical elaboration and standardization.

It is in this last area in particular that the language situation is modifiable and most often must be modified in order to meet the demands of a bilingual education program. The various processes of language planning, language standardization, and language modernization might be considered the focus of a purely sociolinguistic model of bilingual education (e.g., Paulston, 1974). Where in this model we have chosen to make language choice (an aspect of curriculum) the central factor, from the point of view of the sociolinguist, language planning would probably be the key target of involvement.

A bilingual education program can have at least three effects that could be labeled linguistic: language maintenance or language shift or language development (modernization and standardization). The goals of a bilingual program may be transitional bilingualism, partial bilingualism (one form of which is monoliterate bilingualism), or full bilingualism. These linguistic outcomes should be reflected in the public media in terms of a demand for new opportunities to hear and read the language varieties being used in bilingual programs.

The kinds of linguistic goals that are possible depend on the situation. All school systems aim for mastery of the standard language; the nature of the bilingual program depends on the attitude toward the other language. The choice is theoretically limited to maintenance, shift, or revival. If a language is to be maintained, its functions in this regard must be decided, either limited or of equal value with the standard language. Similarly, if a language is to be revived, a decision must be made concerning the domains for which it is intended. Given the choice of linguistic goals, the particular kind of language planning activity required (standardization, development of orthography, lexical elaboration, development of literacy) can be determined.

While it is obvious that linguistic factors are basic to the situation in which bilingual education takes place, and that linguistic areas require modification if a program is to be implemented, it is rare for a linguistic outcome to be the basic motivation for a bilingual program. For the linguist, and for a few other language romantics, the maintenance or revival of a language is a sufficiently important value in itself. For most of those concerned, however, language serves a secondary role either as a symbol or as an instrument for one of the other factors that will be described in later parts of this paper.

Changes like those referred to will not be rapid. Language maintenance or revival can be measured only over a reasonably long period: in a rapid-change situation some indications might turn up within a few years, but the appropriate measures will more often be found outside rather than inside the school.

Sociological Factors

As has been well demonstrated by recent studies in sociolinguistics, the language pattern of a community is a close reflection of its social structure. Whatever distinctions are made within a community, whether on the basis of sex, race, social class, or ethnic group, will almost always be reproduced in linguistic variety. While often this marking will be comparatively subtle, as in the case of social or sexual dialects, it is also very common for it to be reflected in actual language differences. In considering the relevance of these factors for bilingual education, we need to look within a given community at the degree of ethnic or other social integration of the community, at the basic functioning of the school within the community, and at the social status of the speakers of the various languages involved, of the students, and of other people associated with the school.

In terms of goals, the essential contrast is between a model that calls for basic and ultimate assimilation and the model that recognizes pluralism in one form or another: A number of examples will help make clear the general outline of possibilities.

In many areas, there is a degree of social elitism (often reflecting political or economic power) in the standard language. Studies of attitudes to language in Quebec made clear that not only the English-speaking minority but also the French-speaking majority attributed higher status to English than to French and higher status to continental French than to Canadian French (Lambert and Tucker, 1972). Given this fundamental attitudinal situation, even a bilingual program aiming at cultural integration has a long way to go. While there is by now considerable support for French immersion programs that will make English speakers bilingual, there are as yet few signs that the linguistic program is having much effect on the social situation. English-speaking children are learning French well, but they are not learning Canadian French, nor do they seem to be developing the social relations with French Canadians that would be a prelude to an integrated society. In this case, bilingualism does not yet seem to threaten pluralism.

Bilingual programs for immigrants in the United States and Europe work essentially within an assimilatory framework, resulting usually in such a low status for the immigrant language as to discourage its use. A bilingual program is not enough to remedy these social attitudes.

Of considerable importance is the degree to which a school system is an alien or integrated institution. For much of the world, schools of the present kind are something that has been introduced during a period of western colonization. In an extreme case, as on the Navajo reservation, schools have until recently remained essentially alien institutions. Physically, they are differentiated from the rest of the reservation not just by high wire fences but also by a basic difference in design and arrangement of building. Navajos traditionally prefer to live in a reasonably scattered way, each hogan a considerable distance from the next. The cluster of government houses built for teachers around the school compound stands out most clearly. The linguistic isolation has been equally marked: of all institutions of the reservation, only the school has continued to insist on English in all its domains. Similarly, the principal staff of the schools have been Anglos coming from elsewhere to work in reservation schools. A major objective of developing bilingual programs in Navajo schools has been to place Navajos in various roles within the school, first as aides, but then as teachers and even administrators. The greatest sociological effect of this action is to open up the school to the community. It becomes possible for a Navajo parent to go into a school building and find someone to speak to. As a result, the school becomes much more open to community influence. It is seen less and less as an alien institution.

With their economic power, schools are also capable of influencing the social system. In developing societies, the school teacher is often one of a very small group of people who can expect cash wages. With this income can go a change in status. In Samoa, the traditional social system would seem to have been preserved largely by making sure that those people obtaining status in the school system as administrators are themselves chiefs with established social status in the older community. In Ponape in Micronesia, the educational administrators seem to form a new social class different from but respected by the traditional chiefs. In Ponape, a natural alliance in favor of bilingual education seems to have developed between some of these Ponapean administrators and chiefs: for the former, bilingual education is a method of asserting their superiority over the monolingual English-speaking American administrators they are replacing; for the latter, it is a way of providing access for the traditional community to what is clearly a powerful institution.

Economic Factors

Bilingual education can have either long term or short term outcomes. In the long term, schooling may be seen as a preparation for employment. To many parents, learning of the standard language is seen as the principal method of obtaining access to good jobs. Navajo parents want their children to know English because they see that people who speak English have much better jobs than those who do not. Some immigrants and other socially underprivileged minority groups put a great deal of emphasis on school as a method of upward social and economic mobility. Among these groups, there may well be a suspicion that suggests that bilingual programs emphasize less teaching of the standard language and more preserving of the native language, for they suspect that the kind of social pluralism involved will also be accompanied by economic discrimination.

There are, however, short term economic goals that are of considerable importance in many cases. As was mentioned above, the school is often one of the principal employers in an underdeveloped community. Bilingual education provides jobs for members of the community, for it insists on using native speakers rather than bringing teachers from elsewhere. The first programs established under the Bilingual Education Act placed their emphasis on training classroom aides. While there was talk of the possibility of career training for these aides at a time they were not considered a threat to established certified teachers, there was little problem. However, in recent developments, emphasis has moved toward training certified bilingual teachers. The potential impact in such a case as the Navajo reservation is very great. There are over 50,000 Navajo children in school, served by approximately 3,000 teachers. In 1969, no more than 100 of these teachers were Navajos. Any kind of bilingual education program, even a transitional program in the first three grades, would call for the training of a good number of Navajo teachers. The Navajo Tribal Division of Education took as its goal the training of 1,000 Navajo teachers within five or ten years. The economic effect is clear. Generally, the standard of living of Navajos on the reservation is below the poverty level. In order to obtain salaried employment, a Navajo usually has had to be prepared either to leave the reservation or to take a job in one of the developing semi-urban settlements such as Window Rock or Shiprock. The effect of calling for bilingual programs and bilingual teachers in schools throughout the reservation has produced the potential for a thousand jobs for Navajos close to home. The economic effect of such a change will be very great: beyond the economic effect, there will essentially be the development of a significant new middle class throughout the reservation.

Political Factors

In looking at the political factors involved in bilingual education, one may choose to focus on a number of levels. The focus may be international, national, regional, local, or ethnic, depending on the political or linguistic make-up of the community involved. As an example of international focus, one may point out the considerable interest in foreign language teaching and in various forms of elite bilingualism taken within the European economic community. The most common political focus is national: here, the integrational effect of a national language in contrast to the potential disintegration in support of regionalism and regional languages is a common consideration. The move toward community schools has led to even more local political concerns in bilingual education. Finally, one of the effects of the new ethnicity calls for some degree of ethnic education even where an ethnic group is not regionally based.

Two of the four stages of bilingual education proposed by Lewis (1975) are particularly concerned with varying political roles. While the first stage is instrumental and the third individualistic, both the second and fourth are based on an attitude toward national goals. The second, according to Lewis, is the phase of cultural assimilation; the stage at which the principal aim is the creation of one nation. The fourth stage reverses this process in some ways, for it is essentially the phase of pluralism. One of its principal goals is the establishment of equality not only among individuals but also among all groups.

Bilingual education can be used as a method of establishing political power. The example of the Navajos illustrates this. The move for Navajo independence works in a number of domains, but one of the most successful so far has been education. It is not coincidental that each of the independent community-controlled Navajo schools has placed a good deal of emphasis on bilingual education. Nor is it coincidental that the Navajo Education Association and now the Navajo Tribe Division of Education have argued for Navajo control of the educational system as being a goal closely associated with the establishment of bilingual education. Analysis then of changes in the power structure of a community can be an extremely important way of assessing the effect of a bilingual program.

Psychological Factors

Among the psychological factors relevant to establishing a bilingual program or that are affected by it, two main groupings might be considered: those concerned with the students' learning process (the educational-psychological factors) and those concerned with attitude (social-psychological factors).

A good deal of the work in the psychology of bilingualism has been concerned with the effect of bilingualism on the individual. This focus,

Lewis (1975) suggests, came because the studies were made in the United States particularly during what Lewis calls the third phase of bilingual education, the period during which emphasis was on individual effects and on the fullest development of the individual. A great deal of research was carried out to determine whether psychological advantages or disadvantages accrued to being bilingual or to being educated bilingually. In a recent survey in which he looks at bilingual education from a psychological perspective, Norman Segalowitz (1977) comments:

> . . . studies of the effects of bilingualism on measures of intelligence do not indicate any deficits when factors such as social class, educational background, language proficiency and so on are carefully controlled. (p. 156)

Failure to keep these other variables distinct has led to much of the controversy and the existence of studies that make contradictory claims about the intelligence of bilinguals. Similar failure to take into account sociological factors may be at the base of questions raised about the relationship of bilingualism to affective factors. Segalowitz concludes:

> . . . research on the effects of bilingualism on personality and social development suggests that maladjustments observed to accompany bilingualism usually are caused by social factors rather than bilingualism as such. (p. 156)

Essentially, a wide range of differences is possible in a society with two or more languages. A bilingual program can arise from or affect attitudes of the dominant society, of the local community, of the parents, or of the students toward themselves and other groups, toward varieties of language and their speakers, toward education as a whole, and toward bilingual education itself. Studies by Lambert and Tucker (1972) and others in Montreal showed why speakers of French were at that time ready to acquire English while speakers of English were reluctant to acquire French. Each group accepted the higher status of speakers of English and the greater benefits derived from speaking it. Without necessarily changing these basic attitudes, the political reality in Quebec has managed to overcome these attitudinal factors to some extent so that now the vast majority of English-speaking children are being exposed to some version of a French immersion program. There is not yet clear evidence that these bilingual programs are leading to changes in the attitude of English speakers, nor have there yet been reports of attitudinal changes affecting the status of the French language congruent with the legal changes.

When a minority language has been associated for a long time with the lowered status of a minority group, it takes a major change for social attitudes toward it to be altered, particularly if the minority language does not have a public culture such as with a world literature or a major educational system. It takes quite some time for the school and the community to accord the same status in educational affairs to the minority language as to the majority one. The very arguments presented for the preservation of minority language (that it is related to folk culture, that it reflects the warmth of the home) are ones that prepare it for a second-class status in an institution such as school, where formal values (written literature, the modern technological world) have first place.

The major attitudinal claim attributed to bilingual education concerns the pupils' self respect upon discovering that their home language, in which they have invested so many years and with which they have such warm associations, is respected or at least not maligned by the school system. There are frequent claims — though the evidence is uncertain — that improved attitudinal relationship can lead to better educational achievement; at least it is clear that it will lead to a much more pleasant situation with fuller respect for each individual and group making up the school and the community.

Cultural Factors

Attention is focused on the importance of cultural factors by the use of such terms as bilingual/bicultural and bilingual/multicultural education (Spolsky, 1978). The claim is sometimes made that it is not enough to teach in two languages unless the school also recognizes the cultures associated with each language; an additional claim states that it is possible to teach in only one language and still recognize the existence of two or more cultural groups in the community. Arguments like these, I suspect, have more to do with political or educational reality than with the issue of culture itself. The former argument one hears most strongly from people who are not satisfied with bilingual programs' formal teaching of the minority language by non-locals. That teachers are fluent in a variety of the local minority languages is not enough; if they are not members of the community, they are unable to deal adequately with the local culture. This reasoning might be seen then as simply another argument for ethnic or community control of the school. The other approach — that of biculturalism without bilingualism — may arise in cases where few if any of the members of the ethnic or community group qualified to teach in the schools are still fluent speakers of the minority language. One approach to such a situation is, of course, the kind of language revival program I have referred to earlier; a second is for a bicultural program, taught by relatively assimilated members of the minority group but taught in the majority language. It is not the intention of this paper to go into the complexities of cultural questions to be faced within the curriculum. However, it must be pointed out that teaching about the local minority culture, whether in the majority or the minority language, is not the same as finding a way to integrate minority and majority cultures.

Religious Factors

I have already referred to the fact that formal education in a religious context is often involved in teaching a classical language in order to provide access to a sacred text. Religions, like other social institutions, are frequently associated with a specific language. The dissociation of a classical sacred language from religion is considered a major step. Only recently has the Roman Catholic Church accepted vernaculars for the Mass; future historians will be able to judge the effect of this. One of the principles of Nineteenth Century Reform Judaism in Germany was to switch from Hebrew to the vernacular. The principle was retained in Reform Judaism in the United States; but the last twenty years or so, since the creation of the State of Israel, has seen a marked increase in the use of Hebrew even within the Reform movement. Thus, Jewish religious education consists of varying degrees of instruction in the Hebrew language, so that Hebrew School is a normal term for a Jewish religious school whether Reform, Conservative, or Orthodox.

While there are some cases where religious pressure is clearly a factor favoring some variety of bilingual education, the converse can also be true. It is possible for a group to consider it quite inappropriate to bring a sacred language and sacred culture into the profane and alien environment of the school. The paradox is perhaps highlighted most clearly in some Indian pueblos, where very few children still learn the native language at home. In some of these, then, the community — including the more conservative members — is not unwilling to have the school teach the native language so that the children might be better equipped to take part in major religious ceremonies. In other communities, where there has been stronger language maintenance, opposition to the use of the native language in school continues lest the school and the strangers it employs and represents gain access to the religious secrets of the community.

Educational Factors

Of all arguments presented in favor of bilingual education, the most common one concerns the benefit to students. As has been seen, there are probably much stronger reasons behind support for the program. The debate over the effect on students is not quite as serious as one would hope.

It is certainly true that it is difficult to find good hard data bearing on the question of the effect of a bilingual program on the pupil's educational achievement. It is certainly easy to make a good case for the need of a bilingual program when students come to school speaking a language other than the school language. It is hopefully obvious to all that incomprehensible education is immoral as well as illegal: there can be no justification for assuming that children will pick up the school language on their own, no justification for not developing some program that will make it possible for children to learn the standard language and for them to continue to be educated all the time that this is going on. Similarly, very clear arguments can be made for the value of teaching children to read in the language that they speak rather than attempting to teach a new language and initial reading at the same time. As Engle's survey (1975) has made clear, however, it is harder to produce empirical data in support of these claims than it is to make them. Two recent studies deserve mention however. The recent immersion programs in Canada have shown that in appropriate conditions it is possible to develop bilingual programs without evident cognitive disadvantages to the students who become bilingual rather than monolingual. Secondly, studies at Rock Point Community School have shown clear and significant gains in English reading ability for Navajo students whose initial reading work has been in Navajo. As more evidence accumulates, hopefully more clarification of this most vital factor will be obtained.

Conclusion

This sketch has intended to clarify the concept that educational policy adopted in a multilingual society depends on and has ramifications for a multitude of factors beyond those normally considered as related to the school. Any method of assessment that fails to take this complexity into account will miss some of the most vital effects of establishing a bilingual program. Not all factors will be of equal importance in each particular situation, but the full model makes it possible for us to be sure that factors of potential importance have not been left out of account. Each of these areas will need very different kinds of measurement; they will call on skills from many more disciplines than are usually called into play in educational evaluation. But without recognizing the complexity of what we are dealing with, we run the inevitable risk of misguided and distorted evaluation.

REFERENCES

Cooper, Robert L. "An Elaborated Language Testing Model," *Language Learning* (Special Issue), No. 3 (August, 1968), 57-72.

Engle, Patricia L. "The Use of Vernacular Languages in Education: Language Medium in Early School Years for Minority Language Groups," *Papers in Applied Linguistics*. Bilingual Education Series, No. 3. Arlington: Center for Applied Linguistics, 1975.

Fishman, Joshua A. *Advances in Language Planning*. The Hague: Mouton, 1974.

_____. *Advances in the Sociology of Language*. The Hague: Mouton, 1971.

_____. *The Sociology of Language*. Rowley: Newbury House, 1972.

Lambert, Wallace E., and G. Richard Tucker. *Bilingual Education of Children: The St. Lambert Experiment*. Rowley: Newbury House, 1972.

Lewis, E. Glyn. "The Comparative Study of Bilingualism in Education: A Model and a Prospectus of Research." Paper presented at the Bilingual Symposium, Annual Meeting of the Linguistic Society of America, December, 1975.

Paulston, Christina B. "Implications of Language Learning Theory for Language Planning: Concerns in Bilingual Education," *Papers in Applied Linguistics*. Bilingual Education Series, No. 1. Arlington: Center for Applied Linguistics, 1974.

Segalowitz, Norman. "Psychological Perspectives on Bilingual Education," *Frontiers of Bilingual Education,* eds. Bernard Spolsky, and Robert L. Cooper. Rowley: Newbury House, 1977, pp. 119-158.

Spolsky, Bernard. "A Model for the Evaluation of Bilingual Education," *International Review of Education,* in press (a).

_____. "Bilingual Education in the United States," *Proceedings of the 1978 Georgetown Roundtable on Languages and Linguistics,* in press (b).

_____. "Language and Bicultural Education," *Educational Research Quarterly,* II, No. 4 (1978), 20-25.

_____. "Language Testing: Art or Science," *Proceedings of the Fourth International Congress of Applied Linguistics*. Stuttgart: HochschulVerlag, 1977, Vol. III, pp. 7-28.

_____, J. B. Green, and J. Read. "A Model for the Description, Analysis, and Perhaps Evaluation of Bilingual Education," *Language in Sociology,* eds. Albert Verdoodt, and Rolf Kjolseth. Louvain: Editions Pector, 1976, pp. 233-263.

Language Dominance and Pedagogical Considerations

Arnulfo G. Ramírez

This paper reviews some of the previous attempts to assess the language abilities of children in English and Spanish and identifies some of the problems involved in such assessments, such as determining language dominance by surname only or by "free conversations." Zirkel's model of bilingualism is presented along with the Ramírez-Politzer dominance measure. This measure was designed to meet four basic requirements: (1) ability to measure productivity in primary grades and higher level grades, (2) use of an easy scoring system, (3) possibility of measuring Spanish and English comparably, and (4) provision of information on dominance by domain. An example of an individual's bilingual profile resulting from the dominance measure is provided, and pedagogical applications of dominance information are discussed.

U NTIL RECENTLY, the linguistic competence of Spanish/English bilingual pupils in the southwestern United States has been evaluated very subjectively. On a number of occasions these pupils have been classified as Spanish-speaking because of their Spanish surnames. Some have been labeled bilingual because they speak both languages, and some have even been called "alingual" because their English is ungrammatical and their "Spanish is of such an inferior quality that it does not warrant classification as a language" (Carter, 1970, pp. 52-53).

Concrete attempts to judge the language proficiency of bilingual pupils have usually taken the "free conversation approach" in which the tester carries on a natural conversation in English and Spanish with the pupil and then decides on the pupil's degree of bilingualism, or more specifically, on the control of English on the basis of accent, fluency, and the amount of Spanish intrusion. Approaches such as this one do not provide the teacher with a realistic assessment of the total language competence of the bilingual pupil nor do they compare the pupil's relative proficiency in the two languages.

Assessing Language Dominance

The implementation of bilingual education programs has necessitated the development of tests that allow one to assess the language abilities of young children in English (see Appendix, Brengelman and Manning, 1964) and Spanish. In general, it has been simpler to construct easily scored, reliable tests that measure auditory comprehension (see Appendix, Carrow, 1973; Cervenka, 1967) than to develop tests of language production.

One of the most ambitious attempts to measure the language production of bilingual children was undertaken in conjunction with the development of the *Michigan Oral Language Productive Tests* (see Appendix, American Council on the Teaching of Foreign Language, 1970). A discrete-item production test was devised using a combination of pictorial and verbal cues that elicits specific features of standard English grammar missed by speakers of nonstandard dialects and speakers whose dominant language is Spanish. The test is designed for use in kindergarten through the early grade levels. Because of the difficulty of eliciting the expected response by a combination of pictorial and verbal stimuli, the test does require a fairly complex scoring system. It has been criticized for its use of pictorial cues (such as a fishing pole) that may be outside the cultural experience of many children, thus influencing the results.

Burt, Dulay, and Hernández-Chávez (1974), who criticized the *Michigan Oral Language Productive Test*, developed a promising test, the *Bilingual Syntax Measure* (see Appendix). This test primarily assesses the syntactic complexity of sentences produced by children in English and Spanish, and children from kindergarten to the third grade have been tested. Like the *Michigan Oral Language Productive Test*, the *Bilingual Syntax Measure* relies on a combination of pictorial and verbal cues to elicit certain English and Spanish constructions. The choice of constructions is influenced by the sequence in which grammatical morphemes appear in first-language acquisition (Brown, 1973). However, any appropriate response is accepted and analyzed according to a formula that establishes a ratio between the semantic feature used in the child's response and the corresponding adult version, as well as a ratio between the functors used by the child and those that would be used by an adult who speaks standard English or Spanish. The test promises to be a useful research instrument, although again, the scoring system appears rather complex.

The problem of complex scoring procedures for unpredictable responses also besets other bilingual language tests that combine assessments of cognitive and language development in elementary school children. Thus, the language section of the *Language-Cognition Test* (see Appendix, Stemmler, 1967) relies on analyzing the subject's responses according to

basic sentence types, fundamental transformations, type-of-verb constructions, and adjectival usage.

The sociolinguistic concept of domains was introduced recently to tests
(Fishman, 1972). Some evaluators have used children's ability to name
words associated with different spheres of activity such as home, neighborhood, church, and school (see Appendix, Cohen, 1975). A test for oral
proficiency that recognizes different domains has been used in New
Mexico schools in bilingual education programs (see Appendix, Spolsky *et
al.*, 1972). This particular test, however, is designed for general classification rather than precise testing and uses a rating-scale evaluation of communicative competence and self-reporting on the part of the student. It is
not a scorable discrete-item instrument as represented by Manuel's (1950,
see Appendix) *Cooperative Inter-American Tests — Tests of Language
Usage/Pruebas Cooperativas Interamericanas — Pruebas de Uso del Lenguaje.* This latter instrument, however, does not directly test and score the
production of language, nor do its three subscores (active vocabulary,
expression, and total) relate in any way to the question of dominance by
domain.

Depicting Language Dominance

Assessing the relative proficiency of a Spanish/English bilingual pupil
implies an understanding of the concept of bilingualism. Zirkel (1974)
offers a schematic diagram that defines bilingualism in a matrix-like manner and serves as a conceptual model for the determination and depiction of
language dominance (see Figure 1).

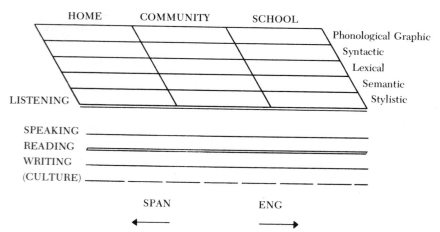

Figure 1. REPRESENTATION OF BILINGUAL DOMINANCE MATRIX
(Zirkel, 1974, p. 12)

Zirkel (1974) describes the diagram shown in Figure 1 as follows:

> The four basic language skills and the cultural substratum are rep-
> resented as a series of continua which are interrelated to the sociolin-
> guistic domains and linguistic levels within a three-dimensional ma-
> trx [*sic*]. Each continuum can be constituted of quantifiable units in
> Spanish and English depending on the dominance measure that is
> utilized. Each dimension could be further analyzed and segmented
> (e.g., listening skill into comprehension and phonetic discrimination;
> speaking skill into pronunciation, intonation, etc.). (p. 12)

Zirkel (1974) notes the complex nature of bilingualism as shown by his
formulation. To illustrate how language dominance information could be
used in the school, he asks the reader to focus at the level of "LISTENING"
(Figure 1) to depict the aural bilingual dominance of first-grade pupils
based on scores of parallel tests of English and Spanish on the Inter-
American Oral vocabulary (Level I) subtest, each test consisting of 25
items.

The pupil's relative degree of bilingualism in terms of aural comprehension can be plotted on a two-dimensional chart, with one dimension
depicting the score on the 25-item Spanish test and the other depicting the
score on the parallel English version (Figure 2). Pupils A1, A2, and A3 can
be classified as Spanish dominant due to their higher scores on the Spanish
test. Pupils B1, B2, and B3 can be referred to as "balanced" bilinguals —
pupil B1 exhibiting a "lower" degree of "balance" than pupil B2 and pupil
B3 having a "higher" degree of "balance" than pupils B2 and B1. Pupils C1,
C2, and C3 can be described as English dominant due to their higher
scores on the English version of the test.

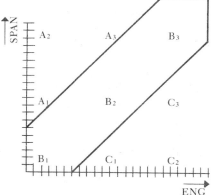

Figure 2. DEPICTION OF AURAL BILINGUAL DOMINANCE:
     SAMPLE CHART
       A = Spanish Dominant   B = Transitional   C = English Dominant
       B3 = Equilingual (or balanced bilingual)
     (Zirkel, 1974, p. 14)

RESULTS OF FIRST GRADE SAMPLE ON PARALLEL O.V. SUBTEST
[INTER-AMERICAN ORAL VOCABULARY]

Pupil	Spanish Score	English Score	Difference Score	Dominance Category
1. Adolfo Jimenez	14	12	+ 2	B
2. Maria Requena	13	5	+ 8	A
3. Alberto Hernandez	6	16	−10	C
4. Cesar Cruz	7	6	+ 1	B
5. Juanita Pizarro	25	17	+ 8	A
6. Etc.				

Zirkel (1974, p. 14) suggests that by using the approach depicted in Figure 2, pupils 1 and 4 could be described as "balanced" bilinguals and could be placed in a traditional (monolingual) English class; pupils 2 and 5 are Spanish dominant and could be placed in a Spanish-dominant class, establishing initial literacy in Spanish; and pupil 3 is English dominant and might have to be taught Spanish as a second language.

The notion of parallel language tests used to depict language dominance has been extended beyond the level of "listening" by researchers at the Center for Educational Research at Stanford (see Appendix, Ramírez, et al., 1976). The CERAS Spanish/English Balance Test was designed with four requirements in mind:

1. The ability to measure productive ability not only in the primary grades but also at higher levels.
2. The possibility of an easy scoring system.
3. The possibility of measuring Spanish and English comparably, thus demonstrating an imbalance in favor of either language.
4. The possibility of giving information concerning dominance by domains (e.g., home, neighborhood, church, school). (Sociolinguistic research has amply demonstrated that knowledge of vocabulary varies according to domain in practically every bilingual speaker. A "general test" of vocabulary knowledge is thus likely to give a fragmentary and probably biased picture of the real language ability of a bilingual speaker.)

The test battery includes parallel Spanish and English versions of (1) a 12-item Pretest, (2) a 32-item Vocabulary-by-Domain Test consisting of four sections — Home, Neighborhood, Church, and School — of eight items each, and (3) a 32-item Grammar Production Test requiring ten different grammatical operations (e.g., change from singular to plural, from affirmative to negative, and from indirect to direct question). A bilingual profile can be established for each pupil on the basis of the pupil's performance on the Vocabulary-by-Domain Test and the Grammar Production Test. These two tests could reveal language dominance according to the four sociolinguistic domains and the relative ability to handle important grammatical operations in the two languages. Figure 3 exemplifies an individual bilingual profile based on the results from both tests:

Vocabulary-by-Domain Test

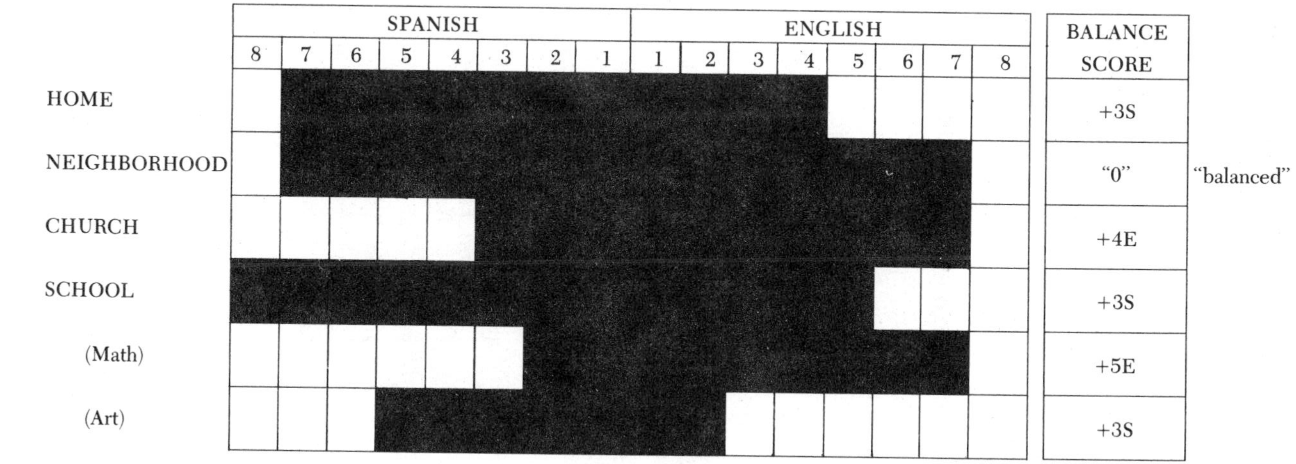

	SPANISH								ENGLISH								BALANCE SCORE
	8	7	6	5	4	3	2	1	1	2	3	4	5	6	7	8	
HOME																	+3S
NEIGHBORHOOD																	"0"
CHURCH																	+4E
SCHOOL																	+3S
(Math)																	+5E
(Art)																	+3S

"balanced"

Grammar Test

Grammar Production Test

CATEGORY	I			II					III		IV				V			VI			VII		VIII			IX			X				WC	NA	T
ITEM	1	2	3	4	5	6	7	8	9	10	11	12	13	14	15	16	17	18	19	20	21	22	23	24	25	26	27	28	29	30	31	32			
S	+	+	√	+	+	+	+	+	+	+	+	+	+	+	+	√	+	+	+	+	+	+	+	+	+	+	+	+	+	+	+	+	28	2	30
E	+	+	+	+	+	+	√	+	+	+	+	+	+	+	+	+	+	+	+	√	+	+	+	+		+	+	+	+	+	+	+	19	2	21

+ = correct   √ = acceptable
NC = Not correct   NA = Not acceptable   T = Total

Figure 3. BILINGUAL PROFILE

Although the concept of vocabulary-by domain presently includes the school domain without relating it to any specific subject matter area, the concept could be used to incorporate the lexicon of content areas such as math, science, social science, humanities, and the arts.

The use of parallel language tests appears to be a useful method for determining and depicting the language dominance of bilingual pupils. However, parallelism in certain sociolinguistic domains may eliminate important elements of cultural differences (e.g., parent/child interaction, parent/parent interaction, work activities in the home, and recreation) that can probably be reflected linguistically but cannot be measured with identical vocabulary items (see Appendix, Ramírez and Politzer, 1975).

Pedagogical Applications of Language Dominance

Educators concerned with bilingual instructional approaches cannot afford to ignore the pedagogical consequences of dominance patterns among bilingual pupils and how these patterns can be altered through curricular design. The most direct application of language dominance information appears to be in the area of literacy. Will a child learn to read more rapidly in the second language if instruction in reading is initially given in the first language? While this question may still be open to debate, many researchers voice opinions similar to the 1953 UNESCO resolution that states as axiomatic that the mother tongue of the pupil is the best medium for teaching reading. A second issue closely associated with literacy centers on the rate that educationally-related skills are learned in the vernacular versus in the second language. Will the child achieve greater general knowledge of other subject matter areas in the second language if instruction is first given in the native language? Results in this area are not in agreement. In math, for example, Treviño (1968) found that Spanish/English-speaking children learned mathematics more effectively if presented bilingually, as did Giles (1969) in Canada with French/English bilinguals. However, Macnamara (1966) found in his Irish study that children's inability to grasp the second language prevented their understanding of more complex reasoning problems associated with arithmetic and recommended that teaching be conducted in the stronger language. Saville and Troike (1971), on the other hand, recommend the teaching of mathematics in the second language.

Language-dominance information can be of practical use to the teacher in making instructional decisions. Zamora (1974) notes that:

> Central to the teaching-learning process are the decisions that a teacher makes — what level of reader a student will read; what math group he will be placed in. . . . Pedagogically, then the crucial issue

> is to make the appropriate *match* or *fit* between the child's dominant
> language and the curriculum. (p. 13)

Although language dominance patterns may seem useful for diagnostic
(placement) purposes and even for measuring change in the dominance
configuration caused by the effects of a particular language program or
curricular design, the language dominance test *per se* will not provide the
curriculum planner all the information needed to decide which content
areas will be taught in which language. When administered to a group of
students at one grade level or to the entire school population, the language
dominance test will be useful inasmuch as the results can serve as an
instructional planning resource.[1]

The criteria for the selection of the content areas and the language
allocation are not always clear. Saville-Troike (1976) uses an argument that
can be called utilitarian in nature when she discusses the teaching of math
and science:

> The decision is often based on available materials in each language,
> especially in intermediate and upper grades. Because mathematics
> and science content is almost always taught in English at advanced
> levels in this country, it is probably best also to use these domains as
> the content for English instruction in the primary grades, so that
> adequate vocabulary for advanced study of these subjects in English
> will be developed. (p. 133)

Cazden *et al.* (1974) uses a domain-free (context-independent) criterion in
selecting science as a curriculum area for second-language development:

> . . . a science program for children which involves both the manipu-
> lation of concrete materials, and then a colloquim in which teachers
> guide children's talk into more and more explicit descriptions of what
> they did and found out, will have a significant effect on the children's
> general referential communication skills when tested experimentally
> out of the science context — e.g. in a two-person communication
> game.
>
> . . . The underlying assumption is that the rules of language usage
> may be learned best by being used in natural communication con-
> texts. Furthermore, the value neutrality of science content and scien-
> tific terminology may be an additional asset in facilitating classroom
> communications. . . . (pp. 16-17)

---

[1]See Appendix A for a class profile established on the basis of pupil performance on the
Grammar Production Subtest (Reduced Version — 20 items) of the *CERAS Spanish/English
Balance Test.*

Bowen (1974) argues:

> . . . that education in any sufficient language is possible, and that the
> choice of the language medium (or media) should be made on the
> basis of psychological or social criteria and not necessarily limited to
> native or strongest language. (p. 14)

Thus, the dichotomy of domain-free and domain-sensitive content areas
may have to be considered more closely. If bilingualism is to be based on
domain-sensitive distribution of the two languages in agreement with the
community's observed behavior and/or ethnic ecology, subject areas such
as social studies, art, and music may be taught in the non-dominant
language and the remainder in the dominant language. However, Jacobson
(1975) reminds us of the shortcomings of such a scheme:

> If the language distribution is culture-conditioned, the student ac-
> quires literate competency in one language to deal with certain
> subjects and in the other language to deal with others. Taken in its
> extreme form, such a program would train children to discuss topics
> related to, say, social studies only in Spanish but not in English and to
> discuss science and math problems in English and not in Spanish. (p.
> 133)

To offer bilingual students a more balanced proficiency in their two languages, Jacobson (1975) suggests the use of a code-alternation teaching
strategy:

> The teacher will . . . teach content once by ably shifting from one to
> the other language. She will avoid compartmentalization and have
> her children approach every aspect of content in both languages,
> stressing at the same time the interactional norms as implemented in
> the community in order for the children to learn how one selects the
> appropriate code for each situation. (p. 134)

The following example dealing with subtraction with numbers illustrates
the technique:

> T: How much is "twenty" minus "eight"?
> S: "Twelve."
> T: And "eighteen" minus "six"?
> S: Also "twelve."
> T: "Twelve" is "*doce*" in Spanish, isn't it?
> S: *Si, maestra.*
> T: *¿Y qué otra palabra puedo usar en vez de "doce" y hablar de la
>   misma cantidad?*
> S: *Una, docena.*

T: *¿Cuántos hay en una docena?*
S: *Doce.*
T: And in half a dozen?
S: Six
   etc.   (Jacobson, 1975, pp. 134-135)

Changing the Language Dominance Configuration

Changing the language dominance configuration of bilinguals at the junior and high school levels may be a radically different proposition from changing dominance patterns of bilinguals at the elementary school level. Adolescents are cognitively superior to elementary school children and are capable of abstract thought, able to grasp the concept of nation, and able to sense and experience group pride. Elkind (1970) notes that adolescents' ability to reason about mental constructions influences their behavior particularly in the area of self-consciousness. Language-related matters may be very important to adolescents. Sociolinguistic questions such as "Who says what, to whom, when, and why?" may intrigue adolescents, and an awareness of the domain-sensitive distribution of the two languages in their home, community, region, and nation may affect their attitude toward their language dominance pattern. Research related to second-language acquisition often cites attitudes and resultant motivations as "important sources of data for theories of second language learning . . ." (Oller and Richards, 1973, p. 233). Gardner (1973) makes these conclusions:

> First, it seems clear that attitudinal-motivational characteristics of the student are important in the acquisition of a second language. Secondly, the nature of these characteristics suggests that a truly successful student (i.e., one who will acquire communicational facility with the language) is motivated to become integrated with the other language community. Thirdly, this integrative motive appears to derive from the attitudinal characteristics in the home and must be fostered by an accepting attitude, by the parents, concerning the other language group. And finally, the process of second language acquisition involves taking on behavioral characteristics of the other language community and the fact that the child will experience resistance from himself and pressures from his own cultural community. (pp. 244-245)

To what extent the attitudinal-motivational factors that appear to be crucial to second-language learning affect adolescent bilingual pupils is not always clear. In one sense, they may not have to learn a second language because they are already bilingual. Their relative proficiency in two languages may vary in that they may have control of all four language skills in English and only listening and comprehension skills in Spanish. The Spanish that Spanish/English bilingual pupils control may not be the same as that taught in the classroom or as that found in school texts.

Depending on a number of factors (e.g., career goals, perceived usefulness of the first and second languages, attitude toward local varieties of language, and motivation to change local allocation of the two languages), adolescent bilinguals may decide to change their language dominance through language study and/or through language study via certain content areas.

In terms of the languages used in the community and the relative status of the two languages at the level of city, region, or nation, it might be useful to classify school subjects into three areas:

1. *domain-free* (e.g., science)
2. *domain-sensitive* (e.g., social studies, music, and art)
3. *career-oriented* (e.g., business and health sciences)

Language instruction could also be classified into two areas:
A. *domain-free*   (e.g., "global knowledge of the language without specifying the particular contexts or functions for which the target language is to be used. . . ." (Cooper and Fishman, 1974, p. 248)
B. *domain-sensitive* (e.g., "realistically contextualized material" which specify "the contexts and purposes for which the student is going to use the target language. . . ." (Cooper and Fishman, 1974, pp. 248, 252)

Keeping in mind all the factors that might affect the language dominance of an individual bilingual (e.g., place of birth, language usage at home, attitude toward the two languages, and opportunity to use the two languages in the greater community), changes in the language dominance configuration brought about by a specific curricular design could be illustrated as shown in Figure 4:

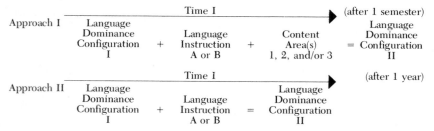

Figure 4. CHANGES IN ADOLESCENT LANGUAGE-DOMINANCE CONFIGURATION

Tucker (1974) argues that a student following instructional Approach I could develop a higher level of proficiency in the second language than a student who follows Approach II, a traditional second-language program that does not include content material. He further claims that:

> The theoretical rationale for such an approach is that the student can most effectively acquire a second language when the task of language learning becomes incidental to the task of communicating with someone (such as a teacher who is usually not a SL specialist but rather a native speaker of the target language) about something (such as geography) which is inherently interesting to the student. (p. 105)

For the Spanish/English bilingual pupil, Approach I might mean rapid development of specific language registers and technical vocabulary associated with certain content areas (e.g., science, social studies, and business). Approach II, which includes domain-sensitive language study, would give the bilingual student the possibility of changing his language-dominance patterns within certain sociolinguistic parameters (e.g., language and topics related to the home, neighborhood, recreation, and work).

Appendix A

Teacher _____   School _____

Grade _____   Date _____

CLASS PROFILE OF BILINGUAL PUPILS

Grammar Production Sub-Test

Grammatical Category

		I		II		III		IV		V		VI		VII		VIII		IX		X		NC	NA	T
		1	2	3	4	5	6	7	8	9	10	11	12	13	14	15	16	17	18	19	20	NC	NA	T
1	S	+	+	+	√	+	√	+	+	√	√	+	+	+	+	√	√	−	√	−	−	10	7	17
	E	+	+	−	−	√	−	√	−	−	√	+	√	+	+	√	√	−	−	−	√	5	7	12
2	S	√	+	+	√	+	√	+	−	−	−	+	√	−	√	−	−	−	−	√	−	5	6	11
	E	+	√	+	√	+	√	+	√	√	√	+	+	+	+	√	√	√	√	+	√	9	11	20
3	S	+	+	+	+	√	+	√	√	+	+	+	+	√	√	+	+	√	√	+	√	12	18	20
	E	+	+	+	√	√	+	+	√	√	−	+	√	√	√	+	+	+	+	√	+	11	8	19
4	S	√	√	+	√	√	√	+	√	√	+	√	+	+	√	+	+	√	√	√	√	7	13	20
	E	+	+	√	√	−	√	−	−	√	−	+	+	√	√	−	−	−	−	−	−	4	6	10
5	S	+	√	√	+	+	+	+	√	√	√	+	+	+	+	√	+	√	√	√	√	10	10	20
	E	+	+	+	√	+	√	+	√	√	+	+	√	+	+	−	+	−	−	√		10	6	16
6	S	+	√	√	+	+	+	+	+	+	√	+	+	√	√	+	√	√	√	+	+	12	8	20
	E	√	√	√	−	−	+	√	√	−	−	−	−	−	−	−	−	−	−	−		0	5	5
7	S	√	√	−	−	−	−	−	−	−	−	−	−	−	−	−	−	−	−	−		0	2	2
	E	+	√	√	+	+	√	√	+	√	√	√	√	√	+	+	+	+	√	+	√	9	11	20
8	S	√	√	+	+	+	+	+	√	√	√	√	+	+	−	+	√	−	−	−		9	7	16
	E	+	+	+	+	+	+	√	√	√	+	√	√	√	√	√	+	+	−	−	−	9	8	17
9	S	+	+	√	√	+	+	−	−	−	−	−	−	−	−	−	−	√	−	√		4	4	8
	E	+	+	+	√	√	+	√	√	√	√	+	+	+	+	+	+	+	+	+	√	13	7	20
10	S	•	•	•																				
	E	•	•	•																				
11	S	•	•	•																				
	E	•	•	•																				
12	S	•	•	•																				
	E	•	•	•																				
13	S	•	•	•																				
	E	•	•	•																				
14	S	•	•	•																				
	E	•	•	•																				

+ = "Correct"   √ = "Acceptable"   − = "Incorrect"

NC = No. correct   NA = No. acceptable   T = Total

Appendix A

CLASS PROFILE OF BILINGUAL PUPILS
Performance on the Grammar Production Test
According to "Levels"

(Spanish/English Ratio)

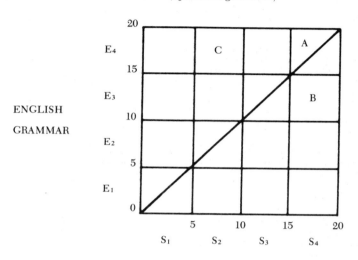

ENGLISH

GRAMMAR

Pupil A
S_4E_4

Pupil B
S_4E_3

Pupil C
S_2E_4

SPANISH GRAMMAR

With this approach, both degree of "balance" and level of performance can be expressed. A subscript can be used to indicate the level (e.g., Spanish (S_3), English $(E_2) = S_3E_2$).

APPENDIX
Tests

American Council on the Teaching of Foreign Language. *Michigan Oral Language Productive Tests*. New York: Modern Language Association Publications Center, 1970.

Brengelman, Frederick H., and J. C. Manning. *Linguistic Capacity Index*. Austin: Southwest Educational Development Laboratory, 1964. (No longer available commercially.)

Burt, Marina K., Heidi C. Dulay, and Eduardo Hernández-Chávez. *The Bilingual Syntax Measure*. New York: Harcourt Brace Jovanovich, 1974.

Carrow, E. *Test for Auditory Comprehension*. Austin: Educational Concepts, 1973.

Cervenka, Edward J. *The Measurement of Bilingualism and Bicultural Socialization of the Child in the School Setting: The Development of Instruments*. Section VI, *Final Report on Head Start Evaluation and Research: 1966-1967* (Contract No. 66-1), to the Institute for Educational Development, by the Staff and Study Directors: Child Development Evaluation and Research Center. Austin: The University of Texas at Austin, August 31, 1967. (Mimeographed.)

Cohen, Andrew D. *A Sociolinguistic Approach to Bilingual Education: Experiments in the American Southwest*. Rowley: Newbury House, 1975.

Manuel, Hershel T. *Cooperative Inter-American Tests – Tests of Language Usage/ Pruebas Cooperativas Interamericanas – Pruebas de Uso del Lenguaje*. Princeton: Cooperative Test Division, Educational Testing Service, 1950.

Ramírez, Arnulfo G., and Robert L. Politzer. "Development of Spanish/English Bilingualism in a Dominant Spanish-Speaking Environment," *Atisbos* (Summer, 1975), 31-52.

_____, et al. *CERAS Spanish/English Balance Test*. Stanford: Center for Educational Research at Stanford, 1976. (To be published by the National Dissemination and Assessment Center, Los Angeles.)

Spolsky, Bernard, Penny Murphy, Wayne Holm, and Allen Ferrel. "Three Functional Tests of Oral Proficiency," *TESOL Quarterly*, VI (September, 1972), 221-235.

Stemmler, Anne O. "The LCT, Language-Cognition Test (Research Edition) — A Test for Educationally Disadvantaged School Beginners, *TESOL Quarterly*, I (December, 1967), 35-43.

REFERENCES

Bowen, J. Donald. "Measuring Language Dominance in Bilinguals." Vol. VIII. *U.C.L.A. Work Papers in Teaching English as a Second Language*, June, 1974, pp. 13-33.

Brown, Roger W. *A First Language; The Early Stages*. Cambridge: Harvard University Press, 1973.

Carter, Thomas P. *Mexican-Americans in School: A History of Educational Neglect*. New York: College Entrance Examination Board, 1970.

Cazden, Courtney B., et al. *Teaching as a Linguistic Process in a Cultural Setting*. Panel Report 5. National Institute of Education Conference on Studies in Teaching, 1974.

Cooper, Robert L., and Joshua A. Fishman. "The Sociology of Second Language Learning and Teaching," *A Sociology of Bilingual Education*, ed. Joshua A. Fishman. Final Report. (Contract No. OECO-73-0588), to the Division of Foreign Studies, Department of Health, Education, and Welfare, United States Office of Education, 1974.

Elkind, David. *Children and Adolescents; Interpretive Essay on Jean Piaget*. New York: Oxford University Press, 1970.

Fishman, Joshua A. *The Sociology of Language: An Interdisciplinary Social Science Approach to Language in Society*. Rowley: Newbury House Publishers, 1972.

Gardner, R. C. "Sociocultural Aspects of Language Study," *Focus on the Learner; Pragmatic Perspective for the Language Teacher*, eds. John W. Oller, Jr., and Jack C. Richards. Rowley: Newbury House Publishers, 1973, pp. 246-250.

Giles, W. H. "Mathematics in Bilingualism: A Pragmatic Approach," *ISA Bulletin*, LV (1969), 19-26.

Jacobson, Rodolfo. "The Dilemma of Bilingual Education Models: Duplication or Compartmentalization," *New Directions in Second Language Learning, Teaching and Bilingual Education*, eds. Marina K. Burt, and Heidi C. Dulay. Washington: TESOL, Georgetown University, 1975, 123-138.

Macnamara, John T. *Bilingualism and Primary Education: A Study of Irish Experience*. Edinburgh: Edinburgh University Press, 1966.

Oller, John W., Jr., and Jack C. Richards, eds. *Focus on the Learner; Pragmatic Perspective for the Language Teacher*. Rowley: Newbury House Publishers, Inc., 1973.

Saville, Muriel R., and Rudolph C. Troike. *A Handbook of Bilingual Education*. Washington: Teachers of English to Speakers of Other Languages, 1971.

Saville-Troike, Muriel. *Foundations for Teaching English as a Second Language: Theory and Method for Multicultural Education*. Englewood Cliffs: Prentice Hall, 1976.

Treviño, Bertha A. G. "An Analysis of the Effectiveness of a Bilingual Program in the Teaching of Mathematics in the Primary Grades," *Dissertation Abstracts*. Vol. XXVIVA, Part I. Austin: The University of Texas at Austin, 1968, p. 521-A to 522-A.

Tucker, G. Richard. "Methods of Second-Language Teaching," *The Canadian Modern Language Review* (Special Number: Bilingualism in Education), XXXI, No. 2 (1974), 102-107.

UNESCO. *The Use of Vernacular Languages in Education*. Monograph on Fundamental Education, No. 8. Paris: UNESCO, 1953.

Zamora, Gloria. "When Spanish is the Native Language." Paper presented at the American Anthropological Association Convention, Mexico City, November, 1974.

Zirkel, Perry A. "A Method for Determining and Depicting Language Dominance," *TESOL Quarterly*, VIII, No. 1 (March, 1974), 7-16.

Some Criteria to Assess Spanish Reading Instructional Materials

Dr. Cornejo's intent is to assist bilingual and monolingual teachers to become more effective instructors when working with the bilingual child by presenting criteria for the selection of Spanish Reading Instructional Materials.

A general discussion concerning the background of the evaluation of reading instructional materials is presented along with a very detailed example of the kinds of considerations that should go into the evaluation of programs as well as materials.

Ricardo J. Cornejo

THE BILINGUAL Education Act of 1967 (Title VII) provided funds for projects to meet the "special educational needs of children who have limited English-speaking ability, who come from environments where the dominant language is one other than English, and who come from low income families" (HEW, 1971, p. 1).

The Act funded local school districts with a high concentration of students speaking languages other than English as their home language. The main emphasis of Title VII has been to make funds available to "exemplary pilot or demonstration projects in bilingual bicultural education" (HEW, 1971, p. 5).

The main goals of these bilingual/bicultural programs have been not only the "cognitive goals of increasing students' competence in both their dominant language and English, but also the affective goals of building self-esteem and pride in both cultures" (HEW, 1971, p. 5).

All Title VII projects have four basic components:

1. instructional program
2. acquisition, adaptation, and development of materials
3. staff development
4. community involvement

This presentation is concerned with component 2, acquisition, adaptation, and development of materials, and specifically, with criteria to select instructional programs to teach Spanish/English reading in bilingual classrooms.

The effectiveness of instructional materials is a key factor in the success or failure of programs in bilingual education. Materials being used in bilingual instruction are supposed to be innovative, unique, and replicable.

It is of the utmost importance that educators and evaluators determine to what extent curriculum components are effective, relevant, and valid in terms of producing specified changes in learners.

The specialists in educational evaluation are becoming increasingly aware of the proliferation of instructional materials in bilingual education. In the last three years more than 100 Spanish reading programs have reached the education market. Among these programs are some that are highly sophisticated, others that are only acceptable, quite a few that are mediocre, and a large number whose existence should make us question why they were written and what motivated people to buy them.

The large number of instructional programs to teach reading in Spanish would lead us to believe that a highly competitive market would increase the quality of the products. Very often, however, the most popular programs are not those with the best content, but those produced by publishers with a highly sophisticated marketing system. Thus, because of the highly diversified quality and quantity of Spanish reading programs it is necessary to determine some criteria to evaluate their effectiveness. As stated by Alkin and Woolley (1970):

> Evaluation is the process of ascertaining the decision areas of concern, selecting appropriate information and collecting and analyzing information in order to report summary data useful to decision-makers in selecting among alternatives.

In line with this definition of evaluation, this paper attempts to offer some criteria to decision-makers for their use in analyzing Spanish reading programs. They are offered in the hope that they will help in the identification of high quality reading materials or in determining the value of those materials already being used by the bilingual programs. Stufflebeam (1973) stated:

> If decision-makers are to make maximum, legitimate use of their opportunities, they must make sound decisions regarding the alternatives available to them. To do this, they must know what alternatives are available and be capable of making sound judgments about the relative merits of the alternatives.

Stufflebeam reinforces the basic concept that decision-makers should have access to reliable data in order to make intelligent decisions about the educational enterprise. As noted by the author, very often these decisions may be shaded by vested interests and various types of biases. Stufflebeam's (1973) reasoning is summarized as follows:

1. the quality of programs depends upon the quality of decisions in and about the programs;
2. the quality of decisions depends upon decision-makers' abilities to identify the alternatives which comprise decision situations and to make sound judgments of these alternatives;
3. making sound judgments requires timely access to valid and reliable information pertaining to the alternatives;
4. the availability of such information requires systematic means to provide it; and
5. the processes necessary for providing this information for decision-making collectively comprise the concept of evaluation. (p. 21)

Providing information to decision-makers does not necessarily mean that this information will be used. The usability of information poses several questions, as noted by Alkin *et al.* (1974):

> Which kinds of evaluative information are useful and which are not? Which kinds of information could be useful but are nevertheless rejected? Which decision-makers actually use evaluative findings to guide decision or policy making and which ignore them or use them only as a matter of form? Under what conditions is evaluation useful and under what conditions is it not useful?

Since the passing of the Bilingual Education Act there has been a proliferation of bilingual materials all over the country. Some institutions and some individuals have made a sincere effort to create innovative curricula for bilingual children; others have revised extant materials (sometimes the revision has not gone beyond changing a dull cover for a brighter one); others have copied extensively from materials from other countries.

How then, can we decide if a reading program is appropriate for bilingual children? A reading program for bilingual children should have, at least, the following general categories identified and adequately presented:

1. Authentic language patterns
2. Appropriate motivational devices
3. Cultural input
4. Sequential development of reading skills
5. Correlation of reading skills in both languages
6. Illustrations representing various cultural groups interacting with target groups

7. Readability according to reading skills of bilingual children
8. Provision for individual differences (bilinguality)
9. A philosophical framework in accordance with current theory and research on bilingualism
10. Content that takes into consideration students' experiences and interests
11. A sound correlation between students' language and language presented in the curriculum
12. Appropriate methods, approaches, and classroom management techniques

Specifically, in assessing Spanish reading materials, several questions need to be addressed.

In the context of this paper, the term "Spanish reading program" refers to a specific curriculum unit, such as the BOLAR system, the Santillana Bilingual Series, the Método Onomatopéyico, the Cartilla Fonética, the Por el Mundo del Cuento y la Aventura, and the Mi Escuela Program.

The following evaluation instrument is a sample of the kinds of considerations that should go into the evaluation of a bilingual program and curriculum materials.

Evaluation of the Instructional Program

A. Identification

1. Title of Program: _____

_____

2. Author(s) or Developer(s): _____

_____

3. Publisher, Location: _____

_____

4. Copyright year: _____

B. Contents and Levels

   1. Subject Matter: _____

        _____

   2. Educational Level(s) (Primary, Intermediate, Secondary, etc.): _____

        _____

   3. Grade Level(s):_____

        _____

C. Author's Rationale for Design and Development of Program:

_____

_____

_____

_____

_____

_____

_____

	Yes	No	No basis for judgment
D. Specific Item Analysis			
1. Assessment			
a. Does the program provide assessment devices?			
b. Are the assessment devices reliable?			
c. Are the assessment devices valid?			
d. Does the program meet standards established by prospective users?			
2. Population to Use the Program			
a. Does the program indicate the intended population?			
b. Could the program be used by populations other than the intended one?			
c. Does the program indicate the age level of students the materials are to serve?			
d. Does the program consider students' interests in its content material and presentation method?			
3. Goals and Objectives			
a. Are the goals stated in terms of a particular educational philosophy?			
b. Does that philosophy represent the ideals of the community whose children will use the program?			
c. Are the objectives clearly stated?			
d. Does the content of the program meet the stated objectives?			
e. Does the assessment component measure these objectives?			
4. Student Activities			
a. Does the program provide effective activities for:			
(1) motivation			
(2) practice			
(3) review			
(4) reinforcement			
(5) follow-up			
(6) enrichment			
5. Classroom Management			
a. Does the program provide activities for:			
(1) group work			
(2) individual work			
(3) a variety of reading techniques			

	Yes	No	No basis for judgment
6. Validation of the Program			
a. Was the program designed according to accepted theories and principles?			
b. Was the program:			
(1) design tested			
(2) pilot tested			
(3) field tested			
(4) validated for a particular population?			
7. Cost Effectiveness			
a. Is the program feasible to implement in terms of costs?			
b. Is the actual cost within the range of the school's financial capacity?			
c. Is the relative cost exorbitant?			
(1) Are there consumable materials that need to be bought every year?			
(2) Are the consumables expensive?			
(3) Are there media materials that could be used for a long period of time?			
(4) Are the teacher's manuals inexpensive?			
(5) Are the materials designed to last?			
8. Language			
a. Does the program consider children's language?			
b. Are skills presented by using language patterns with which children would identify?			
c. Does the program offer dialectal varieties of the language?			
d. Are the materials developed for children representing one particular dialect?			
e. Are the idiomatic expressions in the material appropriate for children who will use them?			
f. If there are slang expressions, are they appropriate for the children who will read them?			
g. Does the program provide examples of dialectal varieties?			
h. Does the program encourage recognition and acceptance of dialectal varieties?			
9. Scope and Sequence-Comprehensiveness			
a. Does the scope of basic pre-reading skills range to higher areas of affective and cognitive skills?			
b. Does the program lead the child from concrete to abstract thinking and reasoning?			

	Yes	No	No basis for judgment
10. Research			
a. Is the program based on research findings?			
b. Is the program based on current theory?			
c. Has the program itself been researched thoroughly?			
11. Method			
a. Does the program follow the procedures of one particular method?			
b. Is the method appropriate to the target audience?			
c. Are the procedures well organized?			
d. Are the techniques carefully delineated?			
e. Are activities in the program relevant to children?			
12. Domains			
a. Does the program offer activities for psychomotor development?			
b. Does the program provide activities for cognitive growth?			
13. Reading skills			
a. Are reading skills sequentially organized?			
b. Is there enough practice of reading skills?			
c. Is there a balance between decoding tasks and activities for comprehension?			
14. Authenticity			
a. Are the reading selections in the program authentic with respect to the language and culture of the children?			
b. Do the selections represent the reading interests of children?			
15. Physical attributes			
a. Is the format appropriate?			
b. Is the binding easy to handle by children?			
c. Is the size appropriate?			
d. Is the print size appropriate?			
16. Viability			
a. Is the program easy to use by inexperienced teachers?			
b. Could it be used by teaching associates?			
c. Could it be used by parents or volunteers?			

	Yes	No	No basis for judgment
17. Quality			
a. Does the program present quality in terms of content?			
b. Is the format appropriate?			
c. Are the illustrations clear and self-explanatory?			
18. Teacher creativity			
a. Does the program provide for teacher innovation?			
b. Does it give the teacher suggestions to prepare creative materials and activities?			
19. Literary quality			
a. Do the reading selections represent quality materials?			
b. Are the reading selections in the upper grade levels chosen from representative literary works?			
20. Continuum			
a. Is the program organized with respect to cognitive developmental cycles?			
b. Does the program provide a continuum from easy to difficult; from concrete to abstract?			
21. Readability			
a. Does the program offer reference to its readability?			
b. Is there a reference to levels of difficulty of the language used in the program?			
22. Vocabulary development			
a. Do the lessons provide a sequential vocabulary development?			
b. Does the vocabulary represent common, generic terminology?			
c. Does the vocabulary represent dialectal variants?			
23. Transfer of skills			
a. Are grapheme-phoneme correspondences in both languages treated appropriately?			
b. Is there an effort to sequence basic language skills in such a way that children transfer reading skills from one language to the other?			

	Yes	No	No basis for judgment
24. Components			
a. Does the program provide:			
(1) teacher's manuals			
(2) workbooks			
(3) readers			
(4) enrichment materials			
(5) audio materials			
(6) visual materials			
(7) audio-visual materials			
25. Motivation and interest			
a. Does the program provide motivational devices?			
b. Do the reading selections reflect children's interest?			
c. Does the program encourage students to read outside the classroom?			
d. Does the program encourage students to develop reading interests?			
26. Bilinguality			
a. Does the program encourage bilingual children to see their bilinguality as a cultural asset?			
b. Are value systems presented?			
c. Is there a reference to diverse cultural values?			
27. Teacher training component			
a. Does the program have a teacher training component?			
b. Does the teacher training component provide information about reading in bilingual settings?			
28. Correlation with content areas			
a. Does the program provide activities to correlate reading skills with other curricular areas?			
29. Review lessons			
a. Are there systematization and review units throughout the program?			
30. Cultural input			
a. Does the program provide insight into other cultural groups?			
b. Does the program foster appreciation, acceptance, and respect toward other cultural groups?			
c. Does the program present content that encourages negative ideas about other groups?			
d. Are the characters in the story stereotyped?			

	Yes	No	No basis for judgment
31. Methodology and instructional approach			
a. Does the program provide adequate methodological instructions?			
b. Are grapheme-phoneme correspondences handled according to basic reading principles?			
c. Is structural analysis handled according to the characteristics of the particular language?			
d. Does the program offer ideas to develop an extensive sight (reading) vocabulary?			
e. Does the program provide the teacher some basic information on child language development?			
32. Literary content			
a. Does the program present literary principles?			
b. Do literary selections represent contemporary views?			
c. Do the literary selections offer a variety of topics?			
d. Does the program encourage students' interest in the literature of their people?			
e. Does the program encourage students to have positive attitudes toward the literary works of authors belonging to their own cultural group?			
33. Verification			
a. Is factual information in the reading program accurate?			
34. Durability			
a. Is the quality of the paper and the binding good enough for the books to last for a reasonable period of time?			
35. Consumables			
a. Does the program have student materials that are consumable?			
36. Relevance			
a. Does the program offer cultural and linguistic experiences which are representative of and relevant to the cultural-linguistic target communities?			

	Yes	No	No basis for judgment
37. Stereotypes			
a. Do illustrations of human beings show ethnic groups in non-stereotyped caricatures?			
b. Are male and female characters presented in equally positive, active, and dynamic activities, rather than traditional stereotyped roles?			
c. Is the program free from:			
(1) cultural biases			
(2) sex biases			
(3) social biases			
(4) political biases			
(5) religious biases			
38. Final assessment and recommendation			
a. In the final analysis, would you recommend this program to teachers in your program?			

39. Rate the program as:
Excellent ☐   Good ☐ Average ☐
Mediocre ☐   Poor ☐
40. State reasons for the rating.

_____

_____

_____

_____

_____

If the variables specified in the preceding evaluation instrument are carefully considered *before* writing curriculum materials, then the chances are much greater that the results will be culturally, educationally, and linguistically appropriate. By following the format *after* the materials have been written in all phases of the evaluation, any errors which may have crept into the initial writing can be corrected in a *systematic* way on the basis of students' responses.

REFERENCES

Alkin, Marvin C., and Dale Woolley. *A Framework for Evaluation of TESOL Programs*. Los Angeles: Center for the Study of Evaluation, UCLA, April, 1970.

Alkin, Marvin C., Jacqueline Kosecoff, Carol Fitz-Gibbon, and Richard Seligman. *Evaluation and Decision Making: The Title VII Experience*. Los Angeles: Center for the Study of Evaluation, UCLA, CSE Monograph Series in Education No. 4, 1974.

Health, Education, and Welfare. *Title VII Manual for Grantees and Applicants*. Washington: Office of Education, 1971.

Stufflebeam, Daniel L. "Toward a Science of Educational Evaluation," *Educational Technology Review Series, Number 11: Evaluation of Education*. Englewood Cliffs: Education Technology Publications, 1973, pp. 20-27.

PART SIX

The National
Network for
Bilingual Education

New Hope for Bilingual Education Through the National Network

Ernest M. Bernal, Jr.

The National Network for Bilingual Education, funded in 1975, consists of Training Resource Centers, Materials Development Centers, and Dissemination and Assessment Centers. The roles and interrelationships of these centers to each other and to Local Education Agencies and Institutions of Higher Education are discussed, as are the functions of the centers in terms of research, development, and evaluation of bilingual education programs. The view is expressed that the Network should provide an integrated view of needs and priorities that can aid Federal funding agencies in their planning and in their ultimate coordination of field programs and basic and applied research programs.

THE NATIONAL Network of Centers for Bilingual Education was originally funded in July, 1975. Eighteen centers were originally selected, constituting a network of seven Training Resource Centers (TRCs), nine Materials Development Centers (MDCs), and two Dissemination and Assessment Centers (DACs).* Their activities, while complementary, are complex but are ultimately designed to service Elementary and Secondary Education Act Title VII projects in Local Education Agencies (LEAs). The Network was founded to increase the capabilities of LEA projects through direct services, improved educational materials and practices, and better program evaluation and pupil assessments.

The thrust of the Network resides clearly in service, research, development, and evaluation. This emphasis necessitates a strong research and development effort, with the LEA projects, teachers, and students firmly fixed as the consuming populations.

Each type of center has some unique functions; an examination of their fundamental interrelationships will provide an overview of the rationale behind the concept of the National Network of Centers for Bilingual Education.

---

*The number of centers increased to 32 in 1976-1977.

Training Resource Centers

The Training Resource Centers (TRCs) serve a clearly defined geographic area and provide all the immediate contacts between other types of centers and the LEA projects in their regions. The TRCs are primarily responsible for providing supportive services to bilingual/bicultural LEA education projects. In addition, they provide services to Institutes of Higher Education (IHEs). TRCs train LEA professional and paraprofessional staff and community members, provide programmatic assistance in planning, and are responsible for taking the materials developed by the MDCs and pilot testing them with cooperating LEA projects and state education agencies. They also maintain an array of bilingual materials available from the DACs so that LEA project personnel in their service region may examine them for possible purchase at cost.

Materials Development Centers

The Materials Development Centers (MDCs) were established to develop high-quality bilingual instructional materials for bilingual education programs in LEAs and IHEs, although other agencies, of course, will have access to them. Specifically, the MDCs develop bilingual/multicultural academic materials in the language of the target groups and bilingual/multicultural training packages for teachers, professionals, and paraprofessionals. The ideal arrangement for MDCs has been deemed by the Office of Bilingual Education (OBE) to be one in which no duplication of effort exists, that is, one in which each MDC has a non-overlapping scope of work in terms of content and grade levels. Thus, two MDCs, each of which is developing materials in the same language, will not address the same grades or subject matter.

MDCs have a strong research and development (R & D) orientation. They are principally responsible for meeting the needs of bilingual programs in specified language groups on a national scale where permitted by the geographic distribution of the language/ethnic group(s) that they address. MDCs conceptualize and design educational materials and strategies for a particular target population and conduct the design and pilot testing of these products so that they may be revised in the light of experience. Additionally, they may develop criterion-referenced tests to accompany the academic or staff training materials.

Design testing, viewed as a rather informal trial of initially designed material for the purpose of obtaining "cleanup" information and other forms of soft data, is characterized by a "hands on review" by students and teachers. Ordinarily, the MDC writing team is very close to this initial test, and the information is fed back in order to make revisions immediately. During this stage, it is not unusual for format as well as content changes to be undertaken and for certain conceptual modifications to be made, such as in the scope and sequence of a curriculum.

A pilot test provides both soft and hard data. Although the Dissemination and Assessment Centers (DACs) may be involved as consultants to the MDCs in the pilot test design, the primary responsibility for the pilot testing of these materials involves the MDC and various TRCs in its implementation. For this reason, MDCs are securing qualified evaluation personnel in addition to professional writing staff members. MDCs train the field personnel of the TRCs in the use of their materials so that they can ensure adequate implementation of these materials by teachers and others in bilingual school settings.

Pilot testing constitutes an intermediate step in development, and the results of these trials are shared among MDCs, TRCs, and DACs. After each step of testing the materials, revisions are made by the MDCs in preparation for the next stage of development.

Dissemination and Assessment Centers

Dissemination and Assessment Centers are responsible for providing a host of research, development, and evaluation (R, D & E) services to TRCs and MDCs. Because of the multitude of services provided by the DACs, their general functions and responsibilities are listed here in outline form:

A. Publication and Dissemination
   1. Assess and select for publication and regional dissemination primarily Title VII project-developed educational products.
   2. Publish and disseminate selected educational products nationally.
   3. Publish and disseminate reviews of educational and psychometric materials.
   4. Collect, publish, and disseminate general information on bilingual/multicultural education.

B. Needs Assessment
   1. Develop assessment instruments and procedures for their administration.
   2. Conduct regional needs assessments.
   3. Specify data analysis procedures.
   4. Analyze and interpret assessment data.

C. Field Testing
   1. Design summative evaluation studies to determine the effectiveness and appropriateness of bilingual/multicultural education products.
   2. Compile, analyze, and interpret field test data for MDCs prior to final revision of bilingual products.

D. Design and Production of Materials
  1. Publish first editions.
  2. Control dissemination of materials and data retrieval in conjunction with TRCs.
  3. Receive voluntary input from users and data retrieval.
  4. Analyze retrieved data.
  5. Cooperate with MDCs on final materials revision.
  6. Publish and disseminate final materials in cooperation with MDCs.
E. Technical Assistance
  1. Provide assistance on evaluation and program implementation.
  2. Train technical specialists in evaluation designs and procedures.
  3. Provide assistance to MDCs in design and pilot testing and formative evaluation techniques.
  4. Provide information on the quality and use of psychometric instruments.
  5. Provide assistance in developing or selecting appropriate instruments.

A review of these functions indicates that the DACs can undertake limited research functions in direct support of the needs of bilingual education projects, particularly when great numbers of these projects evidence the same basic needs. Alternatively, a national bilingual R&D center, which is being contemplated by the National Institute of Education, may assume these research responsibilities.

Conclusion

Many of the functions of the Network are designed specifically to provide the kind of quality control that has long been lacking in the production of bilingual educational materials. In the past, Title VII left materials design and production almost exclusively in the hands of LEAs, which produced materials of varying quality in a cost-inefficient manner, principally for local consumption. The DACs role in negotiating a tailor-made field-test design with each MDC for each major product, together with the cooperating TRCs and LEAs that they identify, includes the production of a limited number of field-test copies. In the past, educators have been painfully aware of the consequences of premature publication of many bilingual materials. This practice will be significantly diminished if not altogether abolished when the materials are developed by the Network.

The dissemination function of the DACs could also include a strong diffusion emphasis. For example, the regular publications emanating from DACs, such as reviews of tests or educational materials (both informational and evaluative), should assist LEA project directors and curriculum adoption personnel not only in making better selection of extant psychometric, educational, and teacher training materials, but also in keeping them abreast of upcoming materials and the dates of their availability. By cooperating with the recently established Bilingual Clearinghouse, a DAC's regional efforts can reach out to bilingual educators nationwide.

The National Network of Centers for Bilingual Education is an effort to systematize what was previously a potpourri of research, development, and evaluation activities. As bilingual education has achieved national attention, its distinctive needs and interests have come to the fore, and general practitioners in research, development, and evaluation can no longer fully serve bilingual education on an *ad hoc* basis. The Network should provide an integrated view of needs and priorities in bilingual education, a view that can be used not only by the Office of Bilingual Education but also by the National Institute of Education and other Federal agencies in their planning and in their ultimate coordination of programs in the field as well as those for basic and applied research.

APPENDIX

Task Force Findings Specifying Remedies
Available for Eliminating Past Educational
Practices Ruled Unlawful Under *Lau* v. *Nichols*

United States Department of Health, Education, and Welfare
Office of the Secretary
1975

TABLE OF CONTENTS

The immediate implementation of the requirements listed within does not apply to those school districts which have had a substantial number of recent school-age Indo-Chinese immigrants whose primary or home language is other than English in the 1975-1976 school year.

I. **Identification of Student's Primary or Home Language**

The first step to be included in a plan submitted by a district found to be in noncompliance with Title VI under *Lau* is the method by which the district will identify the student's primary or home language. A student's primary or home language, for the purpose of this report, is other than English if it meets at least one of the following descriptions:

A. The student's first acquired language is other than English.

B. The language most often spoken by the student is other than English.

C. The language most often spoken in the student's home is other than English, regardless of the language spoken by the student.

These assessments (A-C, above) must be made by persons who can speak and understand the necessary language(s). Then the district must assess the degree of linguistic function or ability of the student(s) so as to place the student(s) in one of the following categories by language:

A. Monolingual speaker of the language other than English (speaks the language other than English exclusively).

B. Predominantly speaks the language other than English (speaks mostly the language other than English, but speaks some English).

C. Bilingual (speaks both the language other than English and English with equal ease).

D. Predominantly speaks English (speaks mostly English, but some of the language other than English).

E. Monolingual speaker of English (speaks English exclusively).

In the event that the student is multilingual (is functional in more than two languages in addition to English), such assessment must be made in all the necessary languages. In order to make the aforementioned assessments the *district must, at a minimum, determine the language most often spoken in the student's home,* regardless of the language spoken by the student, the language most often spoken by the student in the home, and the language spoken by the student in the social setting (by observation).

These assessments must be made by persons who can speak and understand the necessary language(s). An example of the latter would be to determine, by observation, the language used by the student to communicate with peers between classes or in informal situations. These assessments must cross-validate one another (Example: student speaks Spanish at home and Spanish with classmates at lunch). Observers must estimate the frequency of use of each language spoken by the student in these situations.

In the event that the language determinations conflict (Example: student speaks Spanish at home but English with classmates at lunch), *an additional* method must be employed by the district to make such a determination (for example, the district may wish to employ a test of language dominance as a third criterion). In other words, two of the three criteria will cross-validate or the majority of criteria will cross-validate (yield the same language).

Due to staff limitations and priorities, we will require a plan under *Lau* during this initial stage of investigation when the district has 20 or more students of the same language group identified as having a primary or home language other than English. However, a district does have an obligation to serve any student whose primary or home language is other than English.

II. Diagnostic/Prescriptive Approach

The second part of a plan must describe the diagnostic/prescriptive measures to be used to identify the nature and extent of each student's educational needs and then prescribe an educational program utilizing the most effective teaching style to satisfy the diagnosed educational needs. The determination of which teaching style(s) are to be used will be based on a careful review of both the cognitive and affective domains and should include an assessment of the responsiveness of students to different types of cognitive learning styles and incentive motivational styles — e.g., competitive vs. cooperative learning patterns. The diagnostic measures must include diagnoses of problems related to areas or subjects required of other students in the school program *and* prescriptive measures must serve to bring the linguistically/culturally different student(s) to the educational performance level that is expected by the Local Education Agency (LEA) and State of nonminority students. A program designed for students of limited-English-speaking ability must not be operated in a manner so as to solely satisfy a set of objectives divorced or isolated from those educational objectives established for students in the regular school program.

III. Educational Program Selection

In the third step the district must implement the appropriate type(s) of educational program(s) listed in this Section (III, 1-5), dependent upon the degree of linguistic proficiency of the students in question. If none seem applicable, check with your *Lau* coordinator for further action.

1. In the case of the monolingual speaker of the language other than English (speaks the language other than English exclusively).
    A. At the elementary and intermediate levels; any one or a combination of the following programs is acceptable:
        1. Transitional Bilingual Education Program (TBE).
        2. Bilingual/Bicultural Program.
        3. Multilingual/Multicultural Program. (See definitions, page 201.)

In the case of a TBE, the district must provide predictive data that show that such student(s) are ready to make the transition into English and will succeed educationally in content areas and in the educational program(s) in which he/she is to be placed. This is necessary so the district will not prematurely place the linguistically/culturally different student who is not ready to participate effectively in an English language curriculum in the regular school program (conducted exclusively in English).

Because an ESL program does not consider the affective or cognitive development of students in this category and time and maturation variables are different here than for students at the secondary level, an ESL program *is not* appropriate.

    B. At the secondary level:
        Option 1: Such students may receive instruction in subject matter (example: math, science) in the native language(s) and receive English-as-a-Second-Language (ESL) as a class component (see definition, page 201.)
        Option 2: Such students may receive required and elective subject matter (examples: math, science, industrial arts) in the native language(s) and bridge into English while combining English with the native language as appropriate (learning English as a first language, in a natural setting).
        Option 3: Such students may receive ESL or High Intensive Language Training (HILT) (see definition, page 201) in English until they are fully functional in English (can operate equally successfully in school in English) then bridge into the school program for other students.

A district may wish to utilize a TBE, Bilingual/Bicultural, or a Multilingual/Multicultural program in lieu of the three options presented in this section (1.B.). This is permissible. However, if the necessary prerequisite skills in the native language(s) have not been taught to these students, some form of compensatory education in the native language must be provided.

In any case, students in this category (1.B.) must receive instruction in a manner that is expeditiously carried out so that the
student in question will be able to participate to the greatest
extent possible in the regular school program as soon as possible. At no time can a program be selected in this category to
place the students in situations where the method of instruction
will result in a substantial delay in providing them with the necessary English language skills needed by or required of other
students at the time of graduation.

NOTE: You will generally find that students in this category are
recent immigrants.

2. In the case of the predominate speaker of the language other
than English (speaks mostly the language other than English,
but speaks some English):

A. At the elementary level, any one or a combination of the
following programs is acceptable:

1. Transitional Bilingual Education Program (TBE)
2. Bilingual/Bicultural Program
3. Multilingual/Multicultural Program

In the case of a TBE, the district must provide predictive data
which show that such student(s) are ready to make the transition
to English and will educationally succeed in content areas and
the educational program in which he/she is to be placed.

Since an ESL program does not consider the affective or cognitive development of the students in this category and the time
and maturation variables are different here than for students at
the secondary level, an ESL program *is not* appropriate.

B. At the intermediate and high school levels:

The district must provide data relative to the student's
academic achievement and identify those students who have
been in the school system for less than a year. If the stu-
dent(s) who have been in the school system for less than a
year are achieving at grade level or better, the district is not
required to provide additional educational programs. If, however, the students who have been in the school system for a
year or more are underachieving (not achieving at grade
level), (see definition, page 201) the district must submit a
plan to remedy the situation. This may include a smaller class
size, enrichment materials, etc. In either this case or the case
of students who are underachieving and have been in the
school system for less than a year, the remedy must include
any one or a combination of the following: (1) an ESL, (2) a

TBE, (3) a Bilingual/Bicultural Program, (4) a Multilingual/Multicultural Program. *But* such students may not be placed in situations where all instruction is conducted in the native language as may be prescribed for the monolingual speaker of a language other than English if the necessary prerequisite skills in the native language have not been taught. In this case, some form of compensatory education in the native language must be provided.

NOTE: You will generally find that students in this category are not recent immigrants.

3. In the case of the bilingual speaker (speaks both the language other than English and English with equal ease), the district must provide data relative to the student(s) academic achievement. In this case, the treatment is the same at the elementary, intermediate, and secondary levels and differs only in terms of underachievers and those students achieving at grade level or better.

    A. For students who are underachieving, treatment corresponds to the regular program requirements for all racially-ethnically identifiable classes or tracks composed of students who are underachieving, regardless of their language background.

    B. For students who are achieving at grade level or better, the district is not required to provide additional educational programs.

4. In the case of the predominant speaker of English (speaks mostly English, but some of a language other than English), treatment for these students is the same as III.3.

5. In the case of the monolingual speaker of English (speaks English exclusively), treatment for these students is the same as III.3.

NOTE: ESL is a necessary component of all the aforementioned programs. However, an ESL program may not be sufficient as the *only* program operated by a district to respond to the educational needs of all types of students described in this document.

IV. Required and Elective Courses

In the fourth step of such plan the district must show that the required and elective courses are not designed to have a discriminatory effect.

    A. Required courses. Required courses such as American History must not be designed to exclude pertinent minority de-

velopments that have contributed to or influenced such subjects.

B. Elective Courses and Co-curricular Activities. Where a district
has been found out of compliance and operates racially/eth-
nically identifiable elective courses or co-curricular activities,
the plan must address this area by either educationally justifying the racial/ethnic identifiability of these courses or activities, eliminating them, or guaranteeing that these courses
or co-curricular activities will not remain racially/ethnically
identifiable.

There is a prima facie case of discrimination if courses are
racially/ethnically identifiable. Schools must develop strong
incentives and encouragement for minority students to enroll
in electives where minorities have not traditionally enrolled. In
this regard, counselors, principals, and teachers have a most
important role. Title VI compliance questions are raised by
any analysis of counseling practices that indicate that
minorities are being advised in a manner that results in their
being disproportionately channeled into certain subject areas
or courses. A school district must see that all of its students
are encouraged to fully participate and take advantage of all
educational benefits.

Close monitoring is necessary to evaluate to what degree
minorities are, in essence, being discouraged from taking
certain electives and encouraged to take other elective
courses and insist that to eliminate discrimination and to
provide equal educational opportunities, districts must take
affirmative duties to see that minority students are not
excluded from any elective courses and over-included in
others. All newly established elective courses cannot be designed to have a discriminatory effect. This means that a
district cannot, for example, initiate a course in Spanish literature designed exclusively for Spanish-speaking students so
that enrollment in that subject is designed to result in the
exclusion of students whose native language is English but
who could equally benefit from such a course and/or be
designed to result in the removal of the minority students in
question from a general literature course that should be designed to be relevant for all the students served by the district.

V. **Instructional Personnel Requirements (Teacher Requirements)** (See definition, page 201.)

Instructional personnel teaching students in question must be linguistically/culturally familiar with the background of the students to be affected.

The student/teacher ratio for such programs should equal or be less than (fewer students per teacher) the student/teacher ratio for the district. However, corrective action is not required by the district if the number of students in such programs are no more than five greater per teacher than the student/teacher ratio for the district.

If instructional staffing is inadequate to implement program requirements, in-service training, directly related to improving student performance, is acceptable as an immediate and temporary response. Plans for providing this training must include at least the following:

1. Objectives of training (must be directly related to ultimately improving student performance).
2. Methods by which the objective(s) will be achieved.
3. Method for selection of teachers to receive training.
4. Names of personnel doing the training and location of training.
5. Content of training.
6. Evaluation design of training and performance criteria for individuals receiving the training.
7. Proposed timetables.

This temporary in-service training must continue until staff performance criteria has been met.

Another temporary alternative is utilizing paraprofessional persons with the necessary language(s) and cultural background(s). Specific instructional roles of such personnel *must be* included in the plan. Such a plan must show that this personnel will aid in teaching and not be restricted to those areas unrelated to the teaching process (checking roll, issuing tardy cards, etc.).

In addition, the district must include a plan for securing the number of qualified teachers necessary to fully implement the instructional program. Development and training of paraprofessionals may be an important source for the development of bilingual/bicultural teachers.

VI. **Racial/Ethnic Isolation and/or Identifiability of Schools and Classes**

A. Racially/Ethnically Isolated and/or Identifiable Schools:
It is not educationally necessary nor legally permissible to create racially/ethnically identifiable schools in order to respond to student-language characteristics as specified in the programs

described herein.

B. Racially/Ethnically Isolated and/or Identifiable Classes:

The implementation of the aforementioned educational models do not justify the existence of racially/ethically isolated or identifiable classes *per se*. Since there is no conflict in this area as related to the application of the Emergency School Aid Act (ESAA) and existing Title VI regulations, standard application of those regulations is effective.

VII. **Notification to Parents of Students Whose Primary or Home Language Is Other Than English**

A. School districts have the responsibility to effectively notify the parents of the students identified as having a primary or home language other than English of all school activities or notices which are called to the attention of other parents. Such notice, in order to be adequate, must be provided in English and in the necessary language(s) comprehensively paralleling the exact content in English. Be aware that a literal translation may not be sufficient.

B. The district must inform all minority and non-minority parents of all aspects of the programs designed for students of limited-English-speaking ability and that these programs constitute an integral part of the total program.

VIII. **Evaluation**

A "Product and Process" evaluation is to be submitted in the plan. This type of evaluation, in addition to stating the "product" (end result), must include "process evaluation" (periodic evaluation throughout the implementation stage). A description of the *evaluation design* is required. Timelines (target for completion of steps) are an essential component. For the *first three years,* following the implementation of a plan, the district must submit to the OCR Regional Office at the close of 60 days after school starts, a "progress report" that will show the steps which have been completed. For those steps that have not been completed, a narrative from the district is necessary to explain why the targeted completion dates were not met. Another "progress report" is due at the close of 30 days after the last day of the school year in question.

IX. **Definition of Terms**

1. Bilingual/Bicultural Program

A program that utilizes the student's native language (example: Navajo) and cultural factors in instruction, maintaining, and further developing all the necessary skills in the student's native language and culture while introducing, maintaining, and developing all the necessary skills in the second language and culture (example: English). The end result is a student who can function, totally, in both languages and cultures.

2. English-as-a-Second-Language (ESL)
   A structured language acquisition program designed to teach English to students whose native language is not English.

3. High Intensive Language Training (HILT)
   A total immersion program designed to teach students a new language.

4. Multilingual/Multicultural Program
   A program operated under the same principles as a Bilingual/Bicultural Program *except* that more than one language and culture, in addition to English language and culture is treated. The end result is a student who can function, totally, in more than two languages and cultures.

5. Transitional Bilingual Education Program (TBE)
   A program operated in the same manner as a Bilingual/Bicultural Program, except that once the student is fully functional in the second language (English), further instruction in the native language is no longer required.

6. Underachievement
   Underachievement is defined as performance in each subject area (e.g., reading and problem solving) at one or more standard deviations below district norms as determined by some objective measures for non-ethnic/racial minority students. Mental ability scores cannot be utilized for determining grade expectancy.

7. Instructional Personnel
   Persons involved in teaching activities. Such personnel includes, but is not limited to, certified, credentialized teachers, paraprofessionals, teacher aides, parents, community volunteers, and youth tutors.